BY WAY
OF THE HEART

BY WAY
OF THE HEART

*Toward a Holistic
Christian Spirituality*

WILKIE AU, S.J.

PAULIST PRESS
New York/Mahwah

The author gratefully acknowledges permission from Lyle Stuart, Inc. to include excerpts from *The Way of Man According to the Teaching of Hasidism* by Martin Buber, © 1988 by Citadel Press, and from The Christian Century Foundation for excerpts from "Rabbinical Stories: A Primer on Theological Method" by Belden Lane, which appeared in the December 16, 1981 issue of *The Christian Century*.

Cover logo design by Crystal Williams

Book design by Nighthawk Design.

Library of Congress Cataloging-in-Publication Data

Au, Wilkie, 1944-
   By way of the heart: toward a holistic Christian
spirituality/Wilkie Au.
     p.   cm.
   Includes bibliographical references.
   ISBN 0-8091-0436-9:
   1. Spiritual life—Catholic authors.   I. Title.
BX2350.2A8   1990
248—dc20   89-39731
                                           CIP

Published by Paulist Press
997 Macarthur Boulevard
Mahwah, New Jersey 07430

Printed and bound in the
United States of America

DEDICATION

To my mother, Violet Kwai Fah
and in memory of
my father, Tai Hing,
providers of life and
the conditions for faith

CONTENTS

ACKNOWLEDGMENTS

ALTHOUGH THE LABOR of one person, this handiwork bears the touch of many people, who like Socratic midwives, helped in the delivery of this book. I am enormously grateful to them.

I thank Thomas Rausch, S.J., whose encouragement launched my efforts. I am grateful to Gerald McKevitt, S.J., for his friendship which has been a constant support, and for his commitment to scholarship which has been an inspiration. His skillful application of Occam's razor to the manuscript has contributed to a more readable text. I am also indebted to my respected colleague Paul Bernadicou, S.J., for a critical reading of the manuscript. To Priscilla Welles, whose faith in me has been a steady reassurance of the worth of my words, I am deeply grateful. Without their encouragement, this book would never have been born.

I wish to thank Timothy Iglesias for the decisive contribution he has made in the preparation of this work. His perceptive comments helped shape its final form. Special thanks are due to Mary Wilbur for her patient reading of the manuscript in its entirety and her perceptive feedback. I wish to thank others who read selected chapters and provided helpful suggestions: Sr. Margaret Fitzer, S.S.L., and Jesuits William Creed, Kevin Hancock, Matthew Linn, Gerdenio Manuel, and Leo Rock.

I am indebted to Kevin O'Connor and Susan Evans for generously reviewing the proofpages, to Crystal Williams for creating the very fitting cover logo, and, in a special way, to William Johnston for writing the foreword.

Portions of some chapters have appeared in somewhat different form in *Human Development, Chicago Studies,* and *Review for Religious.* I thank the editors for their permission to include those materials here.

Last and by no means least, I am grateful to my Jesuit brothers, especially those with whom I lived and worked at the novitiate at Santa Barbara and the juniorate at Loyola Marymount University, to my former students and counselees, and to my family and friends for their loving support and companionship on the spiritual journey.

W.W.A.

Loyola Marymount University

FOREWORD

As we approach the third millennium it becomes clear that men and women throughout the world are thirsting for prayer. Modern people, tired of controversies and discussions and endless talk, want to experience God in the depths of their being. They long for a holistic spirituality that will do away with division and bring them to union. They long for a spirituality that will unite body and soul, psychology and scripture, east and west—a spirituality that will answer the needs and aspirations of the whole person living in community and walking toward God.

And Wilkie Au has written a modern book of holistic spirituality. He is eminently equipped for such a task. I first met Wilkie in 1978 when he was a newly ordained priest studying and practicing spirituality in Japan. At that time it was abundantly clear that here was a man who could work toward the creation of a holistic spirituality. He was an able psychologist, uniting in himself the roles of counselor and spiritual director. He was educated in the west with a deep interest in Japanese culture, in the poverty of the Philippines and in the vast civilization of mainland China which he subsequently visited in search of his roots. He was steeped in the Bible; he was deeply human; and he was a man of prayer. It was no surprise to me when I later heard that he had been appointed to direct the novices of the Society of Jesus in the path of contemplation in action and to explain to them the modern meaning of chastity, poverty and obedience.

And so *By Way of the Heart: Toward a Holistic Christian Spirituality* comes from the pen of an experienced master. Anyone who reads it will find a sure guide along a path that leads to wholeness, to enlightenment and to God.

William Johnston, S.J.
Sophia University
Tokyo

INTRODUCTION

"YOU HAVE A book in you!" a friend said to me as I left the Jesuit residence at Loyola Marymount University to start a sabbatical. He was referring to my experience: a recently completed term as Jesuit novice director, and before that five years of teaching and counseling adults and students at the university, and training in psychology and spirituality. His encouraging nudge marked the start of what you are reading. Having worked closely with both religious and lay people, I wanted to write something that would benefit all Christians. Thus, the focus of this book is on a common gospel spirituality that is shared by religious and lay alike.

I chose to entitle this work *By Way of the Heart: Toward a Holistic Christian Spirituality* for several reasons. To go to God by way of the heart is to take a path to holiness that is both graceful and human. It is graceful—not strained even in the midst of struggle—because it relies radically on the enabling power of God to achieve its end. While Christian transformation calls for personal responsibility and effort, it can only come about when God replaces our often cold hearts of stone with warm hearts of flesh capable of loving. The way of the heart is also very human because it requires the involvement of the whole self—body and spirit, mind and emotions. The term "heart" is a traditional image for a way of perceiving, feeling, and loving that engages the total person. To St. Augustine, the word signifies "our whole interior and spiritual life, and it includes mind and will, knowledge and love."[1] "Heart," when used to symbolize a spirituality, indicates that following Jesus is not something primarily heady, action-oriented, or moralistic. Rather, it is a matter of being caught up in a dynamic loving relationship with the Lord and others. Thus, Christian habits of the heart are those ways of knowing, valuing, and acting that are appropriate to followers of Jesus. Although the term "holistic" conveys much of what "heart" does, I nevertheless include it in the title because it describes contemporary values which I feel should characterize an integrated spirituality. Finally, "toward" is meant to communicate the incomplete nature of what I present. Clearly, this book does not con-

3

tain a completely developed holistic spirituality, but merely presents a moment of personal synthesis. The process of reflecting on Christian life is never-ending. This work represents one pilgrim's desire to share with his fellow-travelers his observations and insights of the trip up to now.

CONTROVERSIES AND CONTEXT

Two controversial but important issues of Christian life—the relationship between religion and psychology, and between religious and lay people—provide the context for this work. A brief description of them will help to express further the purpose of this book.

First, Christians are short-changing themselves when they "exchange . . . their heritage for a mess of psycho-babble."[2] According to theologian Richard Neuhaus, this statement in the *National Review* reflects the view of a number of thinkers. It exposes a persistent prejudice shared by many Christians: psychology and faith do not mix. For those of us who value the contribution of psychology to spirituality and presume this appreciation to be universal, Neuhaus' report, like a sobering shake, returns us to reality. Some believers are still wary of psychology and worry about the "psychologizing" of religion. Persuaded that the churches have bought tainted goods in being so heavily influenced by modern psychology, some current observers urge them to reappropriate a peculiarly biblical wisdom about mental and spiritual health. Neuhaus reiterates Paul Vitz's argument that the mainstream of contemporary psychology has become, not an ancillary aid to biblical religion, but a substitute for it.[3]

Second, on another polemical front, the argument about the relationship between religious and lay people in the church still flares up. In a widely-circulated journal, an article entitled, "Superiority of the Religious Life," recently appeared. "In the worlds of finance, medicine, the military," the author states, "there is no reason to ascribe superiority to the religious state." But "in the world of holiness and the sacred, there is."[4] These are jolting words for those who thought that Vatican II's emphasis on the universal call to holiness shattered for good all such divisive stratifications of Christians.

To articulate a holistic Christian spirituality based on gospel loves is the purpose of this book. Such a spirituality is meant to strengthen two important alliances: the alliance between the therapeutic and the spiritual, and that between religious and lay spirituality. The therapeutic, which represents what psychology has discovered about healthy human development, can serve spirituality by guarding against any attempt to abandon the human in pursuit of the holy. And by highlighting the gospel values that form the single spirituality offered by Jesus, the holistic approach offered here is intended to bring about a closer unity among members of the one body of Christ. Both alliances are under attack.

PSYCHOLOGY AND RELIGION AS ALLIES

As Neuhaus reports, some modern thinkers suggest that psychology is inherently antagonistic toward the goals and values of religion. In this view, religion and psychology are sworn enemies, determined to destroy one another. Human growth is looked upon as a threat to religious growth, and vice versa. Such views force an unnecessary choice between religious and psychological truth. The problem with this dichotomous mentality is its failure to recognize that truth is a seamless garment and that authentic religion and authentic psychology, each in its own way, shed light on the truth of the human condition. Truth has nothing to fear from itself, whether the truth be of mathematics or physics, physiology or phenomenology, and yes, psychology or religion. It is to the lasting credit of St. Thomas Aquinas, who taught that there is a harmony between faith and reason, between grace and nature, that we recognize there is one author of both, and therefore there can be no contradiction between them. Each, with its own methodology and criteria for determining truth, is a valid, though different, way of knowing.

As a priest and a counselor, I believe that psychological and spiritual health are intimately related and that genuine religion is psychologically healthy. My clinical experience in counseling, as well as in spiritual direction, makes me unsympathetic to alarmist calls to abandon psychology simply because of the excesses of certain true believers of the therapeutic god. In a society where pop psychology is often presented as the panacea for personal problems, abuses will inevitably occur. Nevertheless, when used with intelligence and common sense, psychology can support biblical faith and genuine spiritual development. I hope that the following pages will make clear that spirituality can often find a helpful ally in psychology. Just as authentic human growth cannot be built on a spirituality that denigrates the body or the earthy conditions of human existence, spiritual maturity also has definite psychological prerequisites. For example, love of God and others presupposes a modicum of self-love, just as intimacy with the Lord in prayer requires the ability to be intimate in some prior human relationship. Instead of substituting for religion, psychology can assist pilgrims in their spiritual journey from narcissism to altruism, from egotistic self-realization to self-surrendering love. This book illustrates how psychology and religion can be natural allies in the process by which we are made whole and holy.

THE COMMON VOCATION OF LAY AND RELIGIOUS

The unity between professed religious and lay Christians is being undermined by a prejudice that refuses to die—the myth that a higher spirituality exists for professional religious and priests, and a watered down form for lay Christians in the world. Behind this view lurks the suspicion that secular life is a sort of compromise or halfway measure. Any view that keeps alive the ancient prejudice that looked on monks as total Christians and lay persons as partial Christians misunderstands their common vocation. The spirituality that would stratify Christians into those called to a wholehearted and those called to a halfhearted following of Jesus is incompatible with the spirituality presented here. My dealings with both religious and lay persons have convinced me that both modes of Christian life offer equal opportunities for generous commitment to Christ and rich spiritual development. Lay people, whether called to the married, single, or widowed life, can give themselves totally to God through their devotion to family and friends and their dedication to work and community service. Professed religious can do the same in community life and ministry. Is it belaboring the obvious, then, to say that one can be deeply religious without being a religious?

In purposing a holistic spirituality based on gospel values, I hope to enhance the unity of Christians. While religious life and secular Christian life represent two distinct ways of responding to the radical demands of the gospel, neither constitutes an intrinsically better way of following Christ. Religious life in the church, John Lozano contends, serves as a parable reminding the whole church of the demands that the gospel makes on us all.[5] As such, "the religious life is really no more evangelical than secular Christian life, because the gospel speaks to us of faith, hope, conversion, purity of heart, humility, service and solidarity with the oppressed—none of these are more related to the religious life than they are to secular Christian life."[6] Love, prayer, worship, ministry, and community are the heart of the Christian experience for all. What religious and lay Christians possess in common is far more real, profound, and important than any differences they might have.[7] When Vatican II reaffirmed that the call to holiness is universal, it led to a gradual shedding of elitist interpretations of religious profession that would make it appear to be an intrinsically higher life than the lay state. All Christians, according to the council, are called to strive for the perfection of charity.[8] Consequently, it no longer seems proper to set off religious from others as those with an exclusive vocation to a "state of perfection." This realization has "created a challenge to reinterpret religious life as a way rather than a caste." It also seeks "an understanding of the vows that does not imply a separation of religious from other Christians or exalt them above their sisters and brothers in the Christian community."[9]

A Spiritual Renaissance among Lay and Religious

After more than fifteen years of involvement with the spiritual training of both religious and lay persons, I recognize that both groups share many of the same struggles and problems. Much of what I offer them in spiritual direction and retreats is the same, though adapted to the concrete exigencies of their different lifestyles. A principal concern of this book flows from the common nature of their spiritual journey: How can the spiritual aids traditionally given to professed religious be more equitably shared with the growing number of lay Christians, who individually or in community, seek to deepen their life of faith? This work attempts to open up the rich treasury of Christian spirituality to all Christians who long to take their religious life more seriously, but lack any kind of formal spiritual formation. As the author of a book on a holistic approach to catechesis rightly maintains, "the essential elements of the religious life, which for many centuries were the preserve of a professed few, must once again be made available so that *all* Christians can mature in holiness."[10]

By describing a spirituality that is holistic in its integration of gospel values and its concerns for the humanity of the whole person who is called to spiritual transformation, I hope to contribute to the renaissance taking place today among both lay and religious. Professed religious in increasing numbers are committed to the notion of continuing formation, clearly acknowledging that their development must be actively fostered throughout their lives and not abandoned once they have made a formal profession of vows. Among the laity, this spiritual renewal has taken many forms. Growing numbers of Christians find themselves searching for greater depth in living their religious commitment. I am thinking specifically of directors of religious education, lay spiritual directors, as well as those who are active in myriad forms of lay ministry, charismatic prayer groups and covenant communities, L'Arche houses, and Catholic Worker communities.

AN OVERVIEW

I mentioned earlier that this book originated in my desire to share the insights I have learned from my experience in spiritual direction and psychological counseling. No attempt has been made here to develop a coherent theory of spirituality using the strict methodology of a single discipline. I draw from many sources—scriptural, psychological, personal—to illuminate the multifaceted process of spiritual growth. Some of the material included in this work has already appeared as articles in journals which I indicate in the acknowledgments. While previously published materials have been edited and rewritten for this volume, the major portion of this book appears here for the first time.

A brief overview of the book's structure may be helpful. In Chapter I, I introduce an overall framework based on gospel loves. These biblical values provide a useful context to discuss key issues that affect holistic growth in the spiritual life. While Chapter I presents the general landscape, Chapter II elaborates on each element that contributes to the whole picture. In discussing each gospel value, it is not my intention to be comprehensive, but merely to comment in a way that can enhance its integration into our lives. Then in the remainder of the book, I devote a chapter each to decision-making and life-choice (Chapter III), prayer (Chapter IV), obedience (Chapter V), chastity (Chapter VI), and poverty (Chapter VII).

The first four chapters are obviously equal in their relevance to both religious and lay Christians. Chapters V, VI, and VII discuss the virtues of obedience, chastity, and poverty as gospel values that are important to the lives of all Christians, not only to professed religious. As stated earlier, the religious life of the vows is not different from Christian life. Not that all Christians are called to profess the three vows, but all are nevertheless called to embody the underlying gospel values that the vows represent. If lived in a holistic way, the religious life of the vows can support the vocation of lay Christians who are called to proclaim the same gospel values in the home and the workplace. The religious life can thus be seen as an attempt to articulate explicitly in a lifestyle that which is common to all Christians, that is, the vocation to follow Jesus in his central and all-consuming concern for preaching the good news of the reign of God in our midst.

CHAPTER ONE

A SPIRITUALITY BASED
ON GOSPEL LOVES

"If I have faith in all its fullness, to move mountains, but without love,
then I am nothing at all."
(1 COR 13: 2–3)

LIKE A MAP, a spirituality is useless if it is not based on the existential terrain those following it must traverse. But, even more critical is the realization of travelers that a map is indeed necessary. And this realization results only when they are in touch with their enmeshment, their need for a way out of a perplexing entanglement which blocks progress. Martin Buber, the Jewish theologian, tells a story that brings this truth home nicely.[1]

Buber describes the encounter between a jailed rabbi and the chief jailer. The majestic and quiet face of the rabbi, deep in meditation, touched the jailer deeply. A thoughtful person himself, the jailer began talking with his prisoner and questioning him on various points of scripture. Finally, the guard asked the rabbi,

"How are we to understand that God the all-knowing said to Adam: 'Where art thou?' "
"Do you believe," answered the rav, "that the scriptures are eternal and that every era, every generation and every [one] is included in them?"
"I believe this," said the other.
"Well," said the zaddik[2] "in every era, God calls to every [one]:

11

'Where are you in your world?' So many years and days of those allotted to you have passed, and how far have you gotten in your world?" God says something like this: "You have lived forty-six years. How far along are you?"

When the chief of the gendarmes heard his age mentioned, he pulled himself together, laid his hand on the rav's shoulder, and cried: "Bravo!" But his heart trembled.

Buber goes on to explain that God does not ask the question expecting to learn something new. Rather, God uses the question to confront Adam with the state of his life. God asks the same question of us today to jolt us into examining our lives and taking responsibility for our way of living. This decisive heart-searching is, according to Buber, the beginning of a spiritual way for human beings. So long as we do not face the still, small Voice asking us, "Where art thou," we will forever remain way-less. Adam faced the Voice, perceived his enmeshment, and discovered a way out. The question, "Where art thou?" is like the "red X" on the map of our lives. As on a map of a shopping mall, the "red X" marks the exact location of where we are standing. When we ascertain that point, we can then proceed.

When Christians today face the question, "Where art thou," they find their lives more complicated than ever. Often they feel buffeted by the pressures of life and torn by the competing values that lay unrelenting claims on their limited energy and resources. Inner voices flood their minds with quandaries and concerns:

—"I'd like to develop my prayer life, but I feel so guilty when I take time away from the family."
—"I'd like to volunteer to help out at the downtown shelter for the homeless, but I hardly see the wife and kids as it is, with work being so hectic these days."
—"How do I stay faithful to my duties to my children and husband and still get some time and space for myself? Is it being selfish to tell them that I just have to get away for a couple of hours and that they'll have to fend for themselves for awhile?"

Perplexed by such inner pressures and questions, Christians often experience frustration, guilt, and confusion. They feel the need to clarify their situations and make good choices about how to spend their time and energy.

This demanding existence challenges lay Christians living in a world of "future shock," where the rapidity of change and the crush of choices besiege them daily. But the same situation is increasingly true for professed religious. For them, the increased pace and complexity of their lives were ushered in by Vatican II. By reversing the centuries-long adversary stance of the church in relationship to the world, the council challenged active religious (as opposed to contemplatives) to end their cloistered separation and to place themselves at the heart of the world, where the church felt called to be in solidarity and service to humankind. This relocation placed religious smack in the middle of the world, sharing the same fast and frenzied fate of their fellow Christians. Given this relatively new reality, a spirituality that can, like a map, help orient and guide them in this new terrain of post-Vatican II Christian existence is needed. These days many professed religious find themselves struggling with their own variety of the same quandaries perplexing their lay brothers and sisters:

—"How do I keep from getting over-extended and being burned out, when there's so much to do and such a shortage of help? Let me tell you, the vocation crisis has got me worried!"

—"These days I find myself so exhausted that I don't feel like doing anything when I get home from work. I'm too tired to pray or to get involved in community. But, then, when I skip prayer and withdraw from community I feel lonely and out of sync! What should I do?"

—"I feel the need to stay in touch with good friends, but work at the parish takes up all the time I have."

These inner voices of concern reveal the challenge entailed in living gospel values in the midst of busy lives. Fulfilling the diverse requirements of Christian living in a balanced fashion so that no one aspect is overemphasized to the detriment of others is not an easy task. "A place for everything and everything in its place" suggests a way of achieving harmony. To attain this harmony, an ongoing process of self-monitoring is required. And for this, we need an overall perspective, a way of looking on our lives that provides a sense of the big picture. Only such a framework will enable us to assess whether we are paying adequate attention to the full range of gospel values. A holistic spirituality attempts to tackle the tough task of finding an outlook that will integrate our lives sufficiently to give us a sense of increasing wholeness and guide us in our pursuit of holiness.

Striving for holiness, like taking up exercise, can be hazardous to one's health. If misguided, the pursuit of sanctity can produce immaturity and stunted growth. Wanting to harbor themselves until the storms of life pass by, some people use religion as a safe haven to escape the struggles of adult life which produce growth. While fearful images of God as a stern judge sap zest and spontaneity out of the lives of some Christians, the authoritarian rule of some church leaders perpetuates the childish dependence of others.

Professionals such as priests, ministers, and vowed religious are not exempt from the dangers that come with taking religion too seriously. The caricatures of a "Father Frighteningly Frigid" and a "Sister Severely Stern" illustrate the repressiveness that religious life can produce, even in post-Vatican II times. These caricatures point to only two of a variety of immature religious who form a group of "grumpy children of God" in today's church. We have all met insecure pastors angry at trained volunteers seeking greater involvement in the parish as well as religious whose sexual anxieties make them ineffectual in many pastoral situations. Some people might argue that emotional health should not be absolutized as a Christian value. But all must concede that priests and ministers with emotional hangups often severely impede the spread of God's kingdom, damage lives through the abuse of authority, and undermine collaboration in ministry.

The perils of a religious path also endanger lay Christians. Men and women who take religion seriously can lapse into forms of pious fanaticism and simple-minded fundamentalism that render life burdensome and dull. Those who interpret the Bible literally, for example, often use scripture as a club to beat others into conforming to their inflexible views, and the righteousness of true believers often allows them to condemn others with an ease that would make Jesus blush. A holistic spirituality attempts to safeguard Christians from these myopic extremes.

The holistic approach to the spiritual life suggested in this book will enable both religious and lay people to forge a more vital link between their faith and their daily lives. In this way, they can heal the dichotomy between the human and the holy, the secular and the sacred—a division that has forced so many to be schizophrenic in living out their religious beliefs. In short, this holistic spirituality will help to develop Christians, both religious and lay, who are integrated personalities. Aptly described by Jesuit historian, Hugo Rahner, a mature Christian person is "one who has overcome the pernicious schizophrenia between soul and body, brain and heart, and thus become fully integrated. . . ."[3]

Like Rahner, I believe that a healthy spirituality cannot be built on the ruins of the human person. A healthy spiritual life respects human wholeness and does not pit it in opposition to holiness and religious commitment. Only such a holistic approach can successfully inculcate the habits of the heart that have made the religious path a genuine way to holiness and growth of the total person.

WHAT IS A HOLISTIC APPROACH?

The term "holistic" has in recent years been applied to such diverse fields as medicine, therapy, education, catechesis, and spirituality. In all these applications, the common meaning reflects a concern for wholeness, a desire for integration, and an attempt to understand the connections among the various aspects that constitute a given reality. To capture some of the more significant nuances of the term, let us consider its usage today in a variety of contexts.

Holistic medicine, for example, represents the desire to keep the total person at the center of medical attention, and not to reduce health care to the impersonal treatment of diseased organs or dysfunctional parts. This concern is in reaction to the growing specialization in medical care, and in fear of increased depersonalization due to technological advances. Holistic medicine stresses the organic unity of body and mind, as well as the responsibility and control that individuals have for taking care of their health through proper diet and exercise. Counteracting a certain complacency among some people who feel they are too busy to get the proper amount of nourishment and rest needed for vibrant health, it emphasizes the importance of preventing illness through the cultivation of a well-balanced and harmonious life.

Psychologists also speak of a holistic approach to human development. They stress the importance of acknowledging and developing all the complex aspects that make up the human personality. These include one's body and physical needs, emotions and affective needs, and spirit and religious needs. Psychological health also draws upon the Jungian notion that maturity requires the integration of polar aspects of the psyche and in the Eastern notion of balancing the *yin* and *yang* forces in one's life.

This integration requires a lifetime of effort and reaches a dramatic moment in what has popularly been termed the mid-life crisis. According to Jung, the challenge presented by the afternoon of one's life is to cultivate those aspects of the personality that remain latent and underdeveloped due to their neglect during the morning of one's existence. Thus, the mid-life project requires looking at and owning one's shadow (aspects of the self that had to be repressed for personal reasons in the course of one's history) and growing androgynously through the progressive assimilation of the feminine (*anima*) and masculine (*animus*) principles in the development of one's personality. A holistic approach thus challenges people to go beyond gender stereotypes of what it means to be a male or female and to develop more richly as total personalities.

Human beings, like puzzles, are made up of many parts. Their self-concept allows them to experience themselves as a single entity rather than as a loose collection of unrelated parts. However, unlike a static, prefabricated puzzle with limited parts, the human person is a multifaceted being whose many dimensions are only discovered over the course of a lifetime. When new pieces of the self emerge at different points in life's journey, they demand to be recognized and given their rightful place. Finding a place for these pieces often requires that the present design or self-concept be disassembled so that a more complex pattern capable of incorporating these newly discovered parts can be developed. This dissolution is scary, because it can shatter people's sense of who they are, thus precipitating an identity crisis and creating momentary disequilibrium. Mature growth requires living with this temporary confusion and allowing a more inclusive self-concept to emerge. Threatened by this breakdown of meaning, rigid personalities cling tenaciously to their restricted sense of self and deny these new pieces a legitimate place. In contrast, a holistic approach to development requires that we continually enlarge the images by which we understand ourselves and our world.

Educators have also found the term useful. Holistic education attempts to foster emotional as well as intellectual growth. "Instead of having emotions clash or conflict with intellectual activity," states a leader in the field, "we try to have both work in a harmonious relationship for the ultimate welfare and productivity of the learner."[4] Education is too narrowly viewed when it is reduced to the development of the mind and when it leaves out the cultivation of wonder, irony, and daring to think otherwise, which are essential ingredients for lively engagement in the world.[5] Thus, holistic educators exhort teachers to "take pains not to lose sight of the fact that there is more to 'mind' than knowledge, and more to 'person' than mind."[6] A holistic approach attempts "to pour back some juice into dehydrated educational practices" by blending affectivity and cognition and engaging the senses and the imagination.[7] In a book concerned with "the remaking of American education," the author underscores the vital need for reintegrating thinking, feeling, and sensing in education. "What tomorrow needs," he believes, "is not masses of intellectuals, but masses of educated [persons]—educated to feel and act as well as to think."[8]

In the sphere of formation of faith, contemporary catechesis calls for a holistic approach that goes beyond the classroom model. Holistic catechists argue that only an experiential and participational approach involving the whole person can achieve what *The National Catechetical Directory* describes as the aim of all catechesis: to make a person's faith become living, conscious, and active through the light of instruction.

To attain this objective, effective catechesis cannot merely address the learner's mind, but must "continue the process of developing the individual's full potential: the affective and behavioral as well as the intellectual and the spiritual."[9] Arguing for an integrated approach, one proponent states: "Witness the saints and heroes of our tradition. They were not canonized because of their astuteness or knowledge but because of the evident goodness of their lives. Is this not our goal for religious education? To achieve this goal, a multifaceted, holistic approach is called for."[10]

What, then, does "holistic" connote when used to describe a spirituality and spiritual formation? It should include all the connotations and nuances of the term described above. Like holistic medicine, a holistic spirituality must respect the psychosomatic or body-spirit unity of the person. Like holistic human development, holistic spiritual growth must include the ongoing struggle for integration and wholeness. It must also respect the developmental nature of that lifelong process. Like holistic education, holistic religious formation must go beyond mere theoretical training to engage the whole person in a process of personal transformation. It must also value personal experience as an important teacher and validate trial-and-error learning. And as with holistic catechesis, the aim of an integrated spiritual development is to make a person's faith become a dynamic element affecting every dimension of one's daily life, not merely an intellectual assent to abstract truths.

A holistic spirituality is a religious outlook as well as a way of structuring one's life in order to embody religious values. As a religious orientation, it asks the question, "How is God leading and loving us in all aspects of our lives?" It is holistic insofar as it acknowledges that all aspects of a person's life must be subjected to the transforming influence of the Spirit. In the past, certain spiritualities restricted the scope of the spiritual life to one's relationship to God and the condition of one's soul. In contrast, a holistic spirituality attempts to embrace the totality of a person's existence, including one's relationship with others, with one's work, and with the material world. Defining the spiritual life as coextensive with life itself, it finds every human concern relevant. God's spirit dwells and acts in all aspects of our lives and not merely in such explicitly religious activities as prayer and worship.

Understanding spirituality holistically involves linking it with every aspect of human development—psychological and spiritual, interpersonal and political. "Holism (or wholism) is an aspiration to deal with one's life adequately, giving each significant factor its due.'" Issues revolving around work and leisure, prayer and politics, sex and relationships all clamor for our attention. As a life structure, holistic spirituality is concerned with the question, "Given our limited time, energy, and resources, how can we integrate our Christian lives in a way that provides a sense of growing wholeness and peace?"

A HOLISTIC VIEW OF THE SPIRITUAL LIFE

To view the spiritual life holistically is to assert the truth of two central beliefs: (1) the pursuit of holiness is in no way inimical to healthy human growth; and (2) those who strive to be religious are not exempt from the human condition. They must, like everyone else, work out their growth into wholeness in the context of human struggle. What a Jesuit document states about the vow of chastity applies to the whole of religious life. Chastity "does not diminish our personality nor hamper human contacts and dialogue, but rather expands affectively, unites people as sisters and brothers, and brings them to a fuller charity."[12] Thus, those aspiring to be religious persons, whether as professed or as lay people, must continue to invest in their ongoing human growth. Unless they stay open to expanding as people able to give and to receive love, their quest for religious growth will ironically thwart, rather than stimulate, their cooperation with God in bringing about the universal society of love envisioned by Jesus.

COLLABORATING WITH THE CREATOR

Those who take Christian faith seriously should not denigrate human growth as something merely secular, something unrelated to religious maturity. Because the glory of God, as St. Irenaeus reminds us, is the person fully alive, our vocation as human beings entails a commitment to continuous human growth. Human life is a gift from the creator, who couples the gift of life with a call—a call to us to be co-creators, freely fashioning our lives into something beautiful for God. In this process of ongoing human development, the Lord of creation and the human beings fashioned by God's hand collaborate. Consequently, for people who seek to respond to God, a commitment to growth is more a requirement than a choice. To deny the inner impulse toward continuous growth is tantamount to not responding to God, because "as destiny, as summons, as love, God is present" in our process of becoming.[13] In short, a holistic spirituality sees ongoing human growth as essential to religious maturation. A spiritual life not built on solid human development born of struggle is liable to be superficial and escapist.

GRACE BUILDS ON NATURE

Growth in spiritual maturity depends heavily on integral human development. This truth has long been captured in the Scholastic adage that "grace builds on nature." Leo P. Rock, a former Jesuit novice director, applies this truth to religious formation in a pithy way: "Grace does not substitute for nature, but fulfills it. Healthy, sane personality development is the most fertile soil in which grace can take root and grow. Growth in religious life can best happen in the situation which best fosters personal human growth."[14]

A modern paraphrase of "Grace builds on nature" could be "God meets us where we're at." Sanctity, if it is to be genuine, must be bound up with authentic human life—and thus with the uniqueness, the limited capabilities and potentialities, the emotional maturity of the individual.[15] We may know of some genuinely holy men and women who seem far from psychologically healthy; nevertheless, maturity in spiritual development ordinarily implies maturity at more basic natural and psychological levels.[16] Since God's grace runs along channels of the Lord's own making, generally the Spirit of God respects the natural laws of human development as it interacts with human beings in their struggle towards holiness and wholeness. Thus, any spiritual path that attempts to skirt the natural laws of human development runs the risk of inauthenticity. As a wise old Benedictine abbot in charge of training recruits of varying ages once put it: "You create a monster if you try to put a thirty-year old head on a nineteen-year old body."

On the other hand, nature itself is graced. Because God's grace can be discovered at work within the structure of human development, growth is simultaneously natural development and a surprisingly graceful event. The good news for those struggling to grow spiritually is that God is intimately involved in the process. Far from being indifferent to the struggles of human growth, the transcendent creator of life is mysteriously near to support and sustain that process. Members of Alcoholics Anonymous put it this way: "God always comes to meetings!" God is ever present in us and our world "as the matrix and orientation of [our] coming to be, yet never identified with history nor exhausted by it."[17] Thus, human development is at once both secular and sacred. It involves both nature and grace because the conversions that lead us to greater self-knowledge and re-situate us in regard to our human environment "are not simply psychological but salvational."[18] God is redemptively present in the humanization process.

HOLISTIC GROWTH AND EFFECTIVE MINISTRY

In discussing the relationship between affectivity and sexuality in the life of Jesuits, psychiatrist James J. Gill points out an important reason why a holistic view of spirituality and religious formation must be taken seriously today. There has been a dramatic shift in the nature of effective ministry, he maintains. That shift requires a drastic revision of how lay people and seminarians are trained for apostolic service in the church. In the past, the prominent mode of ministry required that ministers communicate their knowledge (what they knew). Today, effective ministry requires them to share themselves (who they are).

Gill states that people trained for ministry two or three decades ago experienced a formation geared to providing them with knowledge which they could impart and skills by which they could express the truths they were learning about God, people, and the world. They were given to believe that their "spiritual life" was a private matter between themselves and God, and perhaps shared with a spiritual director or superior.

The shift in ministerial emphasis from giving what one knows to sharing who one is requires that ministers today go beyond being impersonal dispensers of "the truth" or distant suppliers of "the answers" to share the problems people face. Today's ministers, whether religious or lay, "are exhorted to 'communicate' with them personally and individually, by listening to their needs, sharing their struggles, allowing them to come to know our deepest attitudes, values, faith experiences, struggles and weakness, and, in brief, giving them a chance to recognize us as 'wounded healers.' "[19] Because of this shift in understanding ministry, those who wish to serve others in ministry hear "a new emphasis on the continuous pursuit of growth, the improvement of our ability to relate to others in Christian friendship, and a deepening of our understanding of ourselves as well as the people we serve."[20] All of these concerns find a place in the model of holistic spirituality that follows.

A Loving Framework

A compelling quality of Jesus' message was its absolute simplicity. When confronting the question set forth by a lawyer hoping to disconcert him, Jesus summarized "the whole Law, and the Prophets also" by recalling the twofold commandment of love: "You must love the Lord your God with all your heart, with all your strength, and with all your mind, and your neighbor as yourself" (Lk 10:25–28; Mt 22:34–40; Mk 12:28–34). Cutting through the morass of pharisaic requirements, Jesus went right to the heart of the matter: love is the sine qua non of religious life. Neither fulfilling the letter of the law, nor fasting and tithing, but simply loving God with our whole being and others as we love ourselves is the bottom line requirement "to inherit eternal life." This truth, so starkly stated, must have been a refreshing moment of clarity for those perplexed by the intricacies of the Mosaic law. With equal force, it can restore perspective to our complicated lives today.

Simplifications can clarify, but they can also distort. The history of thought contains many examples of how complex realities can suffer from over-simplification or distortive reductionism. For example, without denying the powerful force of libidinal energy, one need not buy into a Freudian reductionism that would make sex the sole motivator of all human activities. Similarly, while economic motives in many ways make the world go round, there is sufficient evidence that people are motivated by more than money to resist a theory of economic determinism.

Fortunately, when Jesus reduced "the whole Law, and also the Prophets" to his twofold commandment of love, he was able to clarify without distorting truth and tradition. Because gospel love is multifaceted, it can encompass the complex dimensions of human life and at the same time provide a simple focus. Viewing spirituality from the point of view of gospel love thus allows us to construct an overview for monitoring the quality of our lives and making the difficult choices that competing claims force upon us.

From the twofold commandment of love, we can derive five distinct loves in scripture: love of God, neighborly love (*diakonia*), communal love (*koinonia*), particular love (*philia*), and self-love.[21] These five loves are distinct, but in reality interact and affect each other. For example, self-love makes it possible for one to love others, whether in friend-ship, ministry, or community. Yet, being loved by others also enables one to love oneself. Similarly, loving one's own life as a precious gift forms the foundation for grateful worship and love of God, the giver of that gift. Conversely, self-hatred provides no motive for loving God the creator. These interrelationships illustrate how a constant dialecti-cal interaction exists among these five loves. These gospel loves express themselves through prayer, ministry, community, friendship, and self-esteem. Based on these gospel values, Donald Goergen has described Christian spirituality in a manner that is holistic in its concern for wholeness and balance. Believing it to be a useful basis for our discus-sion, I have built on his basic scheme to create a similar one for a holistic spirituality (see Figure A). My conceptualization is purely a loose framework for sharing some personal thoughts. There will be no attempt to treat it as a formal model by describing precisely each component and the dynamics of its interacting parts. Furthermore, the elucidation of each of the gospel loves represents my personal reflec-tions and understanding, and may or may not coincide with Goergen's own presentation of these same elements in his scheme.

My holistic framework contains the same ten elements suggested by Goergen: the five gospel loves listed above, along with their comple-mentary opposites which must be included for a complete understand-ing of each love. According to Goergen, "we run the risk of misun-derstanding each of the loves unless we raise the question of how that love might be completed and what its complement is."[22] Thus, only in terms of its complement can each gospel love be appreciated in its wholeness. Consequently, self-esteem must be balanced by self-denial; ministry by leisure; friendship by generativity; prayer by humor; and community by solitude.

Goergen's description of Christian spirituality is useful to a holistic approach in two ways. First, it is comprehensive in including all the loves that we must embody as Christians trying to love as Jesus did. It provides the basis of a realistic spirituality, because it reflects the actual issues and tensions that Christians grapple with in their daily lives. It is a useful guide because it maps out the terrain on which we must struggle to find a way towards Christian wholeness. Second, its com-plementary approach encourages us to give each love its proper due and at the same time challenges us to strike the right balance as we try to

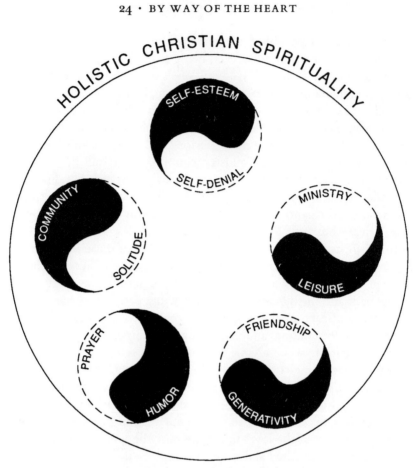

FIGURE A: *Complementary Gospel Values*

incorporate these loves into our nitty-gritty lives. Modeled on Goergen's basic scheme, the representation pictured in Figure A is a way of imaging a holistic Christian spirituality. Utilizing this framework, let us now explore some of the issues involved in living out these biblical loves in an integrated way.

CHAPTER TWO

HOLISTIC SPIRITUALITY: INTEGRATING GOSPEL LOVES

"The silence of prayer orders all the lesser things to go through a door
opening to the one thing, the primary voice of God."[1]
ANN AND BARRY ULANOV, *Primary Speech*

LOVING AS AN ART

Describing love as an art, Erich Fromm asserts that proficiency in loving comes only through practice.[2] The same can be said of the habits of the heart that enable people to imitate the love of Jesus. Christian life can be seen as a practicum or internship for developing those loving habits. Based on gospel loves, holistic spirituality provides a framework that can help all Christians better assess how their love-life is going. They can, for example, ask themselves: "Do I love myself enough so that I can be a person-for-others without betraying my own self out of guilt?" "What is the balance of ministry and leisure in my life?" "In my commitment to community, am I careful to integrate needed solitude to keep my continued involvement fresh and free?" "What is the quality of my life of prayer?" "Does my prayer help me to remain in Jesus and thus increase my fruitfulness in ministry and community?" By posing such questions, a holistic spirituality seeks a path that will integrate our lives sufficiently to give us a sense of increasing wholeness and peace.

There is hope for those who strive for unity in their lives. Martin

Buber discusses this hope in a story about a man struggling to move from being a "divided, complicated, contradictory soul" to being "all of a piece."[3]

> A hasid of the Rabbi of Lublin once fasted from one Sabbath to the next. On Friday afternoon he began to suffer such cruel thirst that he thought he would die. He saw a well, went up to it, and prepared to drink. But instantly he realized that because of one brief hour he had still to endure, he was about to destroy the work of the entire week. He did not drink and went away from the well. Then he was touched by a feeling of pride for having passed this difficult test. When he became aware of it, he said to himself, "Better I go and drink than let my heart fall prey to pride." He went back to the well, but just as he was going to bend down to draw water, he noticed that his thirst had disappeared. When the Sabbath had begun, he entered his teacher's house. "Patchwork!" the rabbi called to him, as he crossed the threshold.[4]

When Buber first heard this story as a youth, he was struck by the harsh manner in which the master treated his earnest, though faltering, disciple. Years later, he came to realize the insight embedded in this tale from tradition. "The object of the reproof is the advance and subsequent retreat; it is the wavering, shilly-shallying character of the man's doing that makes it questionable."[5] Opposed to "patchwork" is work "all of a piece," which Buber suggests can be attained only by "being a united soul." In this, Buber echoes Kierkegaard's advice to his disciple to strive for "purity of heart," which is "to will one thing."[6] Here also the words of Deuteronomy resound: "What does Yahweh your God ask of you? Only this: . . . to love . . . Yahweh your God with all your heart and all your soul" (Deut 10:12). To become "a united soul" and to acquire "purity of heart," one must learn to love all things in God and God in all things.

For Buber, the teaching implied in the rabbi's criticism is hopeful: divine help is available to help persons to unify their souls. The person with the divided, complicated, contradictory soul is not helpless; the core of one's soul, "the divine force in its depths, is capable of acting upon it, changing it, binding the conflicting forces together, amalgamating the diverging elements—is capable of unifying it."[7] Thus, the God who calls us to be whole is also the one who will bring it about. "Deep within them I will plant my Law, writing it on their hearts.

Then I will be their God and they shall be my people. There will be no further need for neighbor to try to teach neighbor, or brother to say to brother, 'Learn to know Yahweh!' No, they will all know me" (Jer 31:33–34). While our own efforts are important and can bring about a certain feeling of wholeness at times they, like the hasid's asceticism, will ultimately not achieve the permanent unity we desire. That unity will arrive gratuitously from the hand of God only after a lifetime of effort on our part. While we wait to enjoy the unity that will finally harmonize the loves of our lives, we are called to work always for that unification. The following discussion of some common issues and difficulties involved in unifying the love of self, neighbor and God is intended to illumine our practice of love.

(A) Self-Esteem and Self-Denial

In discussing gospel loves within a holistic framework, self-love must be looked at first. Some people may quickly take this to reinforce their prejudice that anything labeled "holistic" is simply a clever way of disguising a bourgeois phenomenon narrowly centered on the self. However, self-esteem demands prior consideration because all other loves limp without a footing in self-love. The psychological prerequisite for all other loves, healthy self-regard makes the leap from narcissism to altruism possible. Self-hatred blocks people from loving others and self-rejection often leads to a rejection of God. According to theologian Johannes Metz, a person's self-acceptance is the basis of the Christian creed because assent to God begins with one's sincere assent to oneself, just as sinful flight from God starts in one's flight from oneself.[8] Thus, the serious absence of self-esteem renders people impotent to love and incapable of fulfilling the twofold commandment of Jesus. We have generally overlooked the ethical and religious scope of self-esteem or love of self. Understood correctly, one's "yes" to self "may be regarded as the 'categorical imperative' of the Christian faith: You shall lovingly accept the humanity entrusted to you! . . . You shall embrace yourself!"[9]

Far from achieving self-love with a kind of narcissistic ease, we often find self-acceptance a difficult struggle. We are constantly tempted with self-rejection. Inner voices disturb our peace and tell us that we are not good-looking enough, not smart enough, not rich enough, not talented enough. Advertisements displaying societally acclaimed examples of successful and beautiful people either create or reinforce our inner doubts. On college campuses, the incidences of depression and suicide are growing indications that poor self-worth is a serious problem. Given these conditions, it is not difficult to concur with Metz's insight into why self-love was commanded by God. "Knowing the temptation which humanity itself is," knowing how readily we try to flee the "harsh distress of the human situation," and "knowing how difficult it is to bear with ourselves, we can then understand why God had to prescribe 'self-love' as a virtue and one of the great commandments."[10]

The struggle with self-acceptance is complicated by the fact that it cannot be selective. It is futile to conduct an inventory of ourselves, claiming some parts as good and discarding others as undesirable. Psychologically speaking, healthy self-acceptance cannot be based on denial and projection. Maturity will elude us as long as we try to disown unattractive parts of ourselves and project them onto others. As a popular retreat master used to put it, "Maturity comes when we stop blaming God for making us the way we are!" Only by embracing the totality of who we are as people uniquely fashioned by the Lord can we progress spiritually. Paradoxically, this acceptance, instead of leading to self-complacency, can be the beginning of growthful change. Acceptance allows the walls of self-defensiveness to crumble and permits the pentecostal winds of conversion to blow freely throughout the self. Energies formerly wasted on battling the truth of who we are can be converted to peaceful reconstruction of the self under the guidance of God's spirit. Factored into the reality of Christian self-acceptance is the humble acknowledgment that at every point in our lives we are called to conversion. The Lord's creative power is continually at work in us, who as creatures, are radically unfinished in ourselves, and yet filled with stunning grace. Our personhood is oriented to completions that are received rather than achieved. Capturing the spirit of this truth, a popular poster states, "Please be patient. The Lord is not finished with me yet!"

A Zen master in San Francisco is said to have assigned this mantra to his enlightenment-seeking disciples: "What you are is enough! What you have is enough!" Through repetition and internalization, the mantra was meant to calm the inner storm of self-dissatisfaction. The wisdom of the Zen master's guidance is clear. Because it is easier to say "no" instead of "yes" to ourselves, all asceticism must first be designed to serve this great "yes." But for Christians, no asceticism alone can achieve self-love. Only the Lord's grace can. Unlike Zen Buddhists, Christians must achieve love of self not by any ascetical repetition of spiritual mantras, but by receiving it as a gift from God. At the start of his *Spiritual Exercises,* a set of prayer experiences designed by St. Ignatius of Loyola to share his mystical graces with others, the retreatant is asked to pray for the grace to know in a deeply felt way that "I am limited, yet loved; sinful, yet good."

Ultimately, self-acceptance must be based on an act of faith in the Lord who created us and deemed us to be good. In our self-denigrating way, we too often refuse to believe that "God does not make junk!" Thus we need to experience a conversion in regards to ourselves—a fundamental shift from being self-depreciative to being self-appreciative. Based on the unconditional acceptance of God who delights in us, we are challenged to affirm our radical goodness. Such a conversion will manifest itself psychologically as a growing realization that "I am an important, lovable, useful human being, that people like me, show their affection, and enjoy my presence." Such a conversion would also help me realize that I am an individual with my own needs as well as my own special gifts and talents—a unique identity in the world.

Paul Tillich links this kind of self-acceptance with faith, which he defines as the courage to accept our acceptance despite feelings of unacceptability.[11] This self-affirming faith comes only when a person is struck by God's grace. He described this identity conversion beautifully in a sermon, entitled "You Are Accepted."[12]

> Do you know what it means to be struck by grace? . . . We cannot transform our lives, unless we allow them to be transformed by the stroke of grace. It happens or it does not happen. And certainly it does not happen if we try to force it upon ourselves, just as it shall not happen so long as we think, in our self-complacency, that we have no need of it. Grace strikes us when we are in great pain and restlessness. It strikes us when, year after year, the longed-for perfection of life does not appear, when the old compulsions reign within us as they have for decades, when despair destroys all joy and courage. Sometimes at that moment a shaft of light breaks into our darkness, and it is as though a voice were saying: "You are accepted. You are

accepted," accepted by that which is greater than you, and the name of which you do not know. Do not ask for the name now, perhaps you will find it later. Do not try to do anything now; perhaps later you will do much. Do not seek for anything; do not perform anything; do not intend anything. Simply accept the fact that you are accepted. If that happens to us, we experience grace. . . .

Thus, fulfillment of the gospel commandment to love ourselves is made possible when grace convinces us of our acceptability through our experience of being accepted by one who is greater than ourselves. This identity conversion is a pure gift. We cannot compel ourselves to accept ourselves. We cannot force others to accept themselves. "But sometimes it happens that we receive the power to say 'yes' to ourselves, that peace enters into us and makes us whole, that self-hatred and self-contempt disappear, and that our self is reunited with itself. Then we can say that grace has come upon us."[3] Shug, in Alice Walker's *The Color Purple,* describes the feeling of wholeness that comes with the amazing grace of self-acceptance based on God's love:

> One day when I was feeling like a motherless child, which I was, it come to me: that feeling of being part of everything, not separated at all. I knew that if I cut a tree, my arm would bleed. And I laughed and I cried and I run all round the house. I knew just what it was. In fact, when it happen, you can't miss it.[4]

This conversion that brings about a fundamental shift in attitude can be quite dramatic at times, but generally it is not a once-and-for-all experience. Normally, it is a prolonged process, though its explicit acknowledgment may be concentrated in a few momentous judgments and decisions.[5] Moments of deep consolation in prayer that assure us of God's unshakable love and our absolute lovableness, for example, are important religious experiences, but their impact often diminishes with the passage of time. Thus, Ignatius of Loyola advises people to record these precious moments of graced insight as a support for times when forgetfulness plunges them once again into the chasm of self-doubt.[6] At these moments of desolation, he reminds them to wait in hope for the return of the Lord's affirming visitations.[7]

When people were healed by Jesus, they often found themselves doubly blessed. The grateful leper, for example, was not only cleansed of his unsightly wounds, but was also given back the uniquely human capacity to appreciate and give thanks (Lk 17:11–19). In healing people, Jesus empowered them to reach out to others and to proclaim the Good News. The Gerasene demoniac, screeching out his identity as "legion," was not only healed of his fragmentation and self-destructiveness, but was also given a share in the ministry of Jesus. The cured man "went off and proceeded to spread [*kerussein*] throughout the Decapolis all that Jesus had done for him (Mk 5:20). The verb *kerussein* is used in a technical way in Mark to imply official preaching by a disciple.

As in the case of the demoniac, our unhealed wounds are like binding chains that prevent us from reaching out to others in ministry and community. Pain often imprisons us in caves of isolation and renders us impotent to love others as Jesus did. Thus, a holistic spirituality is misunderstood if it seems in any way to smack of narcissism when encouraging self-esteem among Christians. Ironically, narcissistic behavior often stems from a severe deficit, not an abundance, of self-love. Egotistical preoccupation with keeping the body beautiful or staying in the limelight often derives from a shaky sense of self. Sometimes poor self-worth masquerades itself in seemingly loving behavior, as in the case of a co-dependent spouse who cannot say "no" to his or her addicted partner. This kind of false altruism is deadly for it abets the addiction which should instead be confronted by "tough love," a term used in Alcoholics Anonymous. To deal with an addict with tough love, however, requires a strong sense of self-regard; poor self-worth easily leads a co-dependent into a conspiracy of denial. Another example of poor self-esteem disguising itself as altruism is the compulsive helper (often the adult child of an alcoholic) who is plagued with an excessive sense of responsibility. So, when a holistic spirituality promotes self-love, it is paradoxically encouraging authentic altruism, not narcissism.

Self-love establishes the necessary condition that makes going beyond one's self (self-transcendence) possible. The grace that enables us to accept ourselves, simultaneously stirs up within us an urge to break down the walls that separate us from others. In Tillich's words, "we experience the grace of being able to accept the life of another, even if it be hostile and harmful to us, for, through grace, we know that it belongs to the same God to which we belong, and by which we have been accepted."[18]

The love of self prescribed by Jesus is fully understood only when juxtaposed with the gospel value of self-denial. Unfortunately, the notion of self-denial has suffered so many aberrations throughout the history of Christian spirituality that it frequently triggers off a knee-jerk rejection among some Christians. Brutal scourgings, severe fasts, and other harsh ascetical practices that harm the body have been justified in the name of self-denial. Even such saints as Ignatius of Loyola and Francis of Assisi damaged their health through excessive bodily mortifications which they later regretted. Having been mistakenly accustomed to rationalizing such unchristian views as repression of the body, denigration of sexuality, and devaluation of the earth, self-denial understandably evokes negative feelings among many people. However, no spirituality can be biblically-based and authentically Christian without giving self-denial its proper place. A holistic spirituality must, therefore, reaffirm the value of self-denial while divesting it of distorted meanings.

Since self-denial as the condition of following Christ finds its source in the gospels (Mk 8:34–38; Mt 10:38–39; 16:24–28; Lk 9:23–27; 24:26–27; Jn 12:25), it is best understood in its New Testament context.[19] Here we find that the purpose of Christian self-denial is entirely positive: it is "for my [Jesus'] sake and for the sake of the gospel" (Mk 8:36), that is, for the promotion of the kingdom of God that has come in Christ. Literally, the Greek term for "deny" means to say "no," to negate. The sweeping "no" to one's self which the gospels encourage finds its meaning in the "yes" which one says to Christ by following him and working for the kingdom. The synoptic context does not support any interpretation of self-denial that would direct it primarily against the earthy or sensual, or any particular class of passions. Rather, self-denial is primarily directed against "one's self," in a precise sense: not I as such, but only insofar as "I" stands in the way of witness for Christ and the gospel, insofar as I resist surrendering myself to the concrete demands of the Kingdom of God. Understood in this way, self-denial refers to my selfishness in the here and now, insofar as my choice in this concrete situation wants to say "no" to the will of God. It is not meant to refer "to some abstract condition which is always present within me and against which I must strive in season and out of season."[20] As W.K. Grossouw puts it, "Self-denial must not be associated with hatred of self or even a lust for destroying, subduing, or humiliating self, such as has frequently occurred in the history of religion."[21]

Thus, the object of self-denial is undefined and cannot be known outside of a particular situation. What is to be denied can only be determined in each particular circumstance by a discernment of what in me, in the here and now, is standing in the way of witnessing to Christ and the gospel. These inner obstacles can be anything that I stubbornly want to dispose of by myself, without any regard for how it will impact on proclaiming the gospel. It can involve matters of finances, diet, or relationships. However, it does not apply to any specific material good in and of itself, but only insofar as it is concretely recognized to be an obstacle to giving oneself for Jesus' sake and for the sake of the gospel. From its scriptural context, then, self-denial is most accurately understood as being directed against any form of selfishness that would make a person unavailable for the service of Christ.

To safeguard the radical goodness of the human person, some women spiritual writers prefer to speak of "transcending" rather than "denying" the self. Acknowledging their debt to Karl Rahner, they attempt to evoke the image of the person as a being open to, and capable of communion with, ultimate Mystery. As such, the self to be transcended is good, not evil.[22] In the same vein, theologian Joseph Powers argues that the principal function of religion is to invite each believer to open himself or herself to the basic mystery of our very selves. Far from settling us in security, religion "should be the principal stimulus to a continual transcendence of any or all of the achievements which define a personal or corporate ego."[23] By reassuring us of the enabling presence of God in human life, religion encourages us to reach out to the mystery of being, indeed, to the mystery of being more than our present self.

However, the movement beyond one's self to others in self-transcending love, first requires a healthy sense of self. Once I was asked for advice by a friend struggling with a decision. Anguishing over the plight of Nicaraguans who feared an imminent invasion by American Marines in 1983, she felt moved to join a group of Americans planning to thwart this suspected invasion by laying their bodies down as a human blockade on the border between Honduras and Nicaragua. Aware of her history of low self-worth, I said to her, "My concern is that you don't seem to love your life enough to justify giving it up."

Because we cannot give what we do not have, self-donation presupposes self-possession. This issue is especially problematic for women, who have been socialized to place the needs of others before their own and thus repress awareness of their own rightful needs, or feel guilty and selfish for having them.[24] But the temptation to swallow the self is not limited to women. Men are also susceptible to this trap. The task of spiritual self-transcendence for Christians thus requires that women and men first grow into and claim their conscious and responsible selfhood.

Psychological and spiritual health does not consist in forfeiting a self, but in keeping the process of self-formation flowing, of continually enlarging the images by which we understand ourselves. A holistic spirituality challenges both professed religious and lay Christians not to cling to the "well-being" of the present, but to strive always for the "more-being" contained in future possibilities. In the words of Jesus, "For anyone who wants to save his life will lose it; but anyone who loses his life for my sake, and for the sake of the gospel, will save it" (Mk 8:35–36).

(B) Ministry and Leisure

Self-transcendence for the sake of Christ and the gospel moves us into the heart of Christian ministry. As the expression of love of neighbor, ministry must be a part of every Christian's life. Yet, even after the 1987 Synod on the Laity in Rome, controversy still stalks the question of lay ministry and arguments still abound. Should the term "ministry" be restricted to those with public and stable roles in the church's liturgical and governmental life? Or should it also refer to the wide variety of Christian action that continues Christ's presence in the world today? Some say an exclusive use of the term is divisive and perpetuates the split between the clergy and the lay. Others contend that loosely labeling every good deed a Christian does as "ministry" robs the term of precision and usefulness. What follows here is yet another strong voice chiming in on this heated debate.

Ministry has always been acknowledged to be an essential part of priesthood and religious life. But, until recent years, its important place in the life of lay Christians has not been sufficiently stressed. Two misconceptions have long caused confusion and thereby crippled ministry in the church. The first is that ministry is the exclusive right of ordained priests, professed religious, or other official church ministers.

The second is that lay Christians do not have a direct right to share in the ministry of Jesus, but can enjoy peripheral participation to the extent that they are invited by the hierarchy.

Vatican II has corrected these erroneous notions. According to the council, Christians receive the gift of ministry directly through baptism and confirmation and are directly commissioned by the Lord.[25] Thus, ministry is an essential aspect of being a Christian and not something reserved for a few. Ordination is but one way by which the Christian community officially recognizes the various charisms and ministries needed for the accomplishment of its mission. While reaffirming the special significance of the ordained priesthood as a sacrament, it is important to remember that it is but one ministry among others in the church. Thus, while ordination presupposes ministry, ministry does not necessarily require ordination. By reminding us that the call to serve comes directly from the risen Christ, the council challenges us to acknowledge each person's rightful ministry in the church.

Before leaving them, Jesus commissioned the apostles and the community formed by him to continue his ministry. Just as he was sent by the Father, so he sent his followers to proclaim the good news of God's benevolent reign over a kingdom already begun but not yet flourishing. Participation in the ministry of Jesus means sharing his single-minded commitment to announcing God's saving intervention in human life. Ministry, in its broadest scriptural sense, is any human activity that is seen as a continuation of Jesus' own work for the sake of the kingdom.

The ministry of lay Christians must be understood in a broad and inclusive way. Recently lay involvement in parish ministry has contributed greatly to the grassroots renewal of the local church. But a narrow vision of the laity's role creeps in when excessive emphasis is placed on the work of lay persons *within* the church, in church-related activities. Lay ministry should not be reduced to "official" or "parish" ministry. The recent preoccupation in some places with engaging lay people in parochial and diocesan ministries can lead to a devaluation of the apostolic significance of the ordinary work of Christians in the marketplace and in the home. Many Christians are already acting in ways that embody the risen Jesus' ministry to people today. When they make explicit the connection between what they are doing and the continuation of Christ's actions on behalf of others in the present, their activities can clearly be recognized as ministry.

As the apostle (literally, "the sent one") of God par excellence, Jesus explained his ministry as doing "the works which the Father has granted me to accomplish" (Jn 5:36). His ministry—that is, everything he engaged in to accomplish his mission—can be viewed in three aspects: the kerygmatic, the koinoniac, and the diaconal. In short, Jesus ministered:

(1) by announcing God's forgiveness and acceptance of all (the kerygmatic aspect);
(2) by forming a community that would embody this gracious love of God for all in concrete relationships (the koinoniac aspect);
(3) by performing acts of service and justice that would demonstrate that the kingdom of God has indeed arrived (the diaconal aspect).

These three aspects of Jesus' ministry provide a useful framework for understanding how all Christians can carry on the ministry of Jesus in their daily lives. Like Jesus, Christians in all walks of life can minister by proclaiming the good news (1) through the language of words, (2) through the language of relationships, and (3) through the language of works.

The kerygmatic dimension of lay ministry does not require lay persons to preach in any formal way. Rather, it is a call to all Christians "to share the light of faith."[26] Simply to share one's faith in the ordinary context of one's life is to minister. Thus, sharing the light of faith is not the sole responsibility of catechists, whether professionals or volunteers. Nor should it be restricted to formal teaching in a classroom. Proclaiming the gospel is the proper work of the whole Christian community.

Parents minister to their children kerygmatically when they teach them how to pray or when they hand on their creedal faith. Spouses minister to each other through their words of mutual reassurance during difficult times, and their encouragement to trust in a God who makes all things possible. Friends minister mutually when they share their experiences of the presence of God in their lives. And adult children minister to aging and sick parents when they speak a tender word of trust in a God who always brings good out of everything. In such ways, Christians continue Jesus' joyful proclamation that the Lord of history is a gracious God intimately involved in our lives: to save us, to make us whole, and to bring us to the fullness of life.

Our relationships can also take on the nature of ministry. They can embody God's love in ways that jolt people into realizing that God's earthly reign has already started and is observable in the way Christians treat each other. Parents minister relationally when their unconditional acceptance makes it possible for their children to believe in a God of unconditional love. They also minister when their generous forgiveness enables their children to believe in a God who is freely forgiving of wayward followers. The sexual union of husbands and wives is ministerial when it sparks off intimate insights into the nature of a God who is Love. And the enduring faithfulness of old friends is ministerial when it provides the empirical grounds for believing in the abiding faithfulness of a God who is the Faithful One (Is 49:15–16).

These various embodiments of love among parents, children, and friends enhance our ability to experience God in the community of the church. As Shug puts it in her simple yet wise way in *The Color Purple,* God is most tangibly felt in church when people bring with them the Lord whom they have already experienced in daily life.

> She say, Celie, tell the truth, have you ever found God in church? I never did. I just found a bunch of folks hoping for him to show. Any God I ever felt in church I brought in with me. And I think all the other folks did too. They come to church to *share* God, not find God.
>
> Some folks didn't have him to share, I said. They the ones didn't speak to me while I was there struggling with my big belly and Mr. _____ children.[27]

Shug's words make down-to-earth sense about what ministering through relationships entails. Mark's gospel provides a further illustration in the story of the cure of a leper (1:40–45). Crying out for healing, a leper approaches Jesus. Jesus attends carefully to the afflicted suppliant, to his words and actions. Then, moved with compassion, he reaches out to touch the diseased person. Jesus' touch is therapeutic. The leper is healed. In this episode, we notice a three-fold dynamic that characterizes many of Jesus' ministerial encounters: (1) he is keenly aware of his interpersonal environment, sensitive to the needs of the people around him; (2) he lets what he perceives stir him to compassion; and (3) moved by compassion, he reaches out to help.

Our relationships become ministry when they contain Jesus' compassionate concern and remind others that the risen Jesus is still at work. When we view ministry in this light, the opportunities to minister through our various relationships are unlimited. Through our actions the risen Lord continues today his ministry of freeing and healing people.

The ministry of Jesus today must also take the form of a faith that does justice and is expressed in service, especially on behalf of the poor, the alienated, and the oppressed. This service can occur on three different levels. First, it can take the form of direct aid, as in serving on a food line at a soup kitchen or assisting in a day-care center for children of poor working mothers. Second, it can involve working in union with the poor, as in community organizing, to bring about changes that improve their plight; or it can take the form, for instance, of accompanying displaced Salvadorean peasants who risk physical retaliation by returning to their village. Third, service for the poor and dispossessed such as the work done by the Center of Concern and Network in Washington, D.C., can embrace educational and political action aimed at reforming unjust social structures.

Ministry, the active hands and arms of love, must be directed to all who make up the mystical body, that is, the whole Christ. To love the whole Christ means that no one (be he or she a jobless factory worker or a skid-row dropout, a repentant television evangelist or a bashed-up homosexual) can fall outside the Christian's perimeter of concern. In the parable of the Good Samaritan (Lk 10:25–37), Jesus challenged his followers to expand their understanding of neighbor to include those who do not share the same race, religion, culture or class. Moreover, Christian love of neighbor cannot stop with words; it must be shown in concrete acts of caring. Following the three-fold dynamic of Jesus' own ministerial encounters, the Good Samaritan (truly a lay minister, as opposed to the priest and the Levite) saw the victim, "had compassion, and went to him and bound up his wounds, pouring on oil and wine; then he set him on his beast and brought him to an inn, and took care of him." The Samaritan is a minister in the mode of Jesus. Awareness, compassion, and caring response characterize his service on behalf of a needy neighbor. In short, service takes on the nature of ministry when it is seen as a continuation of the ministry of Jesus for those in need. Such service becomes the observable evidence of Christ's present action and constitutes a nonverbal proclamation of the kingdom in our midst. As with Christ, who identified himself with "the least of these my brethren" (Mt 25:40), our self-identity must continue to grow so that more and more people can find a place within the boundaries of our hearts. More will be said about this important aspect of Christian growth in Chapter VII, which delineates how gospel poverty advances developmental growth by calling for the ongoing expansion of the ways we define ourselves.

To stay vibrant, ministry must be balanced by leisure. How to achieve the kind of leisure that nurtures fruitful ministry confounds many today. Leisure is a difficult thing for some people to legitimize in a society like ours that is so oriented towards work and productivity. At the same time, we are paradoxically a society that *works at* and spends large amounts of time and money for leisure, more than many other societies. In any case, any spirituality that leaves out leisure will lack depth and balance because leisure lies at the heart of prayer, solitude, community, and friendship. Our relationship with ourselves, others, and God requires that quality time be devoted to such "non-productive" activities as prayer and play, solitude and interpersonal sharing. Without leisure we not only jeopardize our humanity, but also endanger the Spirit's work in our lives. Thus leisure must always temper ministry to prevent our spirituality from being lopsided.

Many ministers, both religious and lay, struggle with taking time off for prayer, rest, and recreation. Time off is either such a low priority that it is not regularly scheduled or is taken reluctantly. Often it is spoiled by feelings of guilt and anxiety. Such people make themselves very vulnerable to overwork and the state of joyless exhaustion popularly known as "burnout."[28]

The absence of leisure, especially when it results in burnout and demoralization, can have serious degenerative effects in one's life and ministry. While workers in any field are susceptible to overwork, ministers and others in the helping professions are prime candidates for burnout. Being zealous in the Lord's work and in the service of others is certainly to be praised. Nevertheless, zealous service can often subtly become self-serving, if not monitored by ongoing reflection. A need to be needed, for example, can cause a counselor to spend excessive amounts of time with his clients, thus cultivating immature dependency. Or the need to vent his suppressed anger toward his parents may keep a community organizer always on the firing line against the people at City Hall. Leisure allows for the kind of critical self-awareness that can expose such self-serving behaviors.

Ministers who do not appropriate leisure into their lives can be subtly deluded. St. Ignatius of Loyola, in his famous "Rules for the Discernment of Spirits," talks about how good people are tempted. Unlike those whose orientation is to evil and who are enticed in crude ways, people trying to better their lives are lured in a subtle fashion, under the guise of a good.[29] Working long and grueling hours for others, for example, may initially glitter as gold, appearing as a good. But when it leads to exhaustion and the exclusion of prayer, solitude and in-depth relationships with others, it in fact turns out to be fool's gold. What began as a seeming good, ends as an evil because of the degeneration it causes.

Overwork can be seductive because it often presents itself as a solution to many of the problems that plague us. It offers a respectable rationale to justify escape from facing anguishing personal issues and avoidance of interpersonal difficulties. In reality, it is a pseudo-solution. When left unchecked, excessive work destroys the holistic balance in one's life and leads ultimately to the deterioration of one's inner life and relationships.

Often leading to spiritual dissolution, overwork can be combated best when some of its underlying causes are brought to light. Some people are addicted to their work, know the underlying dynamics of their addiction, and choose to continue in their ways. Other people, however, want to break out of the prison of "workaholism." For these persons, simple awareness of the factors contributing to burnout can help them rearrange unhealthy work patterns. Two categories of causes contribute to workaholism among ministers and helpers. The first relates to obstacles to leisure stemming from unconscious motives. The second deals with obstacles attached to the nature of ministry itself.

Unconscious motivation can destroy the capacity of ministers to keep work in proper balance. For instance, a minister driven by hidden ambition to be promoted to high office or to build up a reputation may be compulsive about work. His or her drivenness is energized more by the spirit of careerism than by the spirit of generous service. Careerism of any kind saps the spirit of ministry from apostolic labor. It causes self-striving to replace service to others. Careerists ask, "What's in this for me?" Christ-like ministers ask, "How can I be of help?"

The unconscious need to compensate for a poor sense of self-worth may also result in workaholic ministers. In such cases, there is an unconscious identification of one's worth with one's performance or an urge to prove one's worth through work. Achievement and success become indispensable props to secure a shaky identity. Dependent on constant affirmation for survival, such fragile egos are easily shaken by the fear of performing poorly or failing. This kind of insecurity, like the dry rot of a forest fire, fuels the consuming flames of exhaustion.

The workaholism of some ministers originates in the need to fill up voids in their affective life. Frustrated celibates, as well as those entangled in unhappy marriages or relationships, are sometimes susceptible to this trap. Sublimating sexual energies into creative outlets in ministry is legitimate and useful. But an excessive investment in work as a way of dealing with the tensions of celibate or married life is ultimately dysfunctional. Rather than alleviating loneliness, overwork exacerbates it. A vicious cycle operates in the lives of many contemporary ministers. They rationalize their workaholism by complaining that community or family living is dead. Then they justify their lack of investment in rectory or family life by protesting that their ministerial labors have drained them of the needed energy and time. The unavoidable truth is this: the building of intimate relationships that could alleviate the loneliness of ministers requires freedom from other kinds of building, that is, work and productivity. It requires leisure and just "wasting time" with others.

Workaholics make dreadful companions. Their drivenness often produces neurotic attitudes and negative emotions. Blind to their unconscious need to compensate for some inner lack, they may be quick to condemn others who do not imitate their compulsive work pattern. Self-righteously, they disdain others for their laziness: "Why don't they do a decent day's work? All they do is sit around and share!" It is common for these same workaholic ministers to complain that: "No one appreciates what I do." This self-pitying attitude quickly leads to bitterness, anger, and alienation.

A second set of obstacles to leisure arises from the nature of ministry itself. John Sanford, an Episcopal priest and Jungian analyst, summarizes succinctly some of the factors that lead to burnout among ministers:[30]

1. *The job of the ministering person is never finished.* Unlike people in other occupations where there is definite termination to tasks, ministers often feel their work is never finished because they face a seemingly unending onslaught of parish functions and persons to counsel. The objective in so many forms of ministry is so open-ended that it leads to the problem of limitless tasks. And the result is that many ministers fail to assess realistically when they have completed an honest day's work so they can close shop for the day and go home. When ministers, like priests and religious, live where they work, the matter is further complicated and the danger of overwork even greater.

2. *The ministering person cannot always tell if his or her work is having any results.* Because the results of a minister's toil are often intangible, a sense of uncertainty can plague ministers, leaving them questioning whether they are actually accomplishing anything. On bad days, self-doubt can be demoralizing and crippling.

3. *The work of the ministering person is repetitive.* The liturgical season or the school calendar contains inevitable annual events. And pastoral care of individuals and families is ongoing; one troubled person terminates counseling only to be replaced by another. And so it goes in many ministries in what can seem like an interminably repetitive cycle. Sometimes, burnout is due more to boredom than physical exhaustion.

4. *The ministering person is dealing constantly with people's expectations.* Not only are ministers burdened by the diverse expectations of a broad constituency, these expectations are often conflicting. Interest groups in parishes and schools, for instance, may make contradictory demands on ministers. Striving to reconcile these expectations will inevitably cause emotional strain. If ministers possess an excessive need to please or rely on the approval of parishioners for retaining their posts, then they will be even more in danger of burnout. Chapter V will deal with the problem of burdensome "shoulds" and suggest ways of dealing with them.

To counteract burnout, two attitudes can restore the proper harmony between work and leisure: first, stronger faith in ourselves as persons made worthwhile by God's love and not by our achievements; second, greater trust in God's power at work in the world today. To awaken to the insight that God has already established our goodness is to diminish the need to prove ourselves. Those who do not feel securely established by God's love struggle to establish themselves in others' minds. Ironically, more prayer and less work would be more productive. Prayer can help them find their identity before God and discover anew that they are the apple of God's eyes. In prayer, we allow our theological identity as individuals utterly loved by God to infuse our often shaky psychological identity.

St. Ignatius' "Contemplation for Attaining Divine Love" offers a theological basis for trust in God's power. For Ignatius, we live in a divine milieu because God pervades all creation. But divinity not only dwells in all things, divine power continues to labor in all creation for our sake. Ignatius asks us "to consider how God works and labors for me in all creatures upon the face of the earth . . . in the heavens, the elements, the plants, the fruits, the cattle . . . [God] gives being, conserves them, confers life and sensation."[31] Because the mighty power of God is always preserving creation in being, ministers can afford to take time off for leisure!

Ministry, for Ignatius, is primarily the action of God. Human beings are given a share in God's action through their call to ministry. At La Storta, about ten kilometers from Rome, Ignatius had a vision of himself being placed by the Father next to Jesus carrying the cross. This vision gave shape to his image of ministry: to minister is to be intimately juxtaposed with Jesus carrying the cross. It is to be invited by God to be closely associated with Jesus, who even now continues to work for the redemption of the world. In ministry, then, God is the principal worker and we are co-workers. As such, we are not indispensable. God's sustaining action will not cease when ministers exercise prudent self-care by taking time off for leisure and solitude. In fact, workaholic ministers who are careless with their health should be told what a religious superior once told a member of his staff: "If you don't stop to admire the daisies, you'll be pushing them up soon."

(C) Friendship and Generativity

Friendship, like leisure, is often sacrificed on the altar of pragmatic concerns. Because keeping in touch with cherished friends is not as pressing as getting the shopping or the office report done, it is usually put off until another time. Unfortunately, convenient times for foster-ing friendships become less and less as the pace of our lives quickens. Friendship for Christians cannot be viewed as a frill that gets elimi-nated when time and resources shrink. The spiritual journey requires close friends—whether they be one's spouse, a spiritual companion, or a life-long comrade. God created Eve so that Adam would not have to struggle through life alone. And Jesus sent the disciples out on their missionary journey in pairs so that their companionship would be a support, especially in those inhospitable towns from which they were advised to leave after shaking the dust from their sandals.

While philosophers throughout the ages have written eloquently of friendship's importance, Jesus affirmed it as a gospel value. In his close ties with Mary and Martha, and especially in his love of Lazarus, Jesus left no room for doubt that Christians who are commanded to love as he did must cherish human friendship. Unfortunately, some Christians still need to be convinced of the value of friendship in Christian living. For example, a spirituality that privatizes one's relationship with God, expressed in a "Jesus-and-me" mentality, easily slips into viewing friendship as superfluous. "With Jesus as my friend, I don't need any-one else" reflects such an outlook. Directly or indirectly, this way of thinking was for years instilled in priests and religious, who were warned that deep human friendship could weaken the intensity of their relationship with Christ and also endanger their vow of chastity. They were cautioned against the dangers of "particular friendships." Because human intimacy is vitally needed for living chastely, the topic of par-ticular friendships will be treated separately in Chapter VI. Here the discussion explores the importance of friendship in Christian living.

Jesus emphasized the value of friendship by having close friends of his own. But more importantly, he used the love of friendship to describe the very meaning of his death on the cross. In the intimate setting of the Last Supper, Jesus explained the significance of the death he was about to face: "[One] can have no greater love than to lay down [one's] life for [one's] friends. You are my friends" (Jn 15:13–14). Jesus clearly saw the meaning of his death as an act of love on behalf of friends.

The raising of Lazarus illustrates this profound truth. When notified of his friend's condition, Jesus was noticeably moved by love for Lazarus. At the sight of Mary's tears and those of the Jews, "Jesus said in great distress, with a sigh that came straight from the heart, 'Where have you put him?' . . . Jesus wept; and the Jews said, 'See how much he loved him!' " (Jn 11:33–35). The raising up of Lazarus, seen in the dramatic unfolding of John's passion narrative, was a highly symbolic act. In committing himself to save his friend, Jesus set in motion his own death. The charged political atmosphere in Jerusalem pressured the chief priests and Pharisees to caucus quickly and decide how to react to the growing excitement Jesus was arousing by "working all these signs." They feared that the swelling popular support for Jesus would threaten the Romans and compel them to "come and destroy the Holy Place and our nation." Thus, the high priest spoke for the group: "You don't seem to have grasped the situation at all; you fail to see that it is better for one man to die for the people, than for the whole nation to be destroyed" (Jn 11:49–50). Johannine irony is operative here, because in a way deeper than the high priest understood, Jesus embraced death himself rather than have all the people destroyed. Jesus' act of love for a friend ended up costing him his life. "From that day they were determined to kill him" (Jn 11:54). Consequently, to love as Jesus did requires a serious commitment to the love of friendship.

Friendship is also an important source of divine revelation, because intimate knowledge of a friend can reveal the face of God. To the apostle Philip's request to "see the Father," Jesus responded, "To have seen me is to have seen the Father, so how can you say, 'Let us see the Father?' " (Jn 14:9–10). Enigmatic as it may sound, Jesus' response comes down to this: He can show us what God is only by the way he reflects God in his own humanity. He can reveal the face of the Father only by showing us his own face.[32] Theologian Monika Hellwig summarizes clearly the truth of how the Father is revealed in our intimate knowledge of a friend: "As Christians, we see Jesus as the unique image of God in humanity. But we also see Jesus as prototypical and inclusive of us all, drawing us into his witness and his ministry of reconciliation and reconstruction, making us in union with himself a kind of temple where God is to be encountered, experienced and brought to others."[33] Therefore, intimate friendships, which embody the love of Christ, can be for us a kind of temple where we can see the face of God.

Hellwig's insight is beautifully illustrated by a story about how two brothers' love for each other transformed their friendship into a temple, where God was made known.

Time before time, when the world was young, two brothers shared a field and a mill, each night dividing evenly the grain they had ground together during the day. One brother lived alone; the other had a wife and a large family. Now the single brother thought to himself one day, "It isn't really fair that we divide the grain evenly. I have only myself to care for, but my brother has children to feed." So each night he secretly took some of his grain to his brother's granary to see that he was never without.

But the married brother said to himself one day, "It isn't really fair that we divide the grain evenly, because I have children to provide for me in my old age, but my brother has no one. What will he do when he's old?" So every night he secretly took some of *his* grain to his brother's granary. As a result, both of them always found their supply of grain mysteriously replenished each morning.

Then one night they met each other halfway between their two houses, suddenly realized what had been happening, and embraced each other in love. The story is that God witnessed their meeting and proclaimed, "This is a holy place—a place of love—and here it is that my temple shall be built." And so it was. The holy place, where God is made known to . . . people, is the place where human beings discover each other in love.[34]

Friendship is a locus of divine revelation because, as this story points out, the Absolute is known in the personal.

Friends reveal God to each other because faith sharing is an important element of Christian friendship. Addressing his disciples in the intimate context of the Last Supper, Jesus tells them, "I call you friends because I have made known to you everything I have learned from my Father" (Jn 15:15b). Here we see that what constitutes a friendship is the intimacy of sharing that takes place in the relationship. As Jesus put it, "I shall not call you servants any more, because a servant does not know his master's business" (v. 15). Jesus honors his disciples as friends precisely by sharing the contents of his communication with God. Sharing one's religious experience and faith is central to Christian friendship.

Thus, all Christians, especially those who tend to devalue human friendship, are challenged to integrate the love of friendship into their spirituality. The exhortation that Jesuits received from their 32nd General Congregation about the importance of friendship is equally significant for other religious and lay ministers. Challenging Jesuits to go beyond colleagueship to friendship, the Congregation directed these words to its members: ". . . it is our community ideal that we should be companions not only in the sense of fellow workers in the apostolate, but truly brothers and friends in the Lord."[35] Being "friends in the Lord" is especially important these days when effective ministry relies increasingly on collaboration among equals.

Friendship among Christians must also bear fruit. In other words, generativity must complement the love of friendship. Psychologist Erik Erikson defined generativity as "the concern for establishing and guiding the next generation."[36] In a less technical sense, generativity simply means being fruitful. It is in this sense that the Talmud states, "Three things one should do in the course of one's life: have a child, plant a tree, and write a book."[37] The intimacy that we share with Jesus and with others must be generative in the sense that it benefits others. The image of the vine and branches makes this point very clear. The metaphor richly captures a dynamic tension that must characterize all relationships of intimacy among Christians. On the one hand, there is the invitation, even exhortation, to "remain in my love" (Jn 15:9). On the other, friendship with Jesus requires that one is open "to go out and to bear fruit" (v. 16). Herein lies the paradoxical nature of Christian friendship: we are called simultaneously to remain with the beloved and to go forth to share that love with others. Christian friendship, in other words, must always be open to the possibility of new life springing forth from it for the sake of the total community and the world.

The love between husband and wife, for example, even while intensely centered on each other, must enrich the lives of others besides. Healthy marriages are those in which the spouses become increasingly good friends and at the same time make themselves a tangible blessing to others. Happy conjugal love has the tendency of transcending the two mates and spilling over into caring actions for their children and those outside the family. Satirist Kurt Vonnegut, in *Cat's Cradle,* termed this kind of love relationship a "karass."[38] A karass is a close-knit unit of love, yet its boundaries are permeable so that others can freely enter in to share its love. In contrast, a "duprass," refers to a relationship in which the partners are so tightly turned in on themselves that no one, not even the children, can break in to share its closeness. Friendships that are generative will resemble a karass, not a duprass.

As a gospel value, generativity pertains to both lay and religious life. One way in which married Christians are generative is when their mutual love issues forth in offspring whom they devotedly nurture. Parenting is often a purifying experience for many. The inevitable struggles that are part of raising children stretch the capacity of parents to love in a sacrificial and gratuitous manner—as Jesus did. In this way, the commitment of parents to generative love is very much part of the process by which parents are made holy and more like Jesus.

Celibates must be equally committed to generative love. While voluntary sexual abstinence precludes producing physical progeny, it should not stifle generativity in celibate lives. Relinquishing the right to bear children need not cripple their ability to love in ways that nurture life. Although Erikson sees generativity being fulfilled directly in parenthood, he also speaks of a sublimated parenthood in which persons willingly direct their caring to those other than their own children. This sublimated parenthood applies to lay people without children of their own, as well as to celibates. Celibates who care for orphans, teach students, and guide others in spiritual direction are in a real way "spiritual fathers and mothers." It is this kind of spiritual progeny that celibate love must generate if it is to remain vital. In their celibate loving, priests and religious must have a sense that they are participating in life and contributing concretely to others' lives. The life-giving quality of their love, not the physical act of procreation, makes for true generativity among those who are celibate for the sake of the kingdom. As with marriage, celibacy can be either sterile or productive. The ideal of celibacy is best seen in a self-forgetful giving that increasingly allows one to love like Jesus—to love in a way that bears fruit for the world.

(D) Prayer and Humor

Prayer, as the human heart reaching out to God, is an essential element of holistic spirituality. Capturing the spirit of prayer, the psalmist says, "Yahweh, hear my voice as I cry! Pity me! Answer me! My heart has said of you, 'Seek [Yahweh's] face.' Yahweh, I do seek your face; do not hide your face from me" (Ps 27:7–8). Prayer reveals a hunger and yearning for God and springs from the felt-realization that human fulfillment can only be found in God. After years of futilely pursuing happiness in worldly pleasures, Augustine came late to realize that "You have made us for yourself, O Lord, and our hearts will remain restless, until they rest in you." The saint's prayer poignantly expresses a central insight into the nature of human happiness: only possessing and being possessed by God can satisfy that deep longing for love implanted in every human heart. Reaching out to God in prayer, therefore, is central to the life of love that Christians are called to live.

In prayer, we are called to let the heart have its sway. The "heart" is that part of us which is drawn toward the Lord by the weight of its own gravity. It is a dormant and undeveloped faculty in many people, and thus needs to be cultivated. Because of the central importance of prayer in the spiritual life of all Christians, Chapter IV will be devoted to holistic approaches to prayer. It is enough for now to assert that prayer is an indispensable part of any spirituality that calls itself Christian.

The conviction in faith that our desire for God in prayer is more than matched by God's desire for us, suggests why prayer should always be accompanied by humor and light-heartedness. The place of humor in the quest for God is well depicted in the amusing story of Zacchaeus, the wealthy tax collector who had to climb a sycamore tree in order to see Jesus pass by because he was too short to see over the crowd. Zacchaeus' encounter with Jesus captures the kind of humor that must complement prayer in a holistic spirituality. It is amusing to imagine an official establishment-figure risking the indignity of clinging to a branch just to glance at an upstart itinerant preacher. The humor of the situation also lies in the incongruity between the awkwardness of Zacchaeus' tree-limb peek at Jesus and the disarming ease of Jesus' presentation of himself to the eager tax collector. Walking straight up to him, Jesus said, with surprising familiarity, "Zacchaeus, come down. Hurry, because I must stay at your house today" (Lk 19:5–6). Jumping off the branch, the diminutive official welcomed Jesus with joy. From being anxious and anonymous, he became joyful and known. And also greatly blessed: "Today salvation has come to this house, because this man too is a son of Abraham; for the Son of Man has come to seek out and save what was lost" (vv. 9–10).

If prayer is the human heart searching for God, humor balances prayer by helping us realize that God, in Jesus, has already "come to seek out and save what was lost." The story of Zacchaeus shows that the human heart's longing for the Lord is matched by a mutuality in the divine heart. Therefore, our search for God can be light-hearted. Our craving for God is to be fulfilled, not frustrated, by the creator who planted it deep within us all. Faith assures us that God searches for us even as we anxiously try to surmount the obstacles that impede our view of the Lord passing by. Humor, then, should alleviate anxiety and foster inner peace. Even in the midst of suffering and trials, we can laugh because we believe that the reign of God is already upon us, that God is present in the world seeking to gift us with salvation.

Humor is holistic because it fosters harmony by preventing us from being too serious about our lives. "Holiness is the capacity to laugh and to play, as well as to pray . . . Only humor allows us to live in this world as though it were not the whole world. Only humor allows us to live in this world from the perspective of that other world which we are building and for which we wait."[39] Humor is linked to our perception of incongruity, flowing from and into prayer. By placing us in the presence of God, prayer provides us the vantage point from which we can see the world from another perspective—the perspective of the coming reign of God—and allows us to relax and to laugh.

(E) Community and Solitude

Another constituent part of holistic spirituality is the love of community. This communal love must begin with the family. A home is meant to provide more than nocturnal storage units for isolated individuals who spend most of the day going their own ways. Rather, it must house a deep affective network of people who choose to gift each other with their caring presence. To build a family into a community where life and love are joyfully shared requires hard work and commitment. Yet, fostering familial life is vitally important for a holistic spirituality because "the love that makes us whole usually begins and ends with our families."[40]

To say that family life is floundering today is not to state a gratuitous opinion. The divorce rate continues to soar, while the reported incidences of incest and sexual abuse involving family members seem to be increasing. Moreover, the notion of a "dysfunctional family" has gained professional currency in the literature dealing with problems of addiction (alcohol, drugs, sex) and emotional maladjustment. Members of therapeutic and support groups (e.g., Adult Children of Alcoholics, Alanon) often share their childhood experiences of growing up in families that deprived them of the right to have feelings, taught them that maintaining facades is more important than facing problems and convinced them that conflict is better handled through avoidance than confrontation. These individuals disclose their painful memories not merely to vent their anger, but also to find healing for childhood wounds that hurt their adult lives. In light of these circumstances, building up family life must be seen as an important part of Christian spirituality. It is a critical aspect of the love of community required by the gospel.

Communal love also identifies the meaning of church membership. To belong to the church is to be part of a community of people who believe in the resurrection of Jesus. It is to experience being gathered into one body bound together by the Lord's love. There is no such thing as a Christian existence that is not a part of an affective network of people who share one faith, one baptism, and one Lord. Recounting the experience of the early church, the *Acts of the Apostles* makes clear that community life is foundational to Christian living. Right at the very beginning of Christianity, the followers of Jesus "remained faithful to the teaching of the apostles, to the brotherhood, to the breaking of bread and to the prayers. . . . The faithful all lived together and owned everything in common. . . . Day by day the Lord added to their community" (2:42; 44; 47). Thus, catechesis today stresses the fact that baptism is the rite of initiation into a community with a vocation to serve the world at large.

The vocation of the Christian community is to be a city on a mountaintop. By its way of life, its quality of care and love, the church is called to be a tangible witness of a communal life that has been transformed by faith in the resurrection of Jesus. Having only the divine cause at heart, the church seeks to have a transforming impact on the world. Thus, while ever seeking to increase the union among its members, the community of the church must not be self-absorbed, but must look outward to its task in the world.

A holistic spirituality strongly encourages commitment to community. Urging is needed because the cost of building community, whether in the family or the neighborhood, is high. Culturally ingrained obstacles militate against the kind of sharing required for interpersonal closeness. Community calls for the kind of self-transcendence talked about earlier that is willing to place the common good over self-interest. It requires a self-sacrificing love that gives of one's self for the sake of union. In an age of rampant individualism, these requirements are difficult to achieve. Insecure about their individual identity and fearful of losing control of their lives through social involvement, many individuals have come to place an excessive priority on independence.

Some observers contend that this tendency has resulted in the breakdown of family and community life in the Western world today. Many years ago Teilhard de Chardin wisely warned that individuals can fulfill or preserve themselves only if they "strive to break down every kind of barrier that prevents separate beings from uniting." Theirs is "the exaltation, not of egotistical autonomy, but of communion with all others!"[41] If community life is to flourish, Christians must drop their hard-shelled isolation and link themselves more closely to others.

Moreover, an over-identification with one's immediate family often hinders the building of community in the church. While the nuclear family is an extremely important social unit, it should not shut us off from investing in the larger extended family and other wider associations. The dream of having a self-contained little household of our own as a protective buffer against the world is inconsistent with the ideal of Christian community. Healthy family life must strike a balance between fostering intimacy within the home and developing life-giving ties outside the domestic walls. As one writer nicely puts it, "The house must be open enough to be ventilated, well enough insulated to retain the warmth of the sun. If the inhabitants have too little connection, they will quickly drift apart. If they live on top of one another, they will come out runty and retarded."[42] Christians must loosen the enclosures that separate them from other families and acknowledge their interdependence for a richer human and Christian existence.

Charismatic households and covenant communities, such as those in South Bend, Indiana, and Kailua, Hawaii, exemplify this kind of community renewal. In a charismatic household, the doors of a nuclear family are opened to non-relatives, who then live as intimate members of the household as if living with their own immediate family. On a larger scale, a charismatic covenant community consists of individuals and families who commit themselves to a regular life of weekly and monthly events including prayer meetings, liturgies, dinners, and social events, as well as common apostolic activities. These charismatic groupings are valuable models. Yet, our imagination must continue to create new forms of interaction that will enable us to integrate concretely the love of community in diverse ways.

As important as community is, it must always make room for solitude. Solitude is time alone for the sake of encountering ourselves. Yahweh's question, "Where art thou?" led Adam to assess his existential state. As such it was an invitation to solitude. That same question is addressed to us today and forms the centerpiece of solitude. By allowing us to get in touch with the currents of our lives, it makes a spiritual life possible. It undergirds a holistic spirituality because it is an essential condition for at-homeness with ourselves and intimacy with God and others. Self-encounter and interpersonal intimacy are impossible if solitude is not a habit in our life. Without a foundation in solitude, a spiritual life is like a house built on sand—shallowly grounded and easily eroded.

Solitude belongs to the inner fabric of community life because it makes self-donation possible. Any in-depth relationship, whether with God or others, requires a solid sense of self. And it is in the silent matrix of solitude that the unique dimensions of the self are fathomed. It is a time for intimacy with one's self. I once received a graphic description of solitude from a most unlikely source, an 11-year-old adolescent. Breaking in on my conversation with his parents about the importance of solitude in all our lives, he asked, "Is it like when I go into my room and sit in the corner by myself and the outside noises (like the banging of the pots in the kitchen) get smaller and the inside noises get bigger?" Listening sensitively to one's inner voices, acquainting oneself with the various parts that constitute the self, and befriending the self as good company—all these things are what solitude makes possible. In turn, these are the very elements that make interpersonal intimacy possible.

Solitude is not the only source of self-knowledge; sharing with others can also increase self-awareness. But sharing without prior solitude runs the risks of being superficial and inconsequential. Groups that encourage faith sharing, like couples in Marriage Encounter and prayer groups, recognize this principle when they structure silent reflection before periods of sharing. Caught off guard, a teenager pressured by his parents to share what was going on in his life retorted in an impertinent, though honest, way: "Let me get back to you when I hear from myself!" If we do not hear from ourselves before we share, our self-disclosure will have all the genuineness and depth of a talk show hack.

Enjoying solitude easily causes guilt in those who view it only in negative terms, as an unjustifiable taking away of time from those who need them. People with low self-worth are very prone to this fallacy. Mothers who cannot leave their families for a refreshing get-away or ministers who are glued to their desks are others who struggle with solitude. The Christian value of solitude, however, possesses a social dimension, and is neither irresponsible nor isolating. Even the solitude of monks, for example, is defensible because it is vitally linked to the lives of others. Thomas Merton pointed this out when he explained that the contemplative withdraws from the world only to listen more intently to the most neglected voices that proceed from its inner depth.[43] Solitude as a gospel value is best fostered when it is seen as something valuable *for* communion rather than as something competing *with* community. It is truly in service of group life because members can return from it restored and better able to contribute to the commonweal.

Time apart provides the space in which intimacy within community can be fostered. When we pray alone or just spend quiet time away from the places where we interact with each other directly, we participate in the growth of community. Getting away like this is not an escape from involvement, because in solitude we take others with us. And there relationships can deepen. In solitude we experience a bond with each other that is deeper and stronger than our own efforts can create. We can humbly acknowledge the truth that community is ultimately not the result of human effort, but the work of God. We admit that it is the Lord, as the source of our unity, who first gathers us together and then keeps us united in the midst of conflict and strife. Thus, time apart teaches us that community is a gift for which gratitude is owed.

Solitude feeds prayer because it allows us to discover "the voice that calls us beyond the limits of human togetherness to a new communion" with a God "who embraces friends and lovers and offers us the freedom to love each other."[44] It provides the place where we can, like Zacchaeus, catch a glimpse of the Lord and allow Jesus to enter our home with his saving love. Prayerful, too, are the times apart that provide us with a certain contemplative distance from our engagements and occupations. This distance enables us to regain a sense of perspective about our lives, which is so often lost in our daily hurly-burly rush. Solitude gives us time to check the balance of loves in our lives and to examine our motivations and behaviors. It offers the chance, for example, to monitor our ministry and ensure that our service stems from love and compassion rather than from inner compulsions, guilt, compensatory needs, or other deficient motives. By sensitizing us to the indwelling spirit, solitude makes us obedient to the guidance of God as we try to live out the twofold commandment of love in our daily lives. For all these reasons, a holistic spirituality embraces solitude as an important complement to community.

HOLISTIC PRACTICE FORMS HABITS OF THE HEART

We are called to love the Lord with our whole heart and with our whole being, and our neighbor as ourselves—as well as we can at each moment of our lives. To be truly holistic, however, our striving to unify the gospel loves discussed in this chapter must be characterized by the following:

1. *It should be developmental.* A developmental understanding views growth as a gradual process that should not run counter to either our human readiness to advance to the next stage or the rhythms of God's grace. Running ahead of ourselves or grace is not spiritually fruitful. A developmental approach also reminds us that the process of growth is ongoing, with the dimensions of our struggle shifting with age and time. For example, the right balance between solitude and community, ministry and leisure will vary with age and life circumstances. The proper balance must be determined at each point of our lives.

2. *It should be experiential.* An experiential approach allows for trial and error and leaves room for mistakes. The concrete balancing of love that Christians are called to possess is a complex matter, unattainable by

the abstract intellect alone. It requires learning by doing, and more often than not relies on an intuitive sense of what is right for a particular occasion or time. Thus, a holistic approach asserts the importance of a confluent approach that brings together the head and the heart, the cognitive and the affective in learning and living.

3. *It should be integrative.* A holistic spirituality is concerned with unified growth that does not develop the spirit and the mind while neglecting the body and the emotions, and vice versa. Neither does it cultivate autonomy at the expense of communion nor group life to the detriment of individuality. It respects the psychosomatic unity of the person at work, at prayer, and in relationships.

4. *It should be transformational.* A holistic spirituality aims for ongoing conversion of individual and group life. Growth entails continual change, not only in our thoughts, but also in our attitudes, feelings, values and behaviors. Holistic prayer, for example, is not effective if it does not make us become more responsibly Christian in our lives of work and love, prayer and politics, sex and social service.

There are no facile methods nor gurus that can tell us ahead of time how to walk in love in all the different situations we encounter.

> To a disciple who was always seeking answers from him the Master said, "You have within yourself the answer to every question you propose—if you only knew how to look for it."
>
> And another day he said, "In the land of the spirit, you cannot walk by the light of someone else's lamp. You want to borrow mine. I'd rather teach you how to make your own."[45]

Throughout our lives, tensions will accompany our efforts to love in a balanced and harmonious way. A holistic Christian spirituality calls for individuals to be faithful to the struggle of loving, to be open to change, and to trust that more important than fixed rules and techniques is the guidance of the ever-present spirit of love. True spirituality consists in walking by the light of that spirit.

CHAPTER THREE

HEART SEARCHING
AND LIFE CHOICE

"By slowly converting our loneliness into a deep solitude, we create that precious space where we can discover the voice telling us about our inner necessity—that is, our vocation."[1]
HENRI NOUWEN, *Reaching Out*

GOSPEL LOVE MUST be embodied in a concrete way of life and work, not merely talked about in a vacuum. When asked "How do we love God and neighbor?" Martin Luther answered: We love and serve God and neighbor "*in community, through vocation.*"[2] Confronting every Christian, therefore, is the central question: "What is my call and purpose in life, my vocation?" In an age of lengthening life span and rapid change, when second and even third careers are increasingly common, this question pertains not only to the young adult starting off in the world, but also to the mid-life person in transition and the early retiree. A story told by Jesuit Anthony de Mello, a spiritual guide from India, succinctly introduces our discussion of life choice and how we go about discovering what God's call might be for us.

> The disciple was a Jew. "What good work shall I do to be acceptable to God?"

> "How should I know?" said the Master. "Your Bible says that Abraham practiced hospitality and God was with him. Elias loved to pray and God was with him. David ruled a kingdom and God was with him too."

"Is there some way I can find my own allotted work?"

"Yes. Search for the deepest inclination of your heart and follow it."[3]

Our "allotted work" is another way of referring to our vocation. In his study of self-actualizing people, psychologist Abraham Maslow discovered that these exemplary human beings often felt a sense of vocation. Their lives of excellence were inspired by an intense desire to contribute to the world in a way that they felt uniquely qualified and called to do. More is involved, however, in a Christian understanding of vocation, which explicitly links vocation with our relationship to God. Old Testament scholar Walter Brueggemann, for instance, defines vocation as finding "a purpose for being in the world that is related to the purposes of God."[4] In a similar way in his *Spiritual Exercises,* St. Ignatius of Loyola taught that our vocational choices should be rooted in the purpose for which we were created: "to praise, reverence and serve God our Lord" and by this means to be saved.[5] Because serving God is the primary vocation of everyone, whatever we choose to do with our lives must lead to the basic end of divine service. Thus, Ignatius states: "My first aim should be to seek to serve God, which is the end, and only after that, if it is more profitable, to have a benefice or marry, for these are means to the end."[6]

VOCATION AS COVENANT PARTNERSHIP

The foundation of any authentic Christian spirituality must rest on a humble acknowledgment of the proper relationship between God and ourselves. God is the gracious and generous giver of all gifts, including the very gift of life. And we are the recipients of these gifts, called to show our gratitude by praising, reverencing and serving the creator. To succeed in this three-fold response of gratitude is to fulfill our vocation as human beings. Or, as developmentalist James Fowler puts it, "human fulfillment means to recognize that we are constituted by the address and calling of God and to respond so as to become partners in God's work in the world."[7] Human actualization can be attained only when we live in reference to God and contribute to God's purposes. As the response of the total self to the Lord's invitation to covenant partnership, a vocation goes far beyond a particular type of job or career.

Rather, it "involves the orchestration of our leisure, our relationships, our work, our private life, our public life, and of the resources we steward, so as to put it all at the disposal of God's purposes in the services of God and the neighbor."[8]

DISCOVERING ONE'S "PARTICULAR WAY"

Within the framework of our common human vocation, however, each of us must ask ourselves: "How specifically am I being called to give myself to God in partnership?" "Given my unique personality, background, and talents, what is my particular way of serving the creator?" Only such questions can help us choose a personal way among a multiplicity of possible ways. Buber makes this point in a story entitled "The Particular Way."

> Rabbi Baer of Radoshitz once said to his teacher the 'Seer' of Lublin: 'Show me one general way to the service of God.' The zaddik replied: 'It is impossible to tell [people] what way they should take. For one way to serve God is through learning, another through prayer, another through fasting, and still another through eating. Everyone should carefully observe what way [one's] heart draws [one] to, and then choose this way with all [one's] strength.'[9]

This chapter suggests how we can better observe our hearts in discerning how we are being drawn by God to serve. Unlike the path that led Dorothy to Oz, there is not a single yellow brick road which each of us must take. Sociologists, for example, claim that a person seeking a spouse can form a happy union with more than one within a large pool of possible partners. The romantic myth that a successful marriage depends on meeting that one special someone is not verified in reality. The same is true with one's vocation in life. Because there are many possible ways of serving God's purposes, the key question is: "Which way am I concretely being drawn by the Lord speaking to my heart?" The issues raised in this chapter reflect my experience with vocational counseling. While much of my own work for the last fifteen years has been with people trying to decide whether they are being called to a professed religious life, the general principles discussed here apply equally to those wondering what career path to follow and whether to marry or remain single. In all cases, vocation discernment must be grounded in a solitude of heart that enables one to encounter the self and the Lord.

SOLITUDE OF HEART AND BEING A SELF

As the zaddik of Buber's story correctly observed, it is impossible to tell individuals what path they should take. Each person must discover his or her own way through a process of heart searching. Mature vocation discernment first requires that individuals take responsibility for their own lives. Some people refuse to stand on their own two feet and, directly or indirectly, communicate the message, "Tell me what to do, how to live." This kind of dependence on others makes discernment impossible, because it detracts from the serious attention that should be given to one's inner life: one's thoughts, feelings, values, aspirations, attractions and repulsions. These inner realities make up the data that can eventually form the basis for a well grounded decision. By turning one's glance inward, solitude provides access to the heart and the valuable data stored within. If our questions and concerns are not tested and matured in solitude, it is unrealistic to expect answers that are really our own.

The poet Rainer Maria Rilke's advice to a young man wondering whether he should be a poet reinforces the importance of solitude of heart for those searching for direction in their lives:

You ask whether your verses are good. You ask me. You have asked others before. You send them to magazines. You compare them with other poems, and you are disturbed when certain editors reject your efforts. Now ... I beg you to give up all that. You are looking outward and that above all you should not do now. Nobody can counsel and help you, nobody. There is only one single way. Go into yourself. Search for the reason that bids you to write; find out whether it is spreading out its roots in the deepest places of your heart, acknowledge to yourself whether you would have to die if it were denied you to write. This above all—ask yourself in the stillest hour of your night: *must* I write? Delve into yourself for a deep answer. And if this should be affirmative, if you may meet this earnest question with a strong and simple "*I must*," then build your life according to this necessity; your life even into its most indifferent and slightest hour must be a sign of this urge and a testimony to it.[10]

Independently, Rilke and Buber voice an inescapable fact of vocation discernment: it entails a heart searching that one must do for oneself. Of course, feedback and advice from others are important. But they can neither supersede nor supplant the kind of solitude of heart that invites a person to befriend his or her inner self. It is in that inner world that people who search are invited to experience the guiding presence of God, who, St. Augustine tells us, is more intimate to us than our most interior parts.

LIBERATING THE HEART

Determining the direction in which our hearts are drawing us is often a difficult undertaking. Because many of us are out of touch with our own inner world and experiences, we are unable to understand our deepest desires. Moreover, others have long ago invaded our hearts and have installed *their* "shoulds" for our lives, claims British psychiatrist R.D. Laing. Our hearts are no longer free, but more like occupied territory. Cultural imperatives, parental "shoulds," and superego dictates often drown out the faint stirrings that suggest what we yearn for.[11] Uncovering the invaluable data of the heart can only occur when the self has been liberated from these foreign "shoulds."

Retaking the heart's territory is crucial in the battle for personal freedom and authentic discernment. The loss of the inside information that the heart can provide is serious because it strips us of the ability to direct our lives according to the interior movements of God and subjects us to the manipulation of exterior forces. A person without access to the data of the heart is like a soldier without a map or a compass. The winds of external pressures, rather than the directives of an intelligent heart, will determine his or her course. Liberating the heart requires dealing with whatever obscures the messages it emits.

A common obstacle to monitoring the spontaneous attractions of the heart is what psychologists call "introjects." Introjects represent the "shoulds" that other people, consciously or not, impose on our lives. These "shoulds" often interfere with our hearing clearly what the "wants" of our hearts are. According to Fritz Perls, the founder of

Gestalt therapy, "An introject . . . consists of material—a way of act-ing, feeling, evaluating—which you have taken into your system of behavior, but which you have not assimilated in such fashion as to make it a genuine part of your organism . . . even though you will resist its dislodgement as if it were something precious, it is actually a for-eign body."[12]

To check for intrusive introjects, we might ask: Are the aspirations of our heart being drowned out by our desire to please our parents or spouse? Do we bury our inner longings by complying submissively to the wishes of others for our lives? Do we hesitate to accept a vocation of altruistic service because the party line among our friends is that there's no room for "good guys" in the real world? Do we betray our heart's desire to create beauty in art and literature because there's no money or security there? Do we turn a deaf ear to the Lord's persistent call, heard in the silent depths of our hearts, to be a priest or professed religious because we fear the disapproval of others? Where and how do we betray the self by not listening with reverence to the voice telling us about our inner necessity—that is, our vocation?

Introjects endanger us in two ways.[13] First, people dominated by introjects never get a chance to develop their own personalities, be-cause they are so busy holding down the foreign bodies lodged in their systems. The more introjects they have saddled themselves with, the less room there is to express or even discover what they themselves are. Second, introjection can bring about personality disintegration. If peo-ple swallow whole two incompatible concepts (their own desires and the conflicting expectations of others, for example), they may find themselves torn to bits in the process of trying to reconcile them. This is not an uncommon experience for many today.

Liberation of the heart not only involves expelling inhibiting intro-jects, but also demands that we face up to inner forces that can be equally destructive of sound vocational choice. Traditionally, these enslaving forces have been called "inordinate attachments." They rep-resent the unruly passions and untamed urges that imperil our freedom of choice and cause us to compromise our ideals. These internal ele-ments are like weeds that can choke the life out of the good seeds of genuine aspirations trying to take root in the soil of our hearts. The garden of every human life contains traces of these destructive weeds, because these disordered desires are part of our weakened human condition. The rich young man of Mark's gospel is a touching illustration of the impeding nature of inordinate attachments. Loved by Jesus and invited to a closer share in his ministry, the young man was unfortunately incapable of an affirmative response and "went away sad, for he was a man of great wealth" (10:22). Contemporary examples of attachments that hinder a free response to God's invitation to partnership are easily found in daily life: take the person who abandons a lifelong dream of being a great scientist or doctor because of a craving for ease or an excessive desire for immediate gratification; or the person who suppresses a deep urge to help the disadvantaged because her desire for worldly prestige makes being a social worker a poor career choice. If left unchecked, these impulses diminish inner freedom and lead easily to the betrayal of self. Self-liberation, therefore, necessitates taming these tendencies that bring disorder to our discernment. Facing them squarely and choosing not to let deficient motives interfere with heartfelt dreams and aspirations are critical to mature vocational choice.

Our heart's deepest desires are like the pearl of great price or the field with the hidden treasure spoken of by Jesus (Mt 13:44–46). Once we identify what these are, we are challenged to sell all we have to possess them. In the same spirit, the poet Rilke says, "What is going on in your innermost being is worthy of your whole love."[4] To mold a life around these deepest aspirations makes a meaningful life possible. To base a life on social expectations and the wishes of others can only lead to fragmentation and patchwork. The challenge of vocation discernment is to discover what is our pearl of great price and then to give our heart and soul to it. To do this is to create the possibility of becoming a "unified soul," a person whose life is "all of one piece" rather than patchwork. The wise "Seer" of Lublin's advice applies to all of us: we must each carefully observe what way our hearts draw us to, and then choose that way with all our strength.

LIBERATING IMAGES OF A GOD WHO CALLS

Another obstacle that commonly interferes with sound choice is a distorted image of God resulting from psychological projection. Projection is a defense mechanism that enables people to disown or deny unwanted feelings, attitudes, and traits by assigning them to others. Chapter V illustrates how projection functions as an impediment to mature Christian obedience. Here the focus is on how projection impedes vocation discernment by destroying the freedom we are all meant to enjoy as children of God.

Just as people tend to project onto others unwanted attitudes and traits that really exist in themselves, so also do they project these attitudes and characteristics onto their mental conception of God. A harsh and puritanical society, for example, will project its dominant qualities and most likely postulate a hard and restrictive god. Or people with tyrannical and domineering parents will often project these constraining qualities onto God and end up with a god that is a suppressor of human freedom and individual autonomy.

A classical example of a distorted image of God based on projection can be seen in the myth of Prometheus, the legendary initiator of human culture. For stealing fire and sharing it with human beings, Prometheus was banished by the gods, who feared the development of human beings as an encroachment. Setting God and human beings in opposition, the Promethean myth reveals how false gods are easily fabricated out of human projection. Prometheus felt obliged to steal what he could not do without because he knew no god who would freely give it to him. He was unable to conceive of such a god, because if he himself had been god, he would have needed fire for himself and would never have shared it with another. "He knew no god that was not an enemy," notes Thomas Merton, "because the gods he knew were only a little stronger than himself, and needed the fire as badly as he needed it."[5] In order to exist, these Promethean gods had to dominate him (for if he himself had been a god, he knew he would have had to control what was weaker than himself). Blinded by his own presuppositions, Prometheus failed to see that fire was his for the asking, a gift of the true God, who created it expressly for human beings.

Integral vocation discernment requires the liberation of God from such inhibiting images that arise from projection. These images destroy our ability to live freely as people loved by God. We must abandon the false image of a power oriented and possessive deity opposed to human desires and development. Instead, we must develop images of God that accentuate the loving generosity of a personal God who not only gifts people with life, but is ever present as a support for the development of that life.

These life-giving images are not new, for they are rooted in the New Testament and reflect the God revealed by Jesus. In the parable of the prodigal son (Lk 15), for example, Jesus portrays God as a forgiving and affirming father. God is like a parent who, without any trace of regret, freely permits us to live our own lives—even though our self-directed journey is often misguided and our return home often tortuous. Unlike the insecure Promethean gods who viewed human development as a danger to divine status, the God whom Jesus called "Abba" perennially supports the human effort to establish a life based on the desires of the heart. Sin and misjudgment may retard our progress. What first appeared to be the pearl of great price may turn out to be a fake. But, as the parable points out, God's graciousness provides many chances. We live in a multiple chance universe, and the effort to root our vocation in authentic, divinely inspired, desires must not be abandoned when faltering steps lead initially to failure. Significant learning sometimes comes only through trial and error. Fortunately for us God, like the father of the prodigal son, allows for trial-and-error learning.

The parable of the prodigal son likens human life to an unrestricted gift which we receive from the hands of a loving God. The creator gives us time and energy, talents and opportunities to serve within a unique vocation that is revealed to us in our own hearts and in prayer. But often we do not experience our life as an unrestricted gift and are unsure that God is really behind us. Afraid to trust our hearts, we hesitate and hedge. Yet like the master in the parable of the talents (Mt 25: 14–30), God has high hopes that we will develop fully our talents and potentialities. Only when we realize that we are given many chances to ascertain God's call will we boldly take risks and try out alternatives. Fear of having only a single chance and of losing it through mistaken choice leads to paralysis and indecision. This fear, as depicted in the parable of the talents, will tempt us to bury our assets rather than invest them with hope for a profitable life. To strive for a vocational existence based on the deep desires of our heart is truly a response to a gracious God's invitation to be co-creators of lives that speak of the marvelous gift and opportunity that human life is.

BALANCING IMAGES OF
TRANSCENDENCE AND IMMANENCE

In searching for liberating images of a God who calls us to vocational existence, we are looking for adult images that do not trivialize our freedom and responsibility. If the Christian faith is to speak to us today, it must reject any view of God that would keep adults infantile. This requires the rejection of images of God that have been built on a pattern of deficient relationships experienced as children. For example, a conception of God that is based upon a fear relationship in childhood is not a satisfactory basis for an adult Christianity. We need images that respect both the dignity of God and of human beings. Many of our unhelpful images stem from a distorted understanding of God's transcendence. When we say that God is a transcendent being, we mean that God is wholly other, distinct from all created beings. While positing a real distinction between ourselves and God, the notion of transcendence in no way implies that God is a distant deity with minimal contact and interest in us. Scripture, after all, presents this transcendent God of ours as the loving creator of Genesis, the faithful liberator of Exodus, and the merciful "Abba" of Jesus. Unfortunately, these biblical images have been eclipsed by aberrant images. The Promethean picture of distant gods antagonistic to humans exemplifies such a misrepresentation. The unequivocal message of Jesus can be reduced to this: the creator of the universe and the Lord of history is forever and unambiguously for us, on our side. This message constitutes the core of the Christian gospel. To obfuscate this central truth is to garble the Good News proclaimed by Jesus.

To rectify such distortions, a reemphasis on images of immanence is needed. "Immanence" comes from the Latin *manere,* meaning "to remain within," as distinct from "to go beyond or outside," which is the root meaning of "transcend." Traditionally predicated of God to express the belief that the divine is to be encountered within the created universe, the notion of divine immanence has been given a variety of interpretations throughout history. In asserting God's immanence, some have slipped into pantheism by holding that God and the universe are one and identical. The church has always rejected all forms of pantheism as unacceptable because it does away with the absolute qualitative distinction between God and the universe. The challenge throughout the ages has been to affirm God's indwelling presence within the world while maintaining that God is wholly other and irreducible to any aspect of creation. "The religious imagination," states theologian William Lynch, "has fought a long struggle to separate God out from everything else in the world while keeping [God] altogether present to the world."[16]

The beneficial use of images of immanence for vocation discernment has been well-delineated by Edith Genet, a religious educator calling for the need to "respect the creative impulse God has put in us."[17] Images of immanence allow us to visualize God, not as a rival, but as a benevolent presence working in us and with us. Made in God's image, we have been endowed with the ability and opportunity to discover our unique way of collaborating with God in covenant partnership. Having no detailed blueprint for our lives, God leaves open many possibilities for choice. St. Paul makes this clear when he speaks of the plan of God as a plan of love in his letter to the Ephesians. "God's plan is to bring all creation together, everything in heaven and on earth, with Christ as head" (Eph 1:10). Speaking of God's will as a divine yearning, a contemporary writer conveys well the Pauline sense of God's will as one of love.

> Unfortunately many people view the will of God as rather like a ten-ton elephant hanging overhead, ready to fall on them . . . Actually the word which we translate into English as *will* comes from both a Hebrew and a Greek word which means *yearning*. It is that yearning which lovers have for one another. Not a yearning of the mind alone or of the heart alone but of the whole being. A yearning which we feel is only a glimmering of the depth of the yearning of God for us.[18]

Thus, the will of God is dynamic, personal love urging us along the path that leads to union with the Lord. As with an ordinary journey, there may be several paths that lead equally well to our destination; or some way may be notably better; or some way may lead us away from our destination. So "the prayer to know God's will," states theologian John Wright, "is a prayer to have this kind of insight about the choices open to me."[19] When we pray "Your will be done," we are not thinking about a script of our lives that God has destined from all eternity.

Rather, we are referring to the choices we must make. And when these lead to union with God, they are compatible with God's plan to unite all creation. "Thus, it may sometimes happen that I will actually be doing God's will, following the guidance of the Holy Spirit, whether I choose this or that."[20] A conversation between Shug and Celie in *The Color Purple* makes this point well:

> "Us worry about God a lot. But once us feel loved by God, us do the best us can to please him with what us like."
> "You telling me God love you, and you ain't never done nothing for him? I mean, not go to church, sing in the choir, feed the preacher and all like that?"
> "But if God love me, Celie, I don't have to do all that. Unless I want to. There's a lot of other things I can do that I speck God likes."[21]

The Christian notion of vocation entails the belief that God calls us to live in certain ways. Yet, God's expectations for our lives are broad; as Shug puts it, "There's a lot of other things I can do that I speck God likes." God calls us, for instance, to imitate the interpersonal love of the trinity through our vocation to be loving human beings. Our vocation as Christians, furthermore, calls us to pattern our lives on the example of Christ to whom we are joined through baptism. Like St. Paul, Christians have been "specifically chosen" to "preach the good news about" Jesus (Gal 1: 15–16). However, the distinctive way each Christian is called to do this is a very personal matter. Through vocation discernment, we try to identify the unique way each of us is called to glorify God in our work or way of life. Because we possess many options and because every "yes" we say implies a "no" to other possibilities, we have to choose with care. God's plan for us is neither a static scenario predetermined from all eternity, nor does it exist independently of our inclinations and desires. Our vocation unfolds through time and is shaped by our choices. The Christian ideal is that we submit these choices to God and benefit from the guidance of grace. In the solitude of our hearts and with the wise counsel of others, we must choose our particular way. Once we choose a way, that way becomes our vocation. Our lives are subsequently shaped by that vocational choice. While our lives could have been different, they would not have been necessarily more in accord with God's will. "In a situation where many choices are possible it does not seem necessary to suppose always that only one of these is according to God's will."[22]

RECONCILING THE EXTERIOR AND THE INTERIOR

Images of immanence highlight the belief that God works through the "natural" processes (our thinking, feeling, fantasizing, and seeking advice) by which we decide on a vocation. When we earnestly and prayerfully rely on these processes to determine a course for our lives, we can be united to God and see God's will active in us. Some people may find this hard to comprehend, if they are used to viewing the will of God as coming from outside themselves or if they see vocation as something decided beforehand by God without any input from the individual involved. In this view, God issues a call and our duty is to respond with confidence and joy. This way of imaging vocation as an exterior call, such as in the cases of Isaiah and Jeremiah, appears in many biblical texts.

However, there are other texts in scripture that suggest an alternative understanding of how God summons people into service. In contrast to an exterior call, this view portrays God's call as embedded in one's heart and emanating from one's life situation. Take, for example, the passage in Exodus about Moses' return to Egypt after a few years in the Arabian peninsula where he got married. In two connecting verses, we see an interesting presentation of contrasting descriptions of the same event.[23]

> Moses went away and returned to his father-in-law Jethro, and said to him, "Give me leave to go back to my relatives in Egypt to see if they are still alive." And Jethro said to Moses, "Go in peace" (Ex 4:18).

The very next verse provides quite a different explanation of how it came about that Moses went to Egypt to check on his family.

> Yahweh said to Moses in Midian, "Go return to Egypt, for all those who wanted to kill you are dead." So Moses took his wife and his son and, putting them on a donkey, started back for the land of Egypt" (Ex 4:19).

The first text, verse 18, leaves the responsibility of the decision to Moses and his understanding of the situation. He assesses things and wants to find out whether his relatives are still alive. The second text, verse 19, belonging to the Yahwist tradition, attributes directly to God the initiative resulting in Moses' return to Egypt. It bypasses Moses' interior process of evaluating his situation and making a decision.

These Old Testament verses represent alternative ways of understanding how God operates in the world. The latter, based on a transcendent image of God, emphasizes the direct intervention of God in directing our lives. The former, based on an immanent image of God, sees the hand of God always at work in the people and events that make up our present reality. Corresponding to these two viewpoints, an understanding of vocation can emphasize either the exterior or the interior aspect of the call.

Similarly, New Testament accounts of the call of the apostles illustrate the same thing. Matthew's gospel, for example, recounts that Jesus, seeing Simon and Andrew, said to them "Follow me" (4:18). In contrast, John's gospel describes the experience of two disciples of John the Baptist being interiorly drawn to follow Jesus. Jesus turned round, saw them following and asked "What do you want?" They answered "Rabbi, where do you live?" "Come and see," replied Jesus (1:35). In Matthew, the initiative is attributed to Jesus. In John, however, the call to follow Jesus is instigated by the prompting of John the Baptist and the disciples' own desire to see for themselves.

Because both approaches have potential pitfalls, sound vocation discernment must balance both views of how God leads us. An overemphasis on vocation as an exterior call can endanger responsible selfhood by fostering the kind of conformity and outer-directedness that easily lead to immaturity. More seriously, an excessive emphasis on an external summons can result in a feeling of being trapped—a feeling that saps all enthusiasm for living and ministering. Without free choice, joyful commitment is impossible. Once a Jesuit priest was approached by a man at a busy shopping mall. "By chance, Father," he asked, "are you a Jesuit?" "Not by chance, sir," the priest responded, "but by choice!" It is this sense of personal freedom that enables people to serve the Lord gladly.

On the other hand, an exclusive reliance on the interior can easily lead to self-deception and delusion. If we are not open to feedback from others in the faith community, our blind spots can lead us into error or lull us into a proud and stubborn sense of certitude that gives the impression that we have a direct line to God. Furthermore, an excessively subjective sense of call may lead to weakened commitment and compromise when difficulties arise. Because discipleship always entails a cost, following Jesus with fidelity, whether in the lay or the religious state, will necessarily involve some hardship and struggle. During these times, our commitment to an interiorly felt sense of vocation can find valuable support in the external ratification of that call by the community.

Concretely, reconciling the interior and exterior requires that we take seriously the data emanating from our heart and life situations, as well as the opinion of others who, by training and charism, can keep our heart searching enlightened and free from self-deceit. Honest and integral discernment of our vocation involves listening to God, speaking both within our hearts and in the world around us. It calls for a sensitivity to our inner desires, as well as an ability to interpret these desires through a process of prayer, reflection, and spiritual direction.

THE ROLE OF DESIRES

Sound Christian decision making dictates not only that we take our desires seriously, but also that we be willing to discuss them with a spiritual guide. Such a person can serve as an objective sounding board and help us avoid the pitfalls of an unbalanced and one-sided interior or exterior approach. According to Thomas Merton, it is important to appreciate the role of desires as indicators of God's will and to be honest about these desires in spiritual direction. Because a real connection frequently exists between our spontaneous desires and God's will for us, he advises people seeking help from a spiritual director to be genuine rather than present a facade.[24] "We have to be able to lay bare the secret aspirations which we cherish in our hearts," he writes, and in this way make ourselves known for who we really are. He stresses the importance of discovering our "holy and spiritual desires" because they "really represent a possibility of *a special, spontaneous and personal gift*" which we alone can make to God.[25] If there is such a gift then most certainly, according to Merton, God asks that gift from us, and "a holy, humble, and sincere desire may be one of the signs that God asks it!"[26] Merton's point is central to vocation discernment: Our deep longings are sometimes very important indications of the will of God for us.

Our discernment is sometimes faulty because we ourselves do not know what we really want. An introject-filled heart or a tyrannical image of God can keep us in the dark about our own desires. Often a legalistic notion of the will of God may lead us to hypocritically falsify our true aspirations. Discernment is drastically undermined when we think that God is a harsh lawgiver, uninterested in our thoughts and desires and concerned only with imposing upon us a rigid, predetermined plan. This attitude is challenged by the fact that we are called to collaborate actively with God in covenant partnership. St. Paul reminds us that "we are fellow workers with God" (I Cor 3:9). As colleagues, we are called to freely contribute to God's kingdom in the world, to advance God's cause. In this collaboration, which is our basic vocation as Christians, we are not merely passive and mechanical instruments. Our loving, spontaneous contributions to God's work are themselves the precious effects of God's grace. "To frustrate this active participation in the work of God," Merton warns, "is *to frustrate what is most dear to [God's] will.*"[27] In a similar vein, E. Edward Kinerk argues, in an essay on the place of desires in the spiritual life, that desires can galvanize our spirituality by generating power and physical energy. If we do not take our desires seriously, "if we are timid about our stronger desires for God and his service, we will have failed to utilize the greatest source of human vitality and passion which God has given us."[28]

The spontaneous desires of our hearts are valuable clues to the will of God for us. Yet, we are often mistrustful of them because we are suspicious of spontaneity. We are "afraid of spontaneity itself," states Merton, "because we have been so warped by the idea that everything spontaneous is 'merely natural' and that for a work to be supernatural it has to go against the grain, it has to frustrate and disgust us. The truth is, of course, quite different."[29] When we fear spontaneity, we mask our desires, sometimes hiding them even from ourselves. This repression of desires hinders the discernment process because only when our desires are brought out of the cave of the unconscious and exposed to the light of day can they be tested. Only through prayerful discernment can we discover which of our desires are authentic indications of God's will and which of them are not, in Brueggemann's phrase, "related to the purposes of God" and therefore incapable of defining a vocation.

THE NATURE OF AUTHENTIC DESIRES

If desires are to give direction to our vocational existence, we need to be able to distinguish between authentic and less authentic ones. In discussing four overlapping presuppositions about desires, Kinerk provides some criteria that can help us sort them out.[30]

First, while all desires are real experiences, they are not all equally authentic. For example, a devout Christian who has been hurt by another might feel both a desire for revenge and a desire to forgive. But he or she would probably judge the desire to forgive as more authentic because the desire to forgive springs from a more profound level of himself or herself. Such a person's reflection might be along the lines of: "I feel more genuinely myself when I picture myself forgiving. And I feel out of sync with the person I want to be when I harbor the desire for revenge." The desire to forgive is more authentic because it more accurately expresses what a devout Christian *really* wants, even though the desire for revenge might be intensely felt. Distinguishing between authentic and less authentic desires involves a groping and fallible process, because it is often difficult for us to know clearly our deeper desires and to separate them from those that are more superficial and ephemeral.

Second, our authentic desires are vocational. What we want is integrally connected with who we are. Insisting that "the question 'Who am I?' can never be answered directly," Kinerk maintains that authentic desires serve essentially to enlighten our hearts. We cannot know ourselves unless we know what we really want. Only by asking the question "What do I want?" do we begin to sense the nature of our unique vocation in life. The more honestly we identify our authentic desires, the more these desires will shape our vocational choice. "What do you want?" is precisely what Jesus asked the first disciples in John's account of their call (Jn 1: 35–39). In their religious quest, the disciples found themselves drawn intuitively to follow Jesus as he passed by them along the river Jordan, where John was baptizing. Jesus aided their vocation discernment precisely by directing them to their desires.

Third, the more authentic our desires, the more they move us to glorify God. All of us experience in some degree a restless yearning for God. Whenever we sincerely respond to this longing we are also responding to the grace of God who has planted that desire in every human being. Our most genuine desires spring ultimately from this level of ourselves. They may not always be expressed in explicitly religious terms, but they always move us towards self-donation to God and others and away from self-centeredness. "At this level," states Kinerk, "the distinction between 'what I desire' and 'what desires God gives me' begins to blur. The more profoundly we reach into ourselves, the more we experience desires which are uniquely our own but also God-given."[31] Thus, heart searching is key to vocation discernment because God is often the source of the desires that emanate from our hearts. Because the danger of self-deception is great, we need to test our desires and our interpretation of them with others who can provide some objectivity. Nevertheless, in no case can these desires be trivialized or disregarded without seriously crippling the process of vocation discernment.

Fourth, authentic desires are always in some way public. This is paradoxical, but nevertheless true. While our desires reflect what is most uniquely personal and idiosyncratic in ourselves, at the same time, when seen at their depths, they stem from communal values, not just individual ones. In Kinerk's words, "Superficial desires—such as those linked with consumerism—demonstrate all too graphically our cultural narcissism, but more authentic desires always lead us out of ourselves and into the human community."[32] Thus, such desires as those to feed the hungry, to clothe the naked, and to utilize our talents in service of others become more compelling than private concerns. These desires are more authentic because they reflect our true nature as social beings.

These insights into the nature of authentic desires are very useful when struggling with life choices. Sound discernment requires not only that we be aware of the data of our hearts, but also that we know how to interpret that data with spiritual sensitivity. If we are not spiritually discriminating, we make ourselves vulnerable to being misled. Distinguishing between authentic and less authentic desires enhances our ability to judge which of our desires are worth building a life upon and which desires should be left dormant.

WHOLEHEARTED WANTING

Distinguishing between "simply wanting something and really want-ing it" can also help us to determine which of our desires should influence the direction of our lives.[33] According to philosopher Robert Johann, the struggle for freedom is not that we do not have ample choices, but that we do not really want what we choose. We contin-ually make choices that we ourselves cannot wholly approve. We make choices that, even as we make them, we realize are at odds with our other interests and desires. Consequently, we are inwardly divided and only halfhearted in our choice. To be free and unconflicted, contends Johann, our wanting must be wholehearted. Wholehearted wanting should be the basis of a life choice.

We must take our desires seriously, since "they provide the only access we have to the worth of things." However, Johann cautions that taking our desires seriously is not the same thing as leaving them to themselves and indulging them as they arise. Because they are simply reactions to present objects, desires arise piecemeal. Our wantings can never be more than fragmentary, so long as they are not examined for their conditions and consequences. If our wanting is to be whole-hearted, what we want has to be grasped not only in itself, but in its connections with the rest of reality. It must be understood and evalu-ated in light of what it portends for our life as a whole. A husband who is committed to being faithful to his wife, for example, may realisti-cally choose not to act out his desire to flirt with a woman colleague or to have a nightcap at her apartment after the office Christmas party. He realizes that his fleeting desire for intimacy with her might well jeopar-dize his deeper desire for marital fidelity. His desire to flirt is not wholehearted because he does not want the possible consequence of sexual involvement with her.

Requiring thought and reflection, wholehearted desiring demands that we step back from immediate goods and pleasures to see where they lead. This means refusing to endorse our initial reactions until their credentials have been checked and validated. We cannot want something wholeheartedly when our minds tell us that we will not want to finish what we have started. In short, the aim of thought is neither to suppress spontaneity nor to substitute for wants and feelings.

Rather, the function of thought is to liberate our desiring from its fascination for fragments and to make wholehearted wanting possible. Reason and emotion are both critical components of holistic decision making. Excluding one or the other seriously detracts from the validity of the process. St. Ignatius, in his *Spiritual Exercises,* teaches how thinking and feeling can work harmoniously in discernment, and at the same time be influenced by God's spirit at work in these human processes.

INTEGRATING REASON, AFFECT, AND RELIGIOUS EXPERIENCE

Ignatius' guidelines for decision making or "election" place heavy emphasis on the integration of thoughts and feelings. Underlying his recommendations is the concern that personal choice be made in the context of one's religious experience. His instructions, consequently, are intended to maximize a person's sensitivity to the influence of God throughout the decision-making process. To alert the person to God's influence, he describes three times or ways in which God can guide the person faced with choice.

The first time occurs when God "so moves and attracts the will that a devout soul without hesitation, or the possibility of hesitation, follows what has been manifested to it."[34] Ignatius cites the example of St. Paul's and St. Matthew's response to Christ's call to illustrate this first time of election. Phenomenologically, this first time can be viewed as a moment of peak religious experience when individuals feel overwhelmed by an inner sense of absolute certainty as to what their decision should be. At such moments, they may experience something deep within click into place, providing them with an intuitive sense of how they must proceed. Or they may perceive such a total congruence between their sense of internal requiredness (what they feel they must do) and God's will (what they think God wants of them) that the course to be followed is unambiguously clear. Quite apart from any deliberation, this personal "moment of truth" can spring suddenly upon the person without any antecedent cause, like a forceful flash of insight, removing any further need for deciding.

The second time of decision making suggested by Ignatius emphasizes the knowledge-bearing capacity of feelings. It occurs when individuals must rely on their affective states of consolation or desolation to detect the influence of God regarding the decision to be made.[35] In the case of people progressing earnestly along the spiritual path,[36] Ignatius understands consolation as a complexus of positive feelings that encourages, supports, and confirms a prospective decision as being "right"; desolation he sees as a complexus of negative feelings that discourages, questions, calls into doubt a prospective decision, suggesting it is not "right." The assumption underlying this second time of election is that one's emotions can be indicators of God's guidance.

The third time of decision making highlights the process of reasoning.[37] Picturing oneself on one's deathbed and recalling one's purpose for existing (that is, "to praise, reverence, and serve God our Lord, and by this means to be saved"),[38] the person is asked to list the pros and cons of various options. This third time presupposes that God's guiding influence can be felt in the process of reasoning. Like the values-clarification exercise which asks people what they would do if they had only a week to live, this Ignatian method relies on the truth that can come at death's door to provide a perspective for present choices. In other words, it asks people to anticipate which decision they would most likely be able to ratify when facing death.

The genius of Ignatius, theologian Michael J. Buckley points out, was not that he counted transpersonal influences, or the attractions of affectivity, or the process of thinking as critical factors in securing the guidance of God. Others also shared this inclusive view.[39] Unique and underivative, however, was Ignatius' explanation of the dynamics of these three, often interrelating, factors within a person's religious experience. "What Ignatius provided," maintains Buckley, "was a structure within which each of these finds a significant place; none is dismissed out of hand. A coordination among them is established so that they reach an integrity of effect and one is taught how to recognize and reply to each."[40]

FEELINGS CAN CONFIRM

The phrase "integrity of effect" aptly describes the desired outcome of Ignatian decision making. Presuming the person is genuinely committed to doing the will of God and is free from inordinate attachments that destroy freedom, the decision is integral if it emanates from an integration of feelings and thoughts. Ignatius sought this integration by building into the second and third times of decision making a complementary dynamic. He directs the person who has made a decision based on the rational approach of the third time to seek affective confirmation by prayerfully attending to his or her feelings as suggested by the second time of election.[41] In other words, following a decision, the person should stay in close touch with the feelings which arise as a result of the decision and determine whether they confirm the rightness of the choice or cast doubt on it. After a period of testing, if positive feelings (e.g., peace, joy, hope, confidence) dominate, it is clear then that affectivity has joined with intelligence to produce an harmonious effect. However, if negative and disturbing feelings (e.g., doubt, fear, anxiety, discouragement) persist, then a closure would seem premature and the person should continue the process until an inner harmony is produced through the alliance of one's thoughts and feelings.

Conversely, a person who makes a decision based on the affective approach of the second time should also seek rational confirmation through a method of the third time. William Peters, in his commentary on the *Spiritual Exercises,* cites the *Directory of 1599* to substantiate this point. He notes that Juan de Polanco, a close friend of Ignatius, called the second time of election "more excellent" than the third, but adds that it might be wise to check the result of an election made in this time by one of the methods of the third.[42]

Clearly, the second time of decision making, based on affectivity, and the third time, based on reasoning, were designed by Ignatius to function in a complementary dynamic. The Ignatian process seeks to ground life choices on felt knowledge, not on theoretical abstractions. This process, according to Ignatian scholar John Futrell, involves paying attention simultaneously to "the continuity of thoughts during reflection, the concomitant feelings constantly reacting to these thoughts—feelings which confirm or call into question the orientation of the reflection—and the growing understanding which involves both the thoughts and feelings—felt knowledge."[43]

WHOLE ORGANISM CONSULTED

Ignatius' approach is an early form of what today is called holistic decision making, which encourages individuals making a decision to rely not only on their mind, but also on the data that come from feelings, senses, bodily sensations and the imagination. Psychologist James Simkin recounts a case that illustrates this approach.[44] Once when working with a man struggling to decide whether to remain in a business venture recently begun with a friend, Simkin asked the client to imagine sticking with his business commitment. As the client tried to imagine as vividly as he could what this option would entail, Simkin directed the person to attend to his bodily sensations. When entertaining the option of remaining with the business, the client experienced his stomach tying up in knots. Then Simkin directed the client to fantasize other alternatives. As the patient did so, he discovered that his stomach began to unravel and relax. The therapist then asked the patient to continue to shuttle between the two different fantasies, while simultaneously paying attention to his bodily reactions. As the patient did so, he began to discover a recurrent pattern: whenever he imagined staying with the business venture, his body was filled with stress; whenever he imagined abandoning the business deal, his body began to relax.

This case cited by Simkin demonstrates how useful the data produced by the imagination, senses, bodily sensations, and feelings can be in decision making. "My total organismic sensing of a situation is more trustworthy than my intellect," states psychologist Carl Rogers in support of a holistic approach.[45] Testifying to this "wisdom of the organism," Rogers states:

> As I gradually come to trust my total reactions more deeply, I find that I can use them to guide my thinking . . . I think of it as trusting the totality of my experience, which I have learned to suspect is wiser than my intellect. It is fallible I am sure, but I believe it to be less fallible than my conscious mind alone.[46]

What psychologists such as Rogers and Simkin say of decision making is equally true of discernment. When thought is made the coin of the realm, other important sources of information, like feelings, bodily reactions, and intuitions, can be overlooked. A purely rational approach to discernment is impoverished because it fails to recognize God's influence in religious and affective experiences. Like holistic decision making, good discernment must take into account one's total, organismic sensing of a situation. A society dominated by science and technology often mistrusts feelings and touts a coldly dispassionate approach as the only intelligent way to decide. Nevertheless, Christian tradition maintains that we must be open to being touched by God in all areas of our lives, because no aspect escapes the influence of Christ's spirit. As Ignatius reminds us, we can encounter God in our cognitive processes, our affective states, as well as in our religious experiences.

MAKING AND KEEPING COMMITMENTS

Successful vocation discernment results in a sense of satisfaction—a feeling that with God's help we have discovered a mission that is worthy of our wholehearted commitment. Some people, however, are blocked from putting closure to their process because of an inability to make a commitment. This incapacity seems to stem from several interrelated myths.

First, there is the myth that "Somewhere there is a problem free lifestyle." When spelled out so explicitly, its obvious falsehood is apparent to all who are in touch with the real world. Nevertheless, this myth subtly deters commitment and encourages an endless search for the perfect lifestyle, job, or mate. The proper question that mature Christians must ask themselves is this: "What vocation will allow me to live out most fully Christ's twofold commandment of love?" This focus on loving will enable us to deal creatively with whatever problems are part of our lives. Facing problems that arise from our efforts to love God and others is a way of becoming holy. It is the Lord's way of transforming our hearts and making us more like Jesus, whose problem-filled life led him to the cross for our sakes. Thus, problems should not be seen as being *in the way* of our vocations, but *the way* by which the Lord calls us to embody his sacrificial love for others. Since no way of life is without its problems, the task is to discern which set of problems bears the most promise for developing our capacity to love and serve as Jesus did.

Second, there is the myth that "Somewhere, this side of the grave, I can have the whole enchilada!" In our clearer moments, we know this is an illusion. But there is a stubborn resistance in many of us to accept the limitations of creaturehood. Often, only a mid-life crisis can extract from us a reluctant and humbling admission that there are real limits to our lives. So often in our weariness and frustration, we are tempted to focus more on the 20 or 30 percent that may be missing in our lives rather than concentrate on the 70 or 80 percent that is there. Because life is a more-or-less situation, total fulfillment will come only when we finally rest in the Lord in the heavenly Jerusalem. Until then, as Augustine so eloquently prayed, our hearts will remain restless. To yield to this fact of faith is the beginning of wisdom and inner peace.

The painful law of human existence is that every choice we make necessarily involves some exclusion. Every "yes" to some choices necessarily involves a "no" to others. Because I say "yes" to being married, I say "no" to the kind of solitude and mobility that a celibate can enjoy. Because I say "yes" to celibate love, I say "no" to the joy of having my own children. Maturity is the ability to live peacefully with limits. The refusal to accept limits makes commitment impossible. In the world of imagination and desires, the absence of limits eliminates the necessity to choose. However, the real world is bound by limits, and it is in this world that we as Christians are called to embody the love of Christ. Maturity consists in making wise and loving choices, not in avoiding commitments.

Third, there is the myth that "Because I'm struggling, I must not be called to live this life." Here it is crucial to distinguish between vocational struggles and developmental struggles. For example, a husband or a wife could mistakenly conclude on the basis of recurrent marital problems that he or she is not being called to married life. Instead of calling into doubt their vocation to marriage, they perhaps should look at growing in ways that would make them better spouses. Or a priest struggling with loneliness could erroneously judge that he does not have the charism of celibacy. Instead of doubting his vocation, perhaps he should look at ways in which he can foster greater intimacy with the Lord and others. Some persistent struggles can suggest that, try as we may, "the shoe does not fit." Other struggles, however, far from indicating that we do not have a vocation, invite us to invest in further growth as we try to remain faithful to our call.

Closely related is another myth that can undermine commitment. Colloquially, it takes the form of "If only I weren't here, I wouldn't be having this problem." This myth tempts people to escape their existential situation with the hope that moving on will solve everything. The difficulty with this approach is that often individuals move on only to discover the same problem in a new setting, as if it were carried there in their back pockets. It seems that their problem is connected more to their way of perceiving, feeling, and behaving than to the concrete situations of their lives. Not to recognize this truth condemns many to a wandering, nomadic life. Seeking a geographic cure for personal struggles results often in disappointment and makes permanent commitment impossible. This is illustrated in the case of people who are always on the move, frantically trying to escape all traces of loneliness. Naturally, their efforts are doomed to failure, because a certain loneliness is inescapable in everyone's life—sometimes experienced most achingly when surrounded by loved ones. Being alone, and sometimes feeling lonely, is a burdensome part of the human condition, for which there will be no final solution short of seeing the Lord face to face. Changing commitments and locations is a dead-end solution to human loneliness.

The phrase "to make a commitment" contains much wisdom when taken literally. Commitments are never given to us already fully developed and ready simply to be enjoyed. We are given precious opportunities to create something worthwhile when we make commitments. But to do this, we must invest—our time, energy, and resources—into *making* a commitment, that is, to actualizing the full potential of a promising reality. Without personal and persevering investment, a commitment can never flower. This is true of commitments made in marriage, friendship, religious life, and the priesthood.

A Jesuit friend tells young couples at their wedding that what they are doing on that day is making an initial installment. By exchanging marriage vows, they are committing themselves to possessing something so precious and costly that they cannot pay for it all at once. They can only "purchase" the fullness of marital love by "buying on time."

Only by making their regular installments in the daily routine of their years together will they be able to achieve the full promise of what they long for on their wedding day. In short, only continual investment can help them "make their commitment" to each other. Something similar can be profitably said to priests on their ordination day and to religious on the day of their profession of vows.

CONCLUSION

"What will this child turn out to be?" This is the question posed by the relatives of John the Baptist (Lk 1:66). It is asked about every person who comes into the world. And no one can answer it except the person himself or herself, when he or she grows old enough to ask: "What shall I be? And what shall I do that I may be myself, that I may use all my God-given talents to live a full life?" When the person asks such questions, he or she is confronting squarely the question of vocation.

Heart searching in solitude and with those who accompany us in our search is the process of vocation discernment. In this process, we must learn to take the data of our heart seriously and realize that our spontaneous desires can be important indications of God's will for us. It is fallacious to think that God's will has nothing to do with our will. We must unlearn the idea that our unique vocation is something our creator peremptorily orders us to do, without any consultation with us. Neither is it something that we decide without any direction from our creator. Theologically, the discernment process presupposes several theological truths: (a) that we can have access to God who dwells in our midst; (b) that God's guiding voice can lead us in the way of a personal vocation, if we listen with solitude of heart and without fear; and (c) that God never coerces us, but always respects our freedom of choice.

God's will reaches us through the Spirit sent to us by the risen Jesus. This Spirit reaches us directly or through others. However, since the means through which Christ touches us by his Spirit are all human, no direction of the Spirit is totally unambiguous until we take the lonely human responsibility of removing the ambiguity by responsible decision. That decision is responsible if it is a sincere response to the Spirit reaching us through all the ways determined by Christ. With regard to any concrete human decision like our life's vocation, the will of God is not "something out there" waiting to be found. By acting responsibly, that is, by responding to the Spirit's lead as best we can, we contribute to bringing about the will of God.

As Christians, we are called to choose our vocations with confidence in the Lord's promise to be with us "always; yes, to the end of time" (Mt 28:20). We know that "by turning everything to their good God cooperates with all those who love the Lord" (Rom 8:28). Finally, we rely on the promise of the Lord for a blessed future: "I know the plans I have in mind for you—it is Yahweh who speaks—plans for peace, not disaster, reserving a future full of hope for you" (Jer 29:11–12).

CHAPTER FOUR

OPEN-HEART PRAYER
AND THE DIVINE

"The mystical lives in the field of daily action."
DIANE M. CONNELLY
All Sickness Is Homesickness

ZACCHAEUS, PERCHED on a sycamore tree looking out for the Lord, is a fitting image of a person at prayer (Lk 19:1–10). Moved by a desire to see Jesus, he positions himself in such a way that the Lord might be revealed to him. We who grapple with prayer easily identify with him. We are often stirred by a similar desire to encounter the Lord, but like Zacchaeus, struggle with knowing how to go about making contact. The short tax collector's inability to see above the crowd is paralleled by our shortsightedness and inability to peer over the many tall concerns and preoccupations that line the path of our busy days, blocking our view of Jesus. Like Zacchaeus, we need to find our own sycamore tree with branches strong and tall enough to lift us above whatever crowds out the Lord and prevents us from seeing him.

The story of Zacchaeus captures the spirit of holistic prayer. Such prayer invites us to look for the Lord close to home, in our own backyards where the Word has "pitched His tent among us" (Jn 1:14). It is essentially earthy. It places more emphasis on our ability to see the Lord in the mundane world of daily life and annual events than on the beatific vision that will be ours later. That is why it insists that when we pray, we must bring all of our actual experiences into prayer, not leave them at the door.

Holistic prayer involves imitating Zacchaeus' resourcefulness and spontaneity. Finding creative ways of making contact with the Word made flesh demands that we be experimental, and not rigid or stodgy in our approaches to prayer. When discouraged about our prayer, the temptation is often to give up completely. Instead of hopeless abandonment, holistic prayer encourages us to try new approaches. Like Zacchaeus, we need the courage to stand apart from the crowd and to try out unaccustomed practices. Sitting on the floor with legs crossed in a Zen posture may not be the way we grew up learning how to pray. Yet, there may be times when we experience so much noisy agitation that the quieting effect of Zen meditation offers the only access to the Lord's small, still voice within. Whatever our condition, we must be committed to doing whatever we need to do to encounter the Lord, even if that means climbing a tree! Sometimes our preconceptions about prayer hinder effective prayer. For example, thinking that we should not bring our strong negative feelings or our struggles with sexual desires into prayer can rob our prayer of all vitality. We may think that in prayer, as in most of our daily relationships, it is inappropriate to be emotionally transparent, to wear our feelings on our sleeves. Or, thinking that prayer should always be dignified and calm may prevent the Spirit from bursting into our hearts with a joy that makes us want to clap and stomp our feet. It does not seem that such self-consciousness deterred Zacchaeus. It may have been a faux pas for an establishment-type like this wealthy, senior tax collector to be so obviously excited about seeing an upstart, itinerant preacher. But Zacchaeus' desire was so strong that it led him to do spontaneously what needed to be done, despite the possibility of social embarrassment.

In prayer, desire to encounter the Lord is primary. Only a deep desire can sustain our efforts. If our desire is weak, our efforts will be unimaginative and short-lived. A guru was once approached by a disciple asking for help in prayer. Agreeing to help, the guru led the eager disciple to a shallow river. Standing next to each other in the river, the guru proceeded to dunk the disciple's head into the water. Quickly, twenty seconds passed, followed by another twenty. Then suddenly, gasping for air, the disciple jerked his head out of the water and faced his guru with bewilderment. Then the master instructed his disciple: "Unless your desire for prayer is as single-minded as your desire for air, you will not succeed."

Desire for prayer is itself a gift from the Lord. Holistic prayer endorses any means that deepens that desire and brings us into more intimate contact with the Lord. Thus, it does not ally itself with any single school of thought or method of prayer. Rather, it encourages the use of whatever works for individuals at different times. We should be hopeful in our prayer because faith reassures us that, as in the case of Zacchaeus, the Lord is also seeking contact with us. Our heart's desire for God is met with divine mutuality.

An important aspect of my ministry has been to help people with their prayer. Because many lay men and women today are asking for help with prayer, I want to make available to them what I have shared with Jesuit novices and other religious in workshops and retreats. Of course, different life circumstances will necessitate some adaptation. Nevertheless, the basic attitudes and approaches to prayer remain the same for all. This chapter may also be helpful to those who share with me the privilege of caring for God's people at prayer.

An Experiential Approach

When Kakichi Sato, 24, of Tokyo first makes his way to Engakuji monastery in Kamakura to learn *zazen* (sitting meditation), the master invites him to learn by doing. After a brief instruction, covering the basics of how to sit, breathe, and focus, the disciple is led into a room and asked to start his practice of Zen. It is in the context of his "sitting" that he receives ongoing instruction on how to improve his practice. Similarly, when Al Noone, 25, of San Jose makes his way to our Jesuit novitiate in Santa Barbara and comes to me for help in prayer, my approach is based mainly on experience and practice.

Al, like most people seeking help in prayer, already possesses prayer experiences which need to be respected and affirmed. So the first way of helping is to invite him to learn from his own experience by reflecting on his history of prayer: How has God communicated with him in the past? What ways has he discovered to be fruitful? What ways unhelpful? Next, I would encourage him to continue praying regularly. Although the ability to pray is essentially a gift of God, only regular practice can develop it into a lasting habit. Practice is important because learners benefit most when they receive instruction in the context of actual experience, and are not just learning in a theoretical and passive way. Finally, I would encourage Al to pay attention to his daily experience and to let his thoughts, feelings, desires, and fantasies flow into his prayer. Personal experience is important because it is the arena of God's present revelation. Thus bringing alert eyes and ears to the events of our day is a good way to start praying. As with Zacchaeus, awareness of the parade of events that constitutes our reality will help us to spot the Lord passing by and attune us to God's saving word being addressed to us.

"THE PLACE ON WHICH YOU STAND IS HOLY GROUND" (EX 3:6)

The story of Moses' encounter with Yahweh before the burning bush (Ex 3:1–6) emphasizes the importance of respecting our experience when praying. One day Moses was tending his flock in the wilderness and came to Horeb, the mountain of God. There Moses saw a flame of fire, coming from the middle of a bush. While the bush was blazing, it was not burning up. Drawn by curiosity, Moses approached the bush. As he drew closer, he heard God call to him from the middle of the bush: "Moses, Moses! . . . Come no nearer . . . Take off your shoes, for the place on which you stand is holy ground. I am the God of your father" (vv. 4–6).

Our present experience is the place where we stand. As with Moses, our personal experience is also holy ground because the Lord is present there. It is where we too are to encounter Yahweh and to hear the Lord of the universe call our name. We must take seriously what Yahweh said to Moses. We should not trample on the holy ground of our experiences, treating them like rough gravel. Rather, we must take off our shoes and reverently tend the fertile soil that is our experience. Only by being attentive to our experiences will we be able to encounter the Lord in the wilderness of our lives. As the authors of a recent book on prayer insist, "The being, the force, the God who came to us in the flesh meets us there in the flesh of our experience, all of it, all of our self and our world, our conscious and unconscious lives."[2]

Our ordinary life is where we will encounter God, for "in fact, he is not far from any of us, since it is in him that we live, and move, and have our being" (Acts 17:28). Since no one of us could exist without God's sustaining love, divine love must be as near as the beat of our hearts. When we view ordinary life with the eyes of faith, every bush can be a burning bush, revealing the Lord's presence. In her poem "Aurora Leigh," the Victorian poet Elizabeth Barrett Browning gives poetic expression to this:

> "Earth's crammed with heaven
> And every common bush afire with God;
> But only he who sees takes off his shoes,
> The rest sit round it and pluck blackberries."[3]

In theological language, what Browning is talking about is the sacramentality of all reality. It is the belief that the gloriously risen Christ reigns over all creation and can use any particle of created matter as a vehicle to embody and manifest God's loving presence. In the words of the Jesuit poet Gerard Manley Hopkins, "The world is charged with the grandeur of God. It will flame out, like shining from shook foil."[4] The word of God is an incarnate word, draped in the richly diverse forms of matter.

Detecting the presence of this omnipresent God in the world of our experience, according to Teilhard de Chardin, is not a matter of seeing extraordinary objects in miraculous apparitions, but of seeing the ordinary things of our experience in a different way. Our faith does not cause us to see different things, but to see things differently. A rabbinical story expresses well the truth that our encounter with spiritual meaning is to be discovered exactly in the earthly context where God has placed us, not in a heavenly city.

> In the hiddenness of time there was a poor man who left his village, weary of his life, longing for a place where he could escape all the struggles of this earth. He set out in search of a magical city—the heavenly city of his dreams, where all things would be perfect. He walked all day and by dusk found himself in a forest, where he decided to spend the night. Eating the crust of bread he had brought, he said his prayers and, just before going to sleep, placed his shoes in the center of the path, pointing them in the direction he would continue the next morning. Little did he imagine that while he slept, a practical joker would come along and turn his shoes around, pointing them back in the direction from which he had come.

The next morning, in all the innocence of folly, he got up, gave thanks to the Lord of the Universe, and started on his way again in the direction that his shoes pointed. For a second time he walked all day, and toward evening finally saw the magical city in the distance. It wasn't as large as he had expected. As he got closer, it looked curiously familiar. But he pressed on, found a street much like his own, knocked on a familiar door, greeted the family he found there —and lived happily ever after in the magical city of his dreams.[5]

Faith does not transport us to a magical city, but enables us to appreciate the significance of what we find at home. Teilhard de Chardin speaks of the radiance of the divine milieu which changes nothing in the relationships between things, but bathes the world with an inward light which leads us to a sense of God's presence. We could say that the great mystery of Christianity is not exactly the appearance, but the transparency of God in the universe. In a word, God is to be recognized not in special visions, but in the way divinity shines forth like shook foil through all creation for all with eyes of faith to see.

God's presence has been homogenized with the ordinary. An affirming word when failure has slain self-confidence, a look of understanding when the death of a spouse has rudely ruptured years of companionship, an ice-breaking word of reconciliation when a bitter family feud seemed destined to last forever—all point to the inspiring Spirit's presence. Other movements of grace are traceable elsewhere, sharpening our instincts of compassion and love: experienced, for example, when we shed our cautious feelings to reach out to AIDS patients or when we work against our sexist resistance to female ministers of communion. Situations like these serve as our burning bush, signalling the presence of the living God.

It has been conjectured that the primary reason why Teilhard touched so many with his message was that he knew how again to make of the universe a temple.[6] His deep faith in the pervasive presence of God in all reality is echoed in his prayer: "Lord, grant that I may see, that I may see *You*, that I may see and feel You *present in all things and animating* all things."[7] This vision of the universe as soaked in divinity is, of course, directly traceable to his roots as a son of Ignatius of Loyola, who defined devotion as the facility to find God in all things.

The consistent testimony of scripture assures us that the Lord who informs every living thing with life is revealed to us in our ordinary experiences. The God of Abraham, Isaac, and Jacob is a God of the living, who mingles with our acquaintances and colleagues. If we open ourselves to life as the arena of divine self-disclosure, we may find the Lord who undergirds our lives with the certainty of dignity and value at any point in our experience. Holistic prayer directs our searching eyes to our experience so that we might recognize the risen Jesus there and proclaim, in the words of the beloved disciple John, "It is the Lord" (Jn 21:7).

BEING TRANSPARENT IN GOD'S PRESENCE

The good news of Christianity is that God's presence is a saving one. The prophet Zephaniah exhorts Zion to shout for joy because "Yahweh, the king of Israel, is in your midst; you have no more evil to fear" (Zep 3:15). Present to save us from whatever threatens us, God is not someone to fear or avoid. A story is told of the French existentialist Jean-Paul Sartre, who as a young boy caught in the midst of a childish prank, cursed when told of God's presence everywhere. Later, Sartre would spell out his belief that the very notion of a God destroys the possibility of human freedom. For him, human freedom can be preserved only if the existence of God is disallowed. Sartre's understanding of God as a negative and restricting reality stands in stark contrast to the Christian view of the loving God whom we are invited to approach in prayer.

In prayer, we are invited to come as we are. Leaving our defenses and facades behind, we try to make ourselves transparent before the Lord. Although past hurts can cause us to hesitate for fear of making ourselves vulnerable, God, nevertheless, invites us with reassuring words to draw near.

> Do not be afraid, for I have redeemed you;
> I have called you by your name, you are mine.
> Should you pass through the sea, I will be with you;
> or through rivers, they will not swallow you up.
> Should you walk through fire, you will not be scorched and the
>   flames will not burn you.
> For I am Yahweh, your God,
> the Holy One of Israel, your savior.

I give Egypt for your ransom . . .
Because you are precious in my eyes,
because you are honored and I love you . . .
Do not be afraid, for I am with you (Is 43:1–5).

Scripture presents God as one who is near and deeply concerned with our existential plight. Like the Lord of the exodus, our liberator sees our oppression and is present to set us free. Like Jesus who multiplied the bread in the desert, our provider sees that we are lost and hungry, like sheep without a shepherd. Our plight always floods God's heart with compassion. The divine intervention on our behalf is available, if we but draw near to the Lord with all that besets us.

In prayer, we must speak all that is in our hearts and minds. If we sit quietly and endure the silence, we will hear all the bits and pieces of ourselves crowding in on ourselves, pleading to be heard. Prayer must begin with this inner racket, because "prayer is noisy with the clamor of all the parts of us demanding to be heard. The clamor is the sound of the great river of being flowing in us."[8] To bring our total selves in transparency to prayer is to let the Lord listen in on this inner racket.

DEVELOPING A PRAYER REPERTORY

Because active people need a repertory of diverse methods to maintain a vibrant prayer life, I suggest various approaches that can be tried. Naturally, the frequency and length of prayer will have to be decided by each person and perhaps determined only after some experimentation. Some people may find that on certain days, they can afford only ten minutes or just the few minutes before turning off the lights at night. On other days, however, they may decide that a longer period of a half-an-hour or more is what they need and desire. The type of prayer engaged in must suit the amount of time that can be set aside for it. For example, a short aspirational or mantric prayer like "Help me, Lord, for I am sinking!" can be rhythmically recited while waiting for the bus or driving, whereas contemplating a scriptural passage with the use of the imagination would require a different setting and length of time. Rigidity can turn a commitment to regular prayer into an oppressive burden; flexibility, which a rich repertory of methods makes possible, is needed to integrate prayer peacefully into the day.

Difficulty in prayer often arises not from waning desire or complacency, but from not knowing what to do when feeling stuck. Sometimes, during these periods of dryness and desolation, there is nothing to do, but to wait on the Lord with patience and hope. However, at other times, trying alternative ways and times for prayer can be helpful. To be fruitful, experiential learning in prayer requires periodic reflection on our practice and occasional assistance from a spiritual guide.

St. Ignatius is very explicit about how help can be given to people on a retreat when their prayer is flat, when "the exercitant is not affected by any spiritual experiences."[9] At such times, he suggests that the director ask the retreatant very detailed questions regarding his or her actual practice. Is the retreatant observing all the guidelines for prayer suggested in the *Exercises?* For example, how are silence and recollection being kept? Are the times set for prayer being faithfully observed? Are the suggested steps in preparation for prayer periods being taken? Is there regular reflection on prayer periods to evaluate what went on? During prayer, are the suggestions for different topics being tried?

Prayer during retreat will naturally be different from prayer in daily life; different forms of prayer also have their own guidelines. The questions suggested by Ignatius are not meant to cover all forms of prayer (for example, less structured and more informal prayer), but they reveal a basic tenet of Christian spirituality: in all things, we must use the available human means to cooperate with God's grace. Although we could not even utter "Abba, Father!" without the support of grace (Rom 8:16), we should not passively presume that our efforts are unimportant. Ignatius' suggestions merely highlight the importance of a generous human response to the gracious initiative of God.

RESPECTING ONE'S RELIGIOUS SENSIBILITIES

When praying, it is important to respect our religious sensibilities; that is, the peculiar ways we find ourselves responsive to the mystery of God's presence. The Lord draws people to intimacy with different strings of love. For example, God attracts some people through the beauty of nature or the wonders of creation. Others feel the allurements of God in the emotional stirrings of their hearts or the penetrating insights of their minds. Music, mandalas, physical movement, and stillness are yet other ways that heighten people's sensitivity to God's ineffable presence. So when praying, it is important to know from past experience how the Lord has dealt uniquely with us. Past experience can be a valuable guide. Since there is no one right way that is equally suitable for all, trying to pray in ways that do not take into account the peculiarly personal manner in which the Lord deals with us can only lead to frustration. Sometimes people do not value their own religious experience enough. They want to pray the way others pray, not in their own way. The prayer methods I will suggest are based on the rich variety of ways by which we perceive and communicate: they employ our mind, imagination, senses, feelings, body, and even our breath. They are offered as possible approaches whose usefulness must be decided by each person on the basis of his or her religious sensibility and past experience of prayer.

THE PSYCHOSOMATIC UNITY OF THE PERSON

An important development in spirituality in recent years is the rediscovery of the body-spirit or psychosomatic unity of the person. Hardly an esoteric concept, the psychosomatic unity of the person can be observed whenever bodily reactions reveal affective states. Blushing, sweaty palms, accelerated heart rate are common examples of these physical manifestations of emotions. Certain forms of psychotherapy, like Gestalt therapy, presuppose the body-spirit unity of persons and rely heavily on body language for an indication of psychological states. Gestalt therapists generally believe that the body conveys how a person feels more truthfully than words, which often conceal as much as they reveal. Another form of therapy based on the psychosomatic unity of the person is called structural reintegration, popularly known as Rolfing. This therapy is based on the assumption that certain undesirable emotions are locked in the person by muscular configurations shaped through years of habitual response. Rolfing attempts to restructure these muscular patterns in order to make new emotional responses possible.

The most direct influence on the renewed appreciation of the body's role in prayer comes from Eastern forms of meditation. Eastern practices such as *zazen* (sitting meditation) or *tai chi chuan* (the slow-motion, Chinese meditational dance) emphasize the close connection between body and spirit. In these exercises, correct posture is considered important because it is believed that bodily calm can engender internal stillness and that exterior concentration can focus the spirit's awareness. These beliefs stem from the view that body and spirit are closely united.

BODILY PRAYER

Praying with our body includes several aspects. First, because of the body-spirit unity of the person, our interior states are expressed, often unconsciously, by our bodily posture and gestures. Consequently, awareness of our body increases an awareness of our inner state. Awareness of our interiority, in turn, can indicate productive directions for our prayer, telling us, for example, what particular form of prayer would be most useful, given our present condition. Being tired or energetic, rushed or relaxed, troubled or calm are factors that should influence how we go about praying. Each time we pray we have to ask what way is best for now: to meditate on scripture, or to recite some formal prayers, or to do some kind of centering prayer, or to recite a mantra like "Jesus, have mercy on me a sinner," or simply to sit in stillness with trust in God's providence.

Second, bodily expression in prayer can sometimes convey what we feel more effectively than words. Examples of such bodily prayer are: kneeling humbly before the Lord; or holding out our hands, palms up, in receptivity to the Spirit; or simply letting our tears tell of our sorrow, fatigue, and frustration. Third, the interior silence we need to hear the often still, subtle voice of the Lord can be induced by the exterior calm and stillness achievable through the various techniques of yoga, Zen, tai chi chuan, body relaxation, and sense awareness exercises.

THE WAY OF IMAGES AND THE IMAGELESS WAY

The journey of prayer for Christians can follow along two distinct paths: the way of images called the *kataphatic* tradition and the imageless way known as the *apophatic* approach. After briefly describing these two basic traditions, I will present methods of prayer based on these two paths.

The kataphatic approach emphasizes the use of images and words, especially those found in scripture, to transport us into the mystery of faith. This approach affirms that divine self-disclosure has occurred in a history that reaches its high point in the person of Jesus Christ. The life, death, and resurrection of Jesus is God's self-manifestation in history. Thus, the way to God is through uncovering the meaning and message of Jesus, who told his apostles: "I am the Way, the Truth and the Life. No one can come to the Father except through me. If you know me, you know my Father too. From this moment you know him and have seen him" (Jn 14:6–7). In the life of Jesus Christ, the Ineffable has expressed itself, disclosing to faith the ultimate meaning and significance of all life. The kataphatic tradition reaffirms our ability to find God in all things. The fingerprints of the divine artist cling indelibly to the works of God's hands and can serve as clues to discovering the divine presence. God can be contacted through images and symbols because the Lord of creation is manifested in created things. Above all, God's face has been shown in Jesus, the living icon of God.

The apophatic approach, on the other hand, emphasizes the ineffable, unknowable mystery of God. Experiencing God is valued over knowing. Because God is the ever-greater God, so wholly other than anything in creation, divinity is best known by negation and elimination. In talking about God, for example, it is more appropriate to say what God is not than to say what God is. Using concepts and images to represent God leads easily to idolatry, the worship of a false God formed in our own image and likeness. Thus, the apophatic approach to prayer is a way of emptying, of letting go of our images and thoughts about God. For example, the anonymous author of *The Cloud of Unknowing,* a classical expression of the apophatic tradition, states: "Thought cannot not comprehend God. And so, I prefer to abandon all

I can know, choosing rather to love."[10] Union with God moves us beyond knowing to loving in darkness. Underscoring that God is infinitely greater than our human capacity to apprehend, the apophatic tradition encourages humble surrender to the mystery of God and total reliance on the divine initiative. As nameless mystery, God can only be loved because God has first loved us.

Both traditions enrich our Christian faith and must be retained for the sake of balance and integrity. The apophatic tradition reminds us that God is always more than the human mind can ever conceive or imagine. Any real knowledge of God must be received as a gift of divine disclosure. As limited creatures, we can only bow in awe and adoration before the infinite mystery of God and wait to be visited. On the other hand, the kataphatic tradition reminds us how blessed we are that the word of God has become flesh and has revealed to us the mystery of God. The Christian God is not the faceless "unknown god" of the Areopagus (Acts 17:23), but the person Jesus intimately addressed as "Abba," loving Father. The Aramaic term "Abba" connotes all the warmth and familiarity that the term "daddy" does. We have been invited by Jesus to address infinite mystery as "Abba." Jesus proclaimed the good news first to Mary Magdalene when he told her, "I am ascending to my Father and your Father, to my God and your God" (Jn 20:17–18). Because of Jesus, we have been made children and heirs. Through him, we now have access to ineffable mystery.

To maintain a healthy balance between the kataphatic and the apophatic in prayer, we need to oscillate rhythmically between worship and iconoclasm. Worship consists in meeting the living God in our religious experience; iconoclasm involves destroying all the concepts and images we construct to articulate our religious experience to ourselves and others. The human processes of knowing and communicating make it necessary for us to conceptualize our insights and symbolize our feelings. When we do this with our religious experiences, we sharpen our understanding of God and improve our ability to share our religious experience with others. Nevertheless, we must always remember that our impoverished words and images can never capture the reality of God. Because our words, no matter how eloquent or poetic, ultimately fail us, we must regularly put aside our theological lexicon and approach the living God with open hands and dependent hearts.

Together the kataphatic and apophatic paths offer Christians a rich repertory of prayer methods. Although these two ways to God are clearly distinct, they can be part of our storehouse of prayer and used at alternate times. Prayer often flounders when we are not resourceful enough to adapt our prayer to concrete situations. Consequently, holistic prayer encourages us to become familiar and facile with as many approaches as possible so that we can flexibly adapt our prayer to different circumstances. It is not my intention here to give an exhaustive list of prayer methods, but merely to illustrate the difference between the kataphatic and apophatic traditions by describing a representative sampling of various prayer forms.

SCRIPTURAL PRAYER

Falling into the kataphatic category, praying with scripture by reading or listening to the Bible has been for centuries an important way of praying. Scripture contains the story of God's saving interaction with humankind, and is full of rich images that can lead us to a greater knowledge and love of God. It is a favorite source of prayer because Christians consider it to be inspired. In the Second Letter to Timothy, the author exhorts his reader to remember "how, ever since you were a child, you have known the holy scriptures—from these you can learn the wisdom that leads to salvation through faith in Christ Jesus. All scripture is inspired by God and can profitably be used for teaching, for refuting error, for guiding people's lives and teaching them to be holy" (3:15–16).

Without getting into a technical discussion of the complex issues regarding the meaning and nature of biblical inspiration, we can say that scripture is inspired in this basic and important sense: it contains within itself the rich power to effect a religious experience in the lives of readers today. Although many different interpretations of inspiration are available, underlying them all is the central conviction that Christ is present in the words of scripture. Thus, perusal of the sacred text can lead to an encounter with Jesus.

There is a simple three-fold method of praying with scripture.[11] First, there is a reading of the text with the dispositions of faith and openness to the power of the Lord's word. After a brief preparation to clear our minds of distractions and to focus our wandering hearts, we read the text slowly with a hunger for the spiritual nourishment contained in the text. Second, there is a period of dwelling with the text, repeating a word, sentence, or phrase. Repetition allows the seed of God's word to sink into the inner soil of our souls. Third, there is a time for praying spontaneously or maintaining a loving silence in response to what the word of God has stirred up in us. This approach to scriptural prayer is reflected in the experience of the prophet Jeremiah: "When your words came, I devoured them: your word was my delight and the joy of my heart; for I was called by your name, Yahweh, God of Sabaoth" (15:16).

IGNATIAN CONTEMPLATION OF SCRIPTURE

St. Ignatius of Loyola has given us a rich way of praying with scripture through the use of the imagination. Called Ignatian contemplation, it has led many to a more intimate relationship with the Lord. The basic thrust of Ignatian contemplation is to dispose us to meet the risen Jesus at the deepest level of our beings, and to actualize this experience by more fully living a committed Christian life. By employing our senses and imaginations, we are asked to immerse ourselves into a gospel mystery so totally that we receive an intimate, felt knowledge of Jesus that goes far beyond something merely abstract and impersonal.

In contemplating a gospel scene, we are invited to move with our imagination and senses directly into the event and relive it as if it were our own experience. This immersion allows the gospel event to spring to life and to become a lively happening in which we participate. When we encounter Jesus this way, he is not a pale figure in a book, but a vibrant person who takes us into the historical events of the gospel mystery and reveals the fullness of its meaning.

In teaching people how to use the method of Ignatian contemplation, I rely on a procedure used by Gestalt therapists when working with dreams. The technique employed in Gestalt dream work contains three steps. First, the client is asked to narrate the contents of the dream, just as he or she would in telling a story or recounting a past experience. Second, the client is asked to shift the narrative into the present tense and describe how the dream would be reenacted, as if staging a play and giving directions to actors about how they should position themselves and what they are supposed to be doing and saying. Third, the client is asked to take the part of the different characters or aspects of the dream. This last step invites the client to fully identify with the people and action contained in the dream.

Dramatization is a key to the Gestalt approach to dreams. Instead of relating a conflict in words and tracing their track to deeper levels, as one might do in analyzing a dream with a psychoanalyst, the Gestalt subject reenacts it by alternately playing out its different parts. Normally several chairs are used and the client shifts back and forth between them as different parts of the conflict are enacted. The patient may first play his overbearing conscience (what Fritz Perls labelled the "top-dog") and yell at an imaginary self in the other chair to do better. Then switching chairs, the client will be the submissive, whining, yet obstinate and wily, "underdog" who limps through life spitefully defying his conscience. The point, of course, is that both parts are really the patient himself, though each is trapped in struggle against the other. By getting the client to give each part its say, he is led to realize vividly that, despite his experience of fragmentation, he is only one organism.

An important goal of Gestalt therapy is to help the client achieve greater wholeness by re-integrating parts of the self that have been divorced from consciousness. According to Gestalt therapy, each element of a dream represents a disowned fragment of one's personality. For example, an angry and violent character in a dream suggests that the client's feelings of anger and violence are being repressed. Or, a taken-for-granted and trampled doormat in a dream may help the client, while identifying with that mat, get in touch with feelings of being abused and unappreciated. As a royal road to the unconscious, dreams call our attention to things that we repress in our waking moments. Awareness of these repressed elements allows us to re-own them and thereby achieve a greater wholeness. Awareness also leads to greater "response-ability" because when we bring these forces which impinge on our lives out of the dark cave of the unconscious, we expand our capacity to deal with them.

The three-step approach of Gestalt dream work is helpful for someone learning how to do Ignatian contemplation. By applying the same three steps to contemplating a mystery of the Bible, we can achieve a progressively deeper immersion into the mystery of faith. An application of this Gestalt procedure to praying with scripture could take this form: First, read the account of an event or mystery in scripture, like the cure of the blind beggar Bartimaeus at the end of the Way section in Mark's gospel (10:46–52). Second, identify with one of the onlookers and describe the action from his or her point of view. Do this as if the event were actually unfolding right now in front of your eyes. Third, insert yourself into the event by identifying with one of the active participants in the scene. As you experience what is happening in the gospel scene, be aware of what you are thinking, sensing, and feeling —your entire subjective response.

The value of this approach is that it can plunge us so deeply into a gospel mystery that we get caught up in a personal encounter with the Lord. As often happens in a psychodrama or a play, there can come a time in contemplation when the artificiality of the put-on identity slips away and the gospel character comes to life in us. Then, it is no longer Bartimaeus the blind beggar who is being summoned to Jesus and being healed. It is the blind person in us who is being led out of the darkness of personal confusion by the Lord's healing touch. It is no longer Bartimaeus who is crying out with desperation for help, but a desperately blind part of us that seeks enlightenment. Then, it is no longer just a study of the historical Jesus interacting with people in biblical times. When our contemplation shifts from imaginative role playing to spontaneous identification, we can get drawn into a graced encounter with the risen Christ today.

Ignatian contemplation can be a powerful way of hearing the word of God being addressed to us in the present. Contemplation, like Gestalt dream therapy, can put us in contact with parts of ourselves that we have unconsciously repressed or consciously suppressed in order to cope with some troubling reality. In either case, disowning parts of ourselves is like saying to members of the family that there is no place for them at home. It is a denial of self that often leads to self-alienation and fragmentation. The struggle for wholeness can be greatly supported by prayer, if we accept our fragmented state and let our struggling parts be addressed by the word of God. When we suppress parts of ourselves, we not only blot them out of our minds, but also exclude them from our prayer—keeping these often wounded parts out of the Lord's healing reach.

In Ignatian contemplation, we can be surprised by the sudden emergence of suppressed parts demanding attention. The attention they need is not only ours, but also the Lord's. Contemplative prayer allows the word of God to address these self-depreciating parts with the good news of the savior's affirming love. In the safety of prayer, for example, these parts, like Nicodemus under the safe cover of darkness, can surface to meet the Lord: the frightened inner child can drop the pretense of worldly self-sufficiency and hear the Lord say to it, "Do not be afraid, for I am with you" (Is 43:5); the chronic worrier of sleepless nights can find consolation in the Lord's assurance that "There is no need to be afraid, little flock, for it has pleased your Father to give you the kingdom" (Lk 12:32); the sexually compulsive part can let its confusion and guilt be dissolved by the unconditional acceptance of Jesus who says to it what he said to the adulterous woman, "Has no one condemned you? . . . Neither do I condemn you" (Jn 8:10–11); or the unfeeling and selfish self can have hope in the Lord's promise that "I shall give you a new heart, and put a new spirit in you; I shall remove the heart of stone from your bodies and give you a heart of flesh instead" (Ezek 36:26–27). By allowing these parts to approach the Lord in the intimacy of prayer, Ignatian contemplation can bring about a powerfully transforming encounter with the living word of God.

The words of theologian William Spohn provide a pithy summary of the value of contemplating scripture through the method of identification with gospel characters:

> As we tangibly and visually move into their narrated encounter with the Lord, we find in ourselves some echo of their response: If Peter could be forgiven, so can I. If the father could welcome home the prodigal son, then my fears of God's anger are without foundation. We learn to "ask for what we want" in these contemplations by the example of these characters in the story. They raise our expectations and open us to hear the Lord's word to us today.[12]

According to Spohn, an important value of Ignatian contemplation is that it trains us to spot the "rhyme," the similarities existing between biblical narratives and our own times. By helping us identify the analogy between biblical situations and our own, it moves us from the memory of God's intervention in the past to a perception of divine intervention in our present crisis. Ignatian contemplation teaches our imaginations how to catch the "rhyme" that can be revelatory for us today.[13]

PRAYING WITH OUR SENSES

Another kataphatic form is praying with our senses. Sense-prayer can be particularly beneficial when we find our minds racing or cluttered with a thousand thoughts. Simple sense awareness exercises can bring about a state of calm attentiveness. For example, by closing one's eyes and concentrating on the various sounds around, one can escape the distracting pull of abstract thought and be transported back to the present moment with greater stillness and awareness. Focusing on sounds, colors, textures, and temperatures is a way of going out of our minds and coming to our senses. Our senses root us in the present and thus enable us to better encounter the Lord in prayer. Effective prayer requires us to be psychologically present to the Lord, not far away in thought.

Sense-prayer is based on the fact that "awareness of the divine begins with wonder."[14] In his *Apology for Wonder,* Sam Keen points out the relationship between wonder and worship, contemplation and celebration. A dominant response to the shock of a wonder-event is the "movement from admiration to contemplation to celebration."[15] By returning us to objects that were given in wonder so that we might prolong admiration and appreciation, contemplation has the capacity to evoke certain affective responses to reality. Admiration generates "gratitude and the impulse to celebrate, or possibly even to worship."[16] Sense-prayer can simply take the form of standing in grateful awe before the dazzling colors of a rose garden or the majestic shapes of Yosemite's stone monuments; it can occur when taking delight in a sunset or marveling over the sparkling beauty of a star-studded sky. A colorful illustration of wonder is the incident recounted in Nikos Kazantzakis' novel, *Zorba the Greek.* One day, Zorba was riding on a donkey with his boss. As they passed an oncoming traveler on another ass, Zorba's eyes were transfixed on the stranger. When chided by his companion for so impolitely gawking at someone, Zorba proclaimed in child-like simplicity his awe over the fact that there are such things in the world as donkeys! To view reality with wonder is to see ordinary things as donkeys with a sense of astonishment—as if seeing them for the first time.

Reality, when regarded with wonder, alludes to something beyond itself. It is this allusion that conveys to us "the awareness of a spiritual dimension of reality, the relatedness of being to transcendent meaning."[7] Perceiving creation with marvel leads naturally to awe—a sense for the reference everywhere to God who is beyond all created things. Praying with our senses can lead to this awe-inspired vision of reality which enables us to find the creator in all things. Sense-prayer can help us to make of the universe a temple, to perceive in the world intimations of the divine, to feel in the rush of the passing the stillness of the eternal, and to sense the ultimate in the simple, common, ordinary experiences of our lives.

Wonder is a sense of radical amazement over the very existence of the material universe. In the words of the philosopher Wittgenstein, "It is not *how* things are in the world that is mystical, but *that* it exists."[18] The source of wonder as radical amazement is the fact that something exists rather than nothing. A blade of grass, for example, does not contain its own adequate explanation or necessary reason for existence. At one time it did not exist and at another time it will cease to exist. It need not be, yet it enjoys the gift of being. Radical amazement is caused by our "sense of perpetual surprise at the fact that there are facts at all."[19] Wonder refers, then, not only to what we see, but also to the very act of seeing as well as to our own selves, to the selves that see and are amazed at our very ability to see. The question that confronts everyone who ponders the existence of being is: "Why is there something rather than nothing?"

Wonder is linked to experiencing the holy because when we regard reality with awe, we open ourselves to receiving "an answer of the heart and mind to the presence of mystery in all things, *an intuition for a meaning that is beyond the mystery,* an awareness of the transcendent worth of the universe."[20] Heschel describes the religious experience that comes through wonder when he states:

> True, the mystery of meaning is silent. There is no speech, there are no words, the voice is not heard. Yet beyond our reasoning and beyond our believing there is a *preconceptual* faculty that senses the

glory, the presence of the Divine. We do not perceive it. We have no knowledge; we only have an awareness. We witness it.[21]

When we pray with our senses, we attempt to enter reverently and gratefully into the garden of creation and there to witness the presence of the divine, who at every moment sustains all things in existence. "God does not die on the day when we cease to believe in a personal deity," states Dag Hammarskjold, "but we die on the day when our lives cease to be illumined by the steady radiance, renewed daily, of a wonder, the source of which is beyond all reason."[22]

THE IMAGELESS WAY

The apophatic tradition is best illustrated by what is called centering prayer, an attempt to experience God shorn of all images. Centering prayer reflects the advice given in *The Cloud of Unknowing* that "in the real contemplative work you must set all this [thinking] aside and cover it over with a cloud of forgetting."[23] Thus, this prayer form eschews the use of the imagination and the mind. In using centering prayer, we try to still our cognitive faculties and eliminate anything that detracts from our focusing on the indwelling presence of the word. Void of thoughts and feelings, the self possesses a greater vacancy for the Lord. By quieting our cognitive processes, we seek to attend singlemindedly to the mystery of God dwelling at the core or center of our being. Because the ineffable mystery cannot be grasped by our limited minds, centering prayer emphasizes the importance of simply waiting in stillness for the Lord's visitation. In prayer, we are called to surrender to the coming of the Lord in whatever fashion the divine chooses to manifest itself.

Perhaps the best way to convey an understanding of centering prayer is to describe how we would go about practicing it. Basil Pennington, the best known proponent of centering prayer in the United States, has delineated three "rules" for centering prayer.[24] He surrounds the word "rules" with quotation marks because he wants to use the term loosely, since the intimate spontaneity of prayer precludes the usefulness of strict rules. The following are his guidelines:

Sit, relax and be quiet.

1. Be in faith and love to God who dwells in the center of your being.

2. Take up a love word and let it be gently present, supporting your being to God in faith-filled love (e.g., "Abba," "Jesus," "Lord," "Love").

3. Whenever you become aware of anything, simply return gently to the Lord with the use of your prayer word.

At the end of the prayer, take several minutes to come out, mentally praying the "Our Father."

Pennington insists that centering prayer should be kept simple: first, in the sense that it should not be a complicated procedure or method; second, in the sense that there is only one, undivided focus, that is the Lord. In centering prayer, we choose God "as the Center of our life, the Center beyond our self-center," states Pennington, and thus we allow the Lord full sway over our lives. "That is the whole prayer . . . it is that simple, that total."[25]

INTEGRATING EASTERN TECHNIQUES

In the last twenty years or so, there have been valuable contributions made by spiritual writers attempting to introduce Eastern approaches into Christian prayer. A decade ago, I was fortunate to spend five months in Japan working with two fellow Jesuits, who have been pioneers in this effort to enrich Christian prayer with Eastern ways. My work with William Johnston, an Irish theologian who has spent close to 40 years in Japan, and with Kakichi Kadowaki, a Japanese philosopher at Sophia University, provided me with many insights, which form the basis of my remarks here.[26]

"Christian Zen" can be described as sitting with faith. This adaptation of sitting meditation (*zazen*) requires that we learn the rudiments of Zen-sitting[27] as any other Zen practitioner, but that we approach the practice with a completely different frame of mind than a non-Christian Zennist would. Zen Buddhism can be accurately understood more as a psychology than a religion. Its devotees seek a sense of harmony with the universe, a feeling of solidarity with everything based on a deep intuition that the underlying unity of all reality makes visible differences merely illusory. This sense of unity allows all tensions and strife, all divisions and conflicts to fall away and to be replaced by inner calm and compassion. The Zen practitioner sits in stillness and silence, waiting for the flash of insight, called *kensho,* that allows him or her to see beneath the superficial level of sensible multiplicity and to perceive the essence of unified reality in its unchanging depths.

When we as Christians practice Zen, however, we do so primarily to encounter the living God, who is the ground of our being. Unlike Zen's merger with the Absolute which destroys all individuality, the union we seek as Christians is interpersonal. We enter into the depths of silence to hear the voice of the risen Lord. With Paul, we believe that "I live now not with my own life but with the life of Christ who lives in me" (Gal 2:20). In practicing Zen as a form of Christian prayer, we seek the peace of the risen Christ, who allows it to be felt in the core of our being. While we try to become proficient in the technical aspects of Zen-sitting, we realize that it is not our technical proficiency that will bring about an enlightening encounter with the risen Christ. Only God's grace can lead us to the light that will shatter the darkness of our lives. So, as in centering prayer, Christian Zen practitioners sit with faith and hope, waiting to be struck by illuminating grace.

Both centering prayer and Christian Zen are a response to the Lord's invitation that we "Be still and know that I am God" (Ps 46:10). Believing that the Lord is capably in charge of the universe, we merely try to sit in God's presence with an attitude of trust and acceptance; we let go of our planning and rely on God's providence. This attitude helps us to live in the present, and not be dragged off from prayer by an anxious and calculating mind. Both approaches to prayer attempt to induce an inner calm that will allow us to be more present to the ever-present God within. The major difference lies in the fact that Zen follows a body of precise and technical rules regarding proper posture and breathing. Centering prayer is less concerned about the techniques of posture and breathing, insisting only that we assume a relaxed position when we sit. The Zen approach is a rich and ancient tradition. While requiring a degree of discipline, its method of inducing spiritual awareness through proper posture, correct breathing, and undivided attention has been proven through the ages. Christians needing more methodic help in prayer to stifle the "monkey mind" which swings distractingly from one cognitive branch to another would well profit from the practice of Christian Zen.

PRAYING WITH OUR BREATH

In Asia, training of the breath is the first step in the spiritual path. Inner stillness is achieved through proper breathing, which is slow, rhythmical, and abdominal. Breathing through our nose, with lips tightly closed, our breathing can be slowed down by simply lengthening our exhalations. Our breathing is ordinarily irregular, dominated by our emotional life and changes in mood. It can become rhythmical simply by our watching or following it. Without trying to change it, we watch our breathing by counting our inhalations or exhalations, or both. Finally, to breathe abdominally, we breathe in such a way that the incoming air swells the muscles of the lower abdomen. When we breathe abdominally, our abdomen expands as we inhale and contracts as we exhale. By sitting with a straight back, so that there is an unobstructed passageway for the flow of air through the body, and by breathing slowly, rhythmically, and abdominally, we can achieve inner and outer stillness.

Praying with our breath can also be very helpful, when words and thoughts are inadequate to express the deep sentiments of our hearts. When lonely or longing for the Lord, we can, by inhaling with faith, take in the divine presence, which sustains us in existence every moment of our lives. Like the air around us, the life-giving Spirit's presence should be seen more as inevitable than as evanescent. As we are reminded in Acts, it is in God that we live, move, breathe, and have our being (17:28). In the upper room, where the fearful apostles huddled together after the crucifixion of Jesus, the risen Christ breathed upon his disciples and passed on his life-giving Spirit (Jn 20:22). Like the apostles, we too can receive the Spirit which Jesus continues to breathe upon his followers today. Because we live in a divine milieu, the Spirit of God is present to us in the air we breathe.

We can also let the Spirit dwelling within help us utter with deep sighs and groans what words simply cannot express. When we pray, it is better to have a heart without words than words without a heart. In a prayer exercise called "breath-communication," Indian Jesuit Anthony de Mello has suggested a simple way of praying with our hearts through breathing.[28] We can breathe in a way that tells of our deep yearning for God by extending our inhalation. We can express our trusting surrender to God's providence by extending our exhalation. Breathing out deeply, we imagine placing our whole selves in God's caring hands. Or we can let the sadness of our hearts be communicated to the Lord by our deep sighs. Communicating with our breath in prayer can also let the Lord know of our love, gratitude, praise, as well as our need for healing, mercy, and love. In faith, we can breathe in what we need from God and breathe out whatever impurities taint our souls: for example, we might imagine ourselves breathing in God's love and breathing out our self-hatred; breathing in the Lord's mercy and breathing out our self-condemnation; breathing in the savior's peace and breathing out our anxiety; and breathing in Jesus' compassion and breathing out our self-righteousness.

MANTRIC PRAYER

Related to breath-prayer is mantric prayer. A mantra is a word or a short phrase of about seven syllables that is rhythmically repeated in prayer in order to focus our attention or to bring about inner stillness. When we repeat a mantra reverently, it becomes part of our internal timing. As one writer puts it, "Synchronized with our breathing, the mantra resonates at a depth that can touch the very essence of our lives . . . helps us to slow down, to journey deep within, to feel the pulse of our inner life, to live from a deeper source."[29]

Synchronizing our breathing with a word or phrase can be easily developed as a form of prayer. For example, we might select a word like "Abba" as a mantra. Then, as we inhale, we mentally say the first syllable, "ab," and then the second syllable, "ba," as we exhale. Doing this in a rhythmical way and with a sense of addressing God as a loving Father can be a simple, yet profound, experience of prayer. Other words such as "Jesus," "Lord," or "Amen" can be used in mantric prayer. Besides such single words, phrases from scripture can also be used. When using phrases in mantric prayer, seven-syllable ones fit most easily into the form. As we inhale, we mentally say the first three words, pause with the fourth word, then finish the phrase as we exhale. Longer or shorter phrases can also be used. The important thing is to be able to find a phrase that can be repeated in a way that synchronizes easily with rhythmic breathing. In any of its variant forms, the well-known Jesus prayer ("Jesus, Son of David, have mercy on me a sinner") can be prayed in a mantric fashion. Some other scriptural examples of helpful mantric phrases are:

There is nothing I shall want. (Source: Ps 23)

A pure heart create for me. (Source: Ps 51)

Give me the joy of your help. (Source: Ps 51)

Live through love in his presence. (Source: Eph 1:3–12)

Your love is better than life. (Source: Ps 63)

You are precious in my eyes. (Source: Is 43:1–5)

I came that they may have life. (Source: Jn 10:1–10)

Be still! Know that I am God. (Source: Ps 46:10)[30]

Besides the Bible, other sources can provide phrases that can be used profitably for mantric prayer. The rosary, for example, can be a form of mantric prayer, if we emphasize the rhythmic repetition of the prayers rather than meditating on the mysteries of Christ's life.

PRAYER AND PERSPECTIVE

Our prayer can become lifeless and dry, if it is disconnected from what is actually going on with us. Such compartmentalized prayer quickly comes to feel irrelevant. The prayer method proposed by St. Ignatius called "the general examination of conscience"[31] addresses this problem by helping active people forge a link between their formal prayer and their daily lives. In recent years, it has been renamed the "awareness examen" or the "consciousness examen."[32] This renaming has been significant because it highlights the value of this prayer for monitoring the quality of our daily lives and for keeping our spiritual growth moving forward.[33] The original name of "examination of conscience" is too often associated in the minds of older Catholics with the negative type of introspection that preceded going to confession.

The awareness or consciousness examen is more helpfully seen in positive terms, as a prayer to gain perspective on our lives. A combination of two Latin words, *per* (through) and *spicere* (to see), "perspective" means being able to see through details for a sense of the total picture and to see through superficial appearances for a deeper appreciation of reality. The examen carves out a few moments of solitude in the midst of a busy day to allow us to reflect on what is going on and where our actions and choices are taking us. It is a form of discernment, because it enables us to look concretely at events and ask: "What is really going on here?" "Where is God in *this* situation?" "How was God there for me in *that* experience?" "What in my present situation is leading me to God and others in love? What is leading me away?" "What is the underlying spirit in my dealings with others?" Such questions invite us to find God in the concrete particularities that make up the reality of our lives.

The examen enables us, with the help of God's illuminating assistance, to stay in touch with the currents and undercurrents of our fast-paced lives. It is often difficult, at the actual time, to know what is really going on (meaning and significance) in what is taking place (occurrence or event). Perhaps, what is really going on in the fierce fight that flares up suddenly between a husband and wife facing imminent separation may be more than meets the eye. A struggle to let go of each other or an unconscious effort to ease the pain of separation may be a truer picture of what is going on than the observable conflict over a small issue. Or, perhaps, their fight is at least a way of making contact, after months of misunderstanding, alienation, and stony silence. Our human lives are filled with many such ambiguous occurrences. We need solitude and distance to gain some understanding of what is really going on in all these situations. The examen is a perspective-providing prayer that allows the Lord's grace to illumine our hearts and minds.

The structure of the awareness examen can take various forms, but essentially consists of five steps. Step 1 is praying for God's enlightenment so that the Spirit will help us see ourselves a bit more as we are seen. Here we are praying for a Spirit-guided insight into our actions and our hearts. Step 2 is praying in gratitude for all the gifts that God has given us. Instead of taking God for granted, we reflect on our many blessings. This reflective thanksgiving can lead eventually to a more spontaneous gratitude as we start to recognize these gifts throughout our day. Step 3 involves a survey of the day in which we pay attention to our feelings, moods, thoughts, and urgings as a way of getting a sense of what is going on in our lives. Step 4 is praying for forgiveness for ways we have not lived up to the twofold commandment of love. And step 5 is asking for the help we need to improve our love of God and all those our lives touch. Meant to be a short prayer of ten to fifteen minutes, done at mid-day and before bed, the examen can serve as a prayerful pause to remind us that the Lord is with us in the activities of our busy days, as well as in the quiet moments we can find for formal prayer.

DEVOTION AS THE FACILITY
TO FIND GOD IN ALL THINGS

In the final analysis prayer is not meant to be a complicated affair, but simply a matter of finding and loving God. St. Teresa once summed it up nicely when she said that "the important thing is not to think much but to love much; and so do that which best stirs you to love."[34]

In prayer, we are called to find and love God in the concrete experiences of our lives. As with Moses before the burning bush, the place where we stand is holy ground. It is there that we find God, not elsewhere. There is a story of a drunkard who was staggering around looking for his missing car keys. To a stranger who ran into him bent over in search, he said, "I lost my keys over there in the dark, but I'm looking for them here because there's more light." We are called to take our experiences to prayer and to recognize the risen Christ in faces and features not his own. Not to turn to our personal experiences in our search for God will cause us to flounder in frustration, like the drunkard searching in the wrong place.

The prayer methods offered in this chapter should serve us as the sycamore branch served Zacchaeus. They are meant to help us spot the Lord in our daily lives and to receive the salvation that our savior wishes to bring to our house this day. If these methods take on an exaggerated importance, they can turn out to be hindrances rather than helps. Techniques in prayer can help dispose us to receive God's self-disclosure and love. But techniques can never replace grace, which alone can help us love the Lord with all our hearts. An ancient Chinese proverb is very instructive here: "Only the fool stares at his finger when it is pointing to the moon." Prayer techniques are like fingers pointing to God. To become preoccupied with them is to be foolishly distracted from our heart's desire.

Finally, we need to appreciate that the only way to know God is to proceed in humility, simplicity, and poverty, enter God's silence, and there in patient prayer wait until divinity reveals itself according to its own good timetable. Often, it seems that we do not wait long enough. Our waiting can be improved through the faithful practice of prayer. To support the life of prayer, I suggest three guiding principles: (1) Adapt your prayer to fit your concrete situation each time you go to pray, to match your mood and physical state, to make your prayer congruent with your existential concerns; (2) Experiment freely and learn from experience what place, posture, and prayer forms work best for you; (3) Trust your intuition and the Spirit's lead in your prayer. Go peacefully where you are drawn by the Spirit of God.

CHAPTER FIVE

IS GOD THE TELLING
INFLUENCE IN MY LIFE?

"God desires our independence—which we attain when, ceasing to strive
for it ourselves, we 'fall' back into God."[1]
DAG HAMMARSKJOLD, *Markings*

"OBEDIENCE" IS A term that disturbs many people, especially when it
is applied to adults. Children should obey; dogs are sent to obedience
school. But, the concept of obedience seems incompatible with notions
of mature adulthood and personal autonomy. How are Christians to
make sense of obedience as a virtue distinguishing their lives as followers of Jesus, who "learnt obedience, Son though he was, through
his sufferings" (Heb 5:8)? Can contemporary Christians embrace obedience as a gospel value, without compromising their maturity as
adults?

Obedience is, fundamentally, our affirmation of the good news that
we are God's very own, chosen to be part of the family of God (Eph
1:14). As the letter to the Ephesians puts it, "God the Father of our Lord
Jesus Christ" has chosen "us in Christ before the world was made to be
holy . . . and to be adopted" children (Eph 1:3–5). The heart of obedience lies in a joyful "yes" to this familial relationship with God.
Through obedience, we humbly acknowledge that we have been created by a loving God and are called to express our gratitude through
loving service. Accepting our nature as creatures, we confess that God
is central to our lives, the *raison d'etre* of our existence.

"The obedience of faith," a phrase used by St. Paul, describes well our acceptance of God as the loving source and destiny of our lives. Speaking about his own role as a missionary to the Gentiles, Paul states in Romans: Through Christ "we have received grace and our apostolic mission of winning the obedience of faith among all the nations for the honor of his name" (1:5). His mission was to bring people to a surrender in faith to God. When we surrender to God in faith, we give up all our illusions about being totally self-sufficient and acknowledge our dependent relationship with a God who is both creator and Lord. In this fundamental sense, obedience is faith, and disobedience is unbelief.

In negative terms, disobedience is a denial of creaturehood. The spirit of disobedience deludes us into thinking that we are wholly self-reliant and a law unto ourselves. Thus, it militates against the kind of loving relationship with God that Jesus proclaimed to be the heart of our fulfillment as human beings. It leads to living a life that is totally devoid of any reference to a higher being from whom we receive all that is good. Disobedience is also human autonomy gone awry because it reflects an attitude of arrogance and domination. If we view human freedom and autonomy as absolute values, we will refuse to acknowledge anything that would interfere with our desire to be in complete control of our lives. This attitude makes us guard our independence like rebellious teenagers and pits us in opposition to God or anyone else who threatens our freedom. It also impedes true interpersonal relationships because people who demand complete control of their lives are likely to treat others as objects. Avoiding closeness to others, such persons betray a deep insecurity about their identity as separate selves. They seem never to have developed an adequate sense of personal autonomy.

AUTONOMY AND OBEDIENCE

The ability to stand on one's own two feet, autonomy involves having a self-assured sense of oneself as unique and distinguishable from others. As such, autonomy is a mark of maturity. The developmental journey from childhood to adulthood requires that children gradually take upon themselves the authority that before had to be exercised by others. Acquiring an autonomous self involves a process called ego development. This process starts with the emergence of a self-concept, which helps infants to set themselves off as distinct from the wider environment of objects and people with whom they perceive themselves initially fused. Then through a sequence of stages, children gradually move from phases of dependence to adult independence. That movement is best understood as a zigzag pattern rather than as a straight line because it involves a struggle, in which there are alternating periods of dependence on parents and rebellion when the child tries to assert his or her independence. The negativity of the "terrible twos" and the stage of adolescent revolt illustrate the struggle. Perhaps the classic expression of the attempted assertion of independence during childhood is the young child who decides to run away from home.

Psychologist Robert Kegan recounts a delightful story that describes the quest for personal autonomy during childhood and the beautiful sensitivity of parents who try to support that struggle for individuality. An eight-year-old boy, deciding one afternoon that he had had it with his parents, declared his intentions to leave home. Trying to be sympathetic, the parents watched him pack a few things into a bag. They told him how much they would miss him and wished him well. As they watched discreetly from a window, their son walked away from the house and fell into playing with some neighborhood friends. Before too long it was dusk. The boy's friends quickly scattered for home and dinner. The parents watched their son as he stood for a long while by himself. He lingered for a long while by his little suitcase and then gradually, dejectedly started back home. Seeing the shame on their son's face and not wanting to humiliate him further, the parents were concerned about what would happen at their reunion. And so they ended up making what is often a wise choice when unsure of exactly what to do. When their son returned, they stayed seated, kept their mouths closed, and offered the boy a gentle undemanding attention. As they watched him sit down in a chair opposite them, they noticed that he too was quiet, pensive, self-absorbed. No one said a word. Finally the family cat dashed across the middle of the room. Looking up, the boy exclaimed, "I see you still have that old cat."[2]

Adult autonomy is achieved when people are both willing and able to leave home and live on their own. Taking responsibility for their own lives, autonomous adults are willing to make judgments and decisions. At the same time, they feel sufficiently confident of their independence to follow directions whenever they feel it is appropriate.

They value their own opinions while remaining open to the opinions of others without feeling threatened. As they grow in self-confidence, they experience a gradually decreasing emotional dependence on parents and others. While such individuals value the support of family and friends, they are confident of their ability to get along reliably well without them.

Furthermore, autonomous adults have their own present motives for doing what they do. Unlike Freudians who emphasize the force of motivational influences from the past, psychologist Gordon Allport states that most normal adult motives are contemporary and no longer related to roots in childhood. "The character of motives," Allport argues, "alters so radically from infancy to maturity that we may speak of adult motives as supplanting the motives of infancy."[3] His notion has been labeled "functional autonomy" to indicate that a habit—for example, practicing the violin at a certain hour each day—need not be tied to a motive from childhood. Although a musician may once have been spurred to mastery of the violin by a need to overcome inferiority feelings, his later love of music becomes functionally autonomous from its origin. According to Allport, the autonomy of an individual's motives is a measure of maturity. Having personal goals and a sense of purpose in life reflects the autonomy that we are all called to achieve in the journey towards adulthood.

A healthy sense of autonomy allows us to enjoy being individuals, while at the same time permitting us to respect the individuality of others. Autonomous persons are able to live peacefully with the inevitable restrictions imposed on personal freedom by the contingencies of group living. The rights of others always place limits on our own freedom. A mark of a healthy sense of autonomy is that it allows people to recognize the corresponding rights and individuality of others in the human community.

People who have not successfully achieved a healthy sense of independent selfhood are likely to struggle with authority and find cooperation with others threatening. They resist authority because anyone who has power over them is perceived as threatening. Reluctant to collaborate, they feel a resistance to going along with plans that others have suggested. They often appear to be irresponsible and willful because they disdain rules and regulations and fight against constraints. Such behavior reveals the dark side of autonomy. When personal autonomy is made an idol it easily leads to sin, disobedience and disorder. According to one writer, "The healthy drive towards autonomy is seduced and vitiated by an unhealthy drive towards egoism and pride."[4] Human autonomy can never be absolute. Yet we are constantly fooled by Satan's promise: "You will be like gods" (Gn 3:5). It is certainly significant that the sin of Adam (humankind) is presented in Genesis as disobedience arising from an overweening desire for autonomy—the very autonomy of God.

JESUS: AUTONOMOUS YET OBEDIENT

The modern problem of obedience requires reconciling personal autonomy with submission to the lordship of God. The example of Jesus, therefore, is key because in his obedient accomplishment of the mission given to him by God, Jesus retained his autonomy and freedom as a mature adult. The primary model of Christian obedience must be that of the adult Jesus. By following the footsteps of Christ, we can integrate autonomy and obedience, initiative and availability, creativity and receptivity.

The gospels clearly portray Jesus as someone with a strong sense of personal autonomy. He possessed a sense of who he was and what he wished to accomplish in life. His deeply rooted sense of identity and purpose allowed him to stay true to his goals, even when misunderstood by his own family, deserted by his early followers, and ridiculed by the religious establishment. In Mark 3:21, we read that his relatives "set out to take charge of him convinced he was out of his mind." Moreover, according to John's gospel, many of Jesus' disciples "left him and stopped going with him" (Jn 6:66), after hearing him proclaim that "if you do not eat the flesh of the Son of man and drink his blood, you will not have life in you" (Jn 6:53). Near the end of his public ministry, Jesus' life was in danger and hence he "no longer went about openly among the Jews" (Jn 11:54). Following the raising of Lazarus and all the excitement stirred up by that event, the chief priests and Pharisees decided that Jesus should be killed to maintain law and order and to reduce the risk of armed intervention by the Romans.

Despite widespread opposition, Jesus pursued his mission with dogged determination. "As the time drew near for him to be taken up to heaven, he resolutely took the road for Jerusalem and sent messengers ahead of him" (Lk 9:51). The Greek text of Luke says literally that Jesus "set his face" towards Jerusalem, a Semitic expression used often in the Old Testament to connote opposition and hostility. Thus, setting his face toward the city where his mission would be fulfilled, is a symbol of Jesus' single-minded determination.

Although all four gospels present Jesus' constant journeying, only the Lukan journey narrative (9:51 to 19:28) delineates the goal so clear before his eyes. Jesus is here portrayed as a man on the move, with a strong sense of mission. The reader gets the sense that Jesus' campaign is stepping into full swing, as he sends out his disciples ahead of him like advance men in a presidential election. There is a sense of urgency, as Jesus' steps lead relentlessly to Jerusalem. On the way, he warns would-be followers that they must tolerate hardships because "the Son of man has nowhere to lay his head" (Lk 9:58). He also admonishes those who want to delay in joining him that there is no time to lose. To one potential follower, he says: "Leave the dead to bury their dead; your duty is to go and spread the news of the kingdom of God" (9:60). And to another who wants first to return home to say goodbye to his family, Jesus says: "Once the hand is laid on the plough, no one who looks back is fit for the kingdom of God" (9:62). These responses sound harsh, unbending, and unreasonable, but they convey well the sense of urgency Jesus felt about his mission. Contemporary readers should not miss here Luke's use of hyperbole, the intentional use of exaggeration to make an effect. As scripture scholar Carroll Stuhlmueller states, "Jesus did not intend to be taken literally, but wanted to stir thought."[5] In any case, the invitation issued by Jesus to join his enterprise challenged the freedom of those who had to decide whether to follow him or not.

That Jesus was an autonomous person is unarguable. He stood his ground firmly and held on unwaveringly to his convictions in the face of bitter opposition. He also kept his granite resolve to pursue his mission, even when slowed down by defections and disbelief. He also had his own motives for pursuing his course of action, which involved a treacherous journey to Jerusalem fraught with personal danger. Jesus makes explicit that he is not a tragic hero whose life is snatched from him by forces beyond his control. Rather, he asserts that "the Father loves me, because I lay down my life in order to take it up again. No one takes it from me; I lay it down of my own free will, and as it is in my power to lay it down, so it is in my power to take it up again; and this is the command I have been given by my Father" (Jn 10:17–18).

Furthermore, the motive for Jesus' sacrificial action was clearly love of the Father. Although aware of outside influences, he remained unswayed by them. "I shall not talk with you any longer, because the prince of this world is on his way. He has no power over me, but the world must be brought to know that I love the Father and that I am doing exactly what the Father told me. Come now, let us go" (Jn 14:30–31). It is evident that Jesus' attachment to the Father motivates him to act. According to New Testament scholar David Stanley, this passage underscores "Jesus' complete freedom from any external coercion in carrying out God's designs for the salvation of the world."[6] "The prince of the world" who is the embodiment of evil had no coercive influence over him. The command that Jesus gives at the end of the passage, "Come, let us go," shows that he was in charge and self-possessed even in the midst of a crisis.

While Jesus exuded a strong sense of independence in all his actions, he was never seduced by the prince of the world into making his personal autonomy an idol. Jesus retained his identity and his freedom while maintaining throughout his life an unswerving attachment to his Father's will. In this, he demonstrated that personal autonomy need not be incompatible with obedience to God.

The supreme importance of obedience in the life of Jesus is illustrated throughout the gospel of John. Consistently, Jesus links his personal identity to his filial relationship with God, whose work he was sent into the world to accomplish.

My food is to do the will of the one who sent me, and to complete his work (Jn 4:34).

I can do nothing by myself; I can only judge as I am told to judge, and my judging is just, because my aim is to do not my own will, but the will of him who sent me (Jn 5:30).

When you have lifted up the Son of man, then you will know that I am he and that I do nothing of myself: what the Father has taught me is what I preach; he who sent me is with me, and has not left me to myself, for I always do what pleases him (Jn 8:28–29).

The world must be brought to know that I love the Father and that I am doing exactly what the Father told me (Jn 14:31).

These texts leave no doubt that Jesus valued obedience to his Father as strongly as he cherished his personal autonomy. Even more important, they convey the truth that his relationship with God formed the basis of his self-understanding. Jesus cannot be understood without reference to the one who sent him. His central identity as son links him inextricably to God as Father. The same is true for us. Our primary identity as creatures links us inextricably to God as creator. "Creatures" and "creator" are co-relative terms. They cannot be properly understood apart from each other, just as "up" cannot be understood apart from "down." This is why St. Ignatius of Loyola taught that the foundation of our spiritual life must be a deep awareness of our basic identity: we are creatures whose very existence depends on the graciousness of a loving creator and Lord. Disobedience, or the denial of creaturehood, leads to a distorted view of human life and separates us from God.

Union with God through Obedience

Obedience, on the other hand, unites us to God in relationship. When we acknowledge with the obedience of faith that every good gift comes from a loving God, our hearts are filled with gratitude and a sense of indebtedness. We want to express our appreciation and to reciprocate love. As theologian Francis Baur states: "The spiritual person is the one who is animated by the giftedness of the universe, fascinated by the giftedness of life, especially one's own life, and hence quickened by the holy urgency to respond to that giftedness."[7] As Christians, our free and loving response to God's graciousness takes the form of loving obedience and service. Furthermore, it is through obedience that we become Jesus' disciples, his brothers and sisters. As the gospels remind us, Jesus calls his true relations those who do the will of his Father in heaven (Mk 3:31–35; Mt 12:46–50; Lk 8:19–21). Finally, at the end of the Sermon on the Mount, Jesus highlights the importance of obedience for all who want to be his followers.

It is not those who say to me, "Lord, Lord," who will enter the kingdom of heaven, but the person who does the will of my Father in heaven. When the day comes many will say to me, "Lord, Lord, did we not prophesy in your name, cast out demons in your name, work many miracles in your name?" Then I shall tell them to their faces: I have never known you; away from me, you evildoers! (Mt 7:21–23)

These are strong words! Jesus alludes to truly great deeds which, one would think, could only be done through divine power. What could be greater than to speak in God's name and to cast out evil from the possessed? Nevertheless, if all of this is not God's will, those who perform such acts are called "evildoers." As this passage underscores so clearly, it is obedience that links our lives to God and makes our actions pleasing to the Lord.

DISTORTED NOTIONS OF OBEDIENCE

Merely doing what one is told, however, is not Christian obedience. In the era before pre-Vatican II, many people had the impression that Christian obedience consisted in childish compliance. This belief was partially influenced by a paternalistic voice from the pulpit telling them that "the duty of Christians is to pray, pay, and obey." Although the council made bishops and priests more sensitive about paternalism and clericalism, distorted notions of obedience persist in the church today. Before discussing the nature of genuine Christian obedience, it would be helpful to expose some false forms.

Obedience, if it is not to impede the adult maturity of Christians, must not be confused with mindless conformity and inaction. None of the following, for example, can be mistaken for authentic obedience: submitting passively to an abusive parent; yielding obsequiously to a tyrannical boss; placating a domineering spouse; or acquiescing fearfully to an authority figure. Christian obedience should not be based on fear, pragmatic necessity, or insecurity; nor should it be motivated by the desire for external approval or the rewards that come to those who quietly conform. All of these deficient motives have ill effects on people's lives. Like the obedience of Jesus, genuine adult obedience must be based on freely chosen motives and centered on the love of God. In imitation of Jesus, we are called to follow the lead of God's spirit which has been given to us to guide our lives.

WHEN GOD IS THE TELLING INFLUENCE IN ONE'S LIFE

Authentic Christian obedience exists when we recognize God's influence upon our lives and when we experience ourselves finding God in what we do. The root meaning of "obedience" is the Latin *oboedire* meaning "to listen." Thus, obedience involves prayerfully attuning ourselves to the word of God in the many ways in which it is addressed to us. God's voice can be heard in many places: in scripture, in the teaching of the church, in other people, in the signs of the times, in our consciences, and in the stirrings of our hearts. Because the whole world is the vocabulary of God, all reality can communicate the Lord's guidance. We must be sensitive to the promptings of the Lord everywhere—in our thoughts, feelings, bodily sensations, as well as in the opinion of others.

In short, Christian obedience consists in listening sensitively to the word of God speaking in our lives and submitting to it in loving trust. This obedient attentiveness can take a variety of forms. It can appear as a basic acceptance of ourselves, or an enthusiastic response to a special calling within the Christian community, or the "Amen" in accepting illness, failure and finally, death. We are obedient Christians when we pray with the prophet Samuel, "Speak, Lord, for your servant is listening" (1 Sam 3:10).

Christian obedience does not always guarantee that we are in fact doing God's will. Nevertheless, our desire to open our lives to the guiding influence of God will inevitably draw us closer to God. Thomas Merton expresses the genuine spirit of Christian obedience beautifully in a prayer.

My Lord God,

I have no idea where I am going.
I do not see the road ahead of me.
I cannot know for certain where it will end.

Nor do I really know myself, and the fact that I think that I am following your will does not mean that I am actually doing so.

But I believe that the desire to please you does in fact please you.

And I hope I have that desire in all that I am doing.

I hope that I will never do anything apart from that desire.

And I know that if I do this you will lead me through the right road though I may know nothing about it.

Therefore, I will trust you always though I may seem to be lost and in the shadow of death.

I will not fear, for you are ever with me, and you will never leave me to face my peril alone.[8]

The Vow of Obedience

In their search for God's will, some Christians feel called to take a vow of obedience within a religious order. Their desire to vow obedience stems from their conviction that the will of God for them can be best found by living within a particular religious group. They believe that the women or men whom they are attracted to join are sufficiently prayerful and in tune with the Spirit that the Lord's will can be authentically mediated for them through the authority structures of that community. They are also convinced that they can better discern the will of God in a group of like-minded and similarly vowed Christians than they could operating alone. Furthermore, they believe that the church, by giving its official stamp of approval to these religious orders, guarantees that the spirituality of these groups represents a fruitful path to holiness. Seen in this light, the vow is merely a means that some Christians use to respond to the call shared by all Christians to live united with God's will.

Obedience as Trust in Divine Providence

An important reason why religious vow obedience is the desire to surrender their lives to the Lord in trust. Representing a generous self-offering, the vow is taken with the hope that the Lord, in accept-ing this gift, will enter more fully into their lives to dispose and shape them according to the divine pleasure. In relinquishing control, those who vow obedience testify to their belief that God desires what is best for them and can be trusted.

"God always throws a better party!" is another way of expressing this underlying attitude. A Jesuit friend once shared a part of his life story with me that concretely illustrates how God's providence often works through the human dynamics of obedience. When he was a young seminarian living in New York in the early 1950s, about to start the study of theology in preparation for ordination, he received a severe disappointment. Instead of being assigned to Woodstock College, Maryland, then the preeminent Jesuit school of theology in America, he was sent across the country to Alma College, a Jesuit theologate isolated in the mountains of northern California. This assignment cre-ated a crisis of obedience for him. For a bright and sophisticated New Yorker, being shipped off to the West was like being banished to a cultural wasteland. But, firmly committed to his vow of obedience, he reluctantly went West and spent four years there.

More than thirty years later, after returning to New York, his health had deteriorated to the point where his doctors urged him to return to California. At that point, he was forced to abandon his niche in New York and start anew. But to his surprise, he quickly discovered a new home in a distant country. Uprooted though he was, he was not lonely or isolated. In California, he was given a warm welcome by his old classmates from Alma College and quickly made to feel at home. In retrospect, he realized that his disappointing assignment to California thirty years prior had laid the groundwork for a future blessing. His subsequent life in Los Angeles was filled with happiness in community and obvious success in ministry. Shortly before his death, he shared his story with me to illustrate the importance of trusting in God's provi-dence working within the framework of religious obedience. Some-times the wisdom of God's ways may not be immediately evident. But when the other shoe finally drops, it becomes clear that the God to whom we vow obedience is indeed a faithful and trustworthy Lord.

A Talmudic story about a certain Rabbi Akiba illustrates well how Yahweh has a way of wringing good out of bad situations and how we must trust in a God whose ways are not always our ways.

In the turbulent first century, the rabbi once traveled in a strange country where mystery still dwelt. He had taken with him three possessions—an ass, a rooster, and a lamp—and had stopped at night in a village where he hoped to find lodging. When the people there drove him out, he was forced to spend the night in a forest nearby. But Rabbi Akiba bore all pains with ease, being heard always to say, "All that God does is done well." So he found a tree under which to stop, lit his lamp, and prepared to study Torah briefly before going to sleep. But a fierce wind suddenly blew out the flame, leaving him with no choice but to rest. Later that night wild animals came through and chased away his rooster. Still later, thieves passed by and took his ass. Yet in each case, Rabbi Akiba simply responded by saying, "All that God does is done well."

The next morning he returned to the village where he had stopped the night before, only to learn that enemy soldiers had come by in the night, killing everyone in their beds. Had he been permitted to stay there, he too would have died. He learned also that the raiding army had traveled through the same part of the forest where he had slept. If they had seen the light of his lamp, if the rooster had crowed, or if the ass had brayed, again he would have been killed. And how did Rabbi Akiba respond? He simply replied as he always did, "All that God does is done well."[9]

Trust in divine providence, however, does not remove the need for personal responsibility. Allowing room for God to act graciously on our behalf is an important aspect of Christian obedience. Nevertheless, it must be balanced by an active component, which requires that we use all our human resources and talents to further God's desires for us. Without creative human initiative, religious obedience can become irresponsible and immature.

PERSONAL RESPONSIBILITY AND MATURE OBEDIENCE

The renewal of religious life since Vatican II has certainly challenged men and women to live their vows in ways that do not impede personal maturity. Twenty years ago, John Courtney Murray spelled out this challenge in a talk to fellow Jesuits. He warned that religious obedience poses a real danger to personal development if it fosters the abdication of responsibility for one's life choices. Obedience is a perilous path to personal maturity because this vow, if poorly lived out, produces people "who to a degree are purposeless, their lives not consciously and strongly patterned, not inwardly directed toward a determined goal with all the organized power of the whole self."[10] The vow can provide an escape from bruising encounters with oneself, with one's own powers and the problems of their full exercise towards the achievement of a determined purpose.

Vowed religious can succumb to the trap posed by obedience by being overly submissive to authority figures in order to gain acceptance or to enjoy a kind of infantile dependence free from the anguish of personal decision making. Those who manifest these forms of immature behavior often justify their way of acting in spiritual terms, thus disguising what they are actually doing. When they say that they "just want to follow God's (or the superior's) will," it is sometimes simply a rationalization to defend their unwillingness to take responsibility for themselves. This becomes obvious when the superior has no strong feelings or particular preference about what should happen, and in fact would like the religious to assume some independent initiative and to indicate a clear preference.

Acknowledging this threat to maturity, a document on Jesuit formation makes clear that "the more the novices are stimulated to assume responsibilities with prudent and discerning charity, the more successfully will they acquire spiritual maturity and the more freely will they adhere to their vocation."[11] Mature obedience is unattainable apart from the constant cultivation of a spirit of initiative and responsibility.[12]

RESPONSIBLE OBEDIENCE THROUGH A DISCERNMENT PROCESS

To foster personal responsibility within the framework of religious obedience, I have used the following eight-step model to teach novices a way of practicing discernment:

Step 1: Identify the decision to be made or the issue to be resolved.

Step 2: Examine the underlying values or concerns (human, Christian, religious, and Jesuit) involved.

Step 3: Take time to pray over the matter, paying attention to how one is being drawn or led.

Step 4: Discuss the matter with a spiritual director.

Step 5: Dialogue with the superior and engage in a mutual search for God's will in the matter.

Step 6: Strive for a state of Ignatian "indifference," that is, a state of inner freedom and balance which allows one antecedently not to incline more towards one option than to another, but to allow one's preference to be shaped by the single criterion of what will be most to God's glory. This state of equipoise makes possible the acceptance of whatever decision or resolution is finally determined to be for God's greater glory.

If a person is unable to achieve "indifference," discussing the matter in spiritual direction can bring valuable self-knowledge and clarity about how best to proceed in the search for God's will. Perhaps, more prayer and dialogue with the superior regarding conflicting values and perspectives may be needed before a peaceful closure and decision can be arrived at.

Step 7: Accept the superior's decision with trust in God's providence at work within the dynamics of religious obedience.

Step 8: Stay open to the emerging data of ongoing experience to check for confirmation. In a study of Ignatian obedience, John Futrell states that "the principal means of confirmation of the decisions of the superior . . . are the mutual contentment of himself and his companions and the proof of living experience."[3] If there is serious doubt that the superior's decision truly reflects God's will, the process of prayer, consultation, and dialogue must begin again.

This discernment process promotes personal responsibility and growth because it requires the active participation of those seeking God's will. In coming to a decision, they must work with their religious superior, rather than have things fully decided or resolved for them from above. Step 1 requires them to invest in the process by defining the parameters of the issue from their personal point of view. Step 2 involves a process of values clarification in which they state the values that are at stake in the decision. Steps 3 and 4 give them the chance to critique these values, both alone in prayer and together with a spiritual director. Steps 2, 3, and 4 press them to ask an important twofold question: "Am I free to pursue my values?" and "Are they worth the pursuit?" By requiring them to come to some kind of tentative decision before dialoguing with their superior, these steps deepen their sense of being a self, because decision making forces people to claim their desires and convictions. Finally, if attained, the spiritual attitude of Ignatian indifference provides them with the inner freedom that guarantees that their act of autonomous choice can be integrated with religious obedience. For in the end, Ignatian indifference allows them to accept whatever is decided with both a sense of having done their part as responsible adults and of being faithful to their commitment to obedience.

THE DISCERNMENT PROCESS IN LAY LIFE

This discernment model, while useful to those in religious life, can also be fruitfully employed by lay people. The first three steps can be followed just as described. Steps 1 and 2 clarify the issues and values involved by requiring reflection and thought. Step 3 moves beyond thought to prayer: we ask for God's guidance and try to be sensitive to how we are being drawn when the matter is brought to prayer. Here it is important to remember what was said in Chapter III regarding the interplay of reason, affect, and religious experience in the decision making process. God can influence us through our thoughts as well as through our feelings of consolation and desolation in prayer. Because discerning the movements of God can often be a complex task requiring assistance, Step 4 calls for getting help by sharing our deliberation with a spiritual companion. This spiritual guide could be a trusted friend, counselor, or minister. The important thing is that it be a person who is committed to finding God's will and being honest and persevering in the search. Because we are capable of being deceived, especially when trying to decide on matters that are deeply personal and emotional, we need help to be objective and honest.

Step 5, which asks the religious to discern the matter with her or his superior, contains an important element that lay persons should also factor into their discernment. It is the element of communication with those who will be intimately affected by the decision being made. Too often decisions that affect spouses, children, and other loved ones are made unilaterally, without engaging the participation of those who have a right to be involved. These decisions, for example, may pertain to changing jobs, selling the house and moving, or caring for aging parents. Religious involve their superior in the discernment process because the superior represents the community, which is the central interpersonal matrix of religious life. Lay Christians, too, must make an effort whenever appropriate to ensure that important decisions are not made alone, but shared with the significant people in their lives.

By calling for Ignatian indifference, Step 6 contains an important aspect of discernment that applies equally to lay and religious life. By indifference Ignatius meant a radical openness to doing only what best leads to one's holiness and God's glory. It entails a strong attachment to God as the only absolute value in reality; everything in creation is seen as having only relative worth. Unfortunately, "indifference" is a bad choice of a word to convey Ignatius' meaning, since it often connotes apathy and complacency. The notion has nothing to do with the absence of feelings, nor does it mean disinterest in people and situations. In the Genesis account of God's testing of Abraham's obedience, we have a clear illustration of Ignatian indifference. Although he deeply loved Isaac, the long hoped-for fulfillment of a covenant promise, Abraham possessed the freedom and trust to let go of his dear son if that was what God required. Without doubt, God was the telling influence in his life. Similarly, indifference invites Christians to make God the telling influence in all their desires, decisions, and actions. Indifference is an inner freedom to choose only what leads them closer to God and to achieving their purpose in life.

Step 7 calls for the religious to accept the superior's decision with trust in God's providence at work within the dynamics of religious obedience. For lay persons, this step requires them to trust in God and to decide, even in the absence of certitude. Sometimes fears and doubts can paralyze people and cause them to procrastinate in making important decisions. Christians are called to live boldly and decisively. They must act, even though their carefully discerned decisions may remain clouded by uncertainty. They are called to trust in God's power at work bringing good out of everything. As St. Paul says in Romans: "We know that by turning everything to their good God cooperates with all those who love him" with all those who have been called according to God's purpose (8:28). Finally, both religious and lay persons must be alert to their ongoing experience to verify whether their decision was good or not. If there is serious doubt that a decision truly reflects God's will, they must repeat the process by taking the matter up again in prayer, reflection, and dialogue.

PROJECTION AS AN OBSTACLE
TO MATURE OBEDIENCE

God and others (parents, spouses, religious superiors, employers) are sometimes made accountable for the decisions of people who refuse to take responsibility for their lives as autonomous adults. These responsibility-shirking individuals make God or other authority figures accountable for choices that stem less from a process of spiritual discernment, and more from an unconscious distortion that blurs the distinction between the self and others. When the distinction between self and others is lost sight of, the danger of abdicating personal responsibility is great. A common cause of this confusion between self and others is projection, a defense mechanism that allows people to disown or deny unwanted feelings, attitudes, and traits by assigning them to others. Whereas repression appeared to be the most used defense during Freud's time, psychologist James Simkin speculates that projection is now by far the most commonly encountered defense.[14] People unconsciously project onto other persons those attitudes, attributes, and traits that they find unacceptable in themselves or are unwilling to claim as their own. They then blame and castigate the other person for whatever they do not like in themselves.

Projection is an obstacle to mature obedience when it fosters passivity and encourages Christians to blame others for what happens to them. Blaming others greatly impedes their active engagement in the process of desiring, discerning, and choosing—all legitimate aspects of the process by which they can come to know and do the will of God. The following are examples of possible projection:

—"I'm in a rut, but superiors won't let me take the risks of changing ministry or trying something new." (To probe for possible projection here, the clarifying question is: Is the unwillingness to risk actually coming from superiors, or is the person attributing his or her own unwillingness to superiors?)

—"I've no time to relax because my wife/husband expects so much from me." (Here the clarifying question is: Whose expectations are preventing the individual from getting proper rest, his or her own or the spouse's?)

—"I know I made a bad choice, but God expects us to live with our mistakes, no matter what." (Once again, the question is: Whose expectation is it really? God's or the individual's?)

PROJECTION AND DISTORTED IMAGES OF GOD

Just as we project unwanted attitudes and emotions unto others, we also project them onto our image of God. Speaking of this kind of projected image of God, J.B. Phillips states, in *Your God Is Too Small,* "A harsh and puritanical society will project its dominant qualities and probably postulate a hard and puritanical god. A lax and easy-going society will probably produce a god with about as much moral authority as Father Christmas."[5] The psychological phenomenon of projection, therefore, exposes us to the danger of imaging a god with attitudes, feelings, and traits like our own—and with the same blind spots.

The resulting images are naturally distorted and consequently easily destroy the possibility of mature Christian obedience. For example, when our dominant image of God is that of a merciless tyrant, our corresponding response of obedience can only be servile. When our dominant image is that of resident policeman, then our response can only be fearful; when it is that of a judge, then our obedience can only be guilt-ridden. And when it is that of a demanding parent, obedience tends to be infantile and childish. The connection between our father or parent-image of early childhood and our later conception of God is obvious, especially in those of us who exhibit an abnormal fear of authority or an apprehensive attitude towards God. Destroying the possibility of a free and loving surrender to God's influence, this fear can often be traced to the tyranny of a dominating parent. When it is not recognized as the result of a false image of God and is permitted to dominate our religious consciousness, it undermines Christian obedience which has nothing to do with being fearful, servile, childish, and guilt-ridden.

GLORIFIED SELF-IMAGE

Related to projection, another obstacle to mature obedience arises from a compulsiveness rooted in one's self-image. Psychologist Karen Horney describes how some personalities, in order to make up for deep feelings of inadequacy, inferiority, and insignificance, gradually and unconsciously create in their imaginations an idealized image of themselves. In the process, they endow themselves with unlimited powers and develop an overrated or glorified self-image. They come eventually to identify themselves with their idealized image. Then, instead of remaining a visionary image which they secretly cherish, "the idealized image becomes an idealized self." In other words, they imperceptibly become this image. This brings about an alienation from self because, according to Horney

> this idealized self becomes more real to [the neurotic] than his real self, not primarily because it is more appealing but because it answers all his stringent needs. This transfer of his center of gravity is an entirely inward process; there is no observable or conspicuous outward change in him. The change is in his feelings about himself.[16]

Horney terms this process of self-idealization a "comprehensive neurotic solution" because it promises implicitly to satisfy all the inner needs that have arisen in an individual at a given time. Furthermore, "it promises not only a riddance from . . . painful and unbearable feelings (feeling lost, anxious, inferior, and divided), but in addition an ultimately mysterious fulfillment" of oneself and one's life.[17] It is no wonder that this idealized self has such a tenacious hold on the person. These promises shift the person's energies from driving toward self-realization to illusory actualizing of an idealized self. Such a person often exhibits the need for perfection which aims at nothing short of molding the whole personality into the idealized self. This drive for perfection is sought through a complicated system of "shoulds" and taboos. Horney describes the emergence of "the tyranny of the should" in the neurotic personality:

> . . . the neurotic sets to work to mold himself into a supreme being of his own making. He holds before his soul his image of perfection and

unconsciously tells himself: "Forget about the disgraceful creature you actually are; this is how you should be; and to be this idealized self is all that matters. You should be able to endure everything, to understand everything, to like everybody, to be always productive" —to mention only a few of these inner dictates. Since they are inexorable, I call them "the tyranny of the should."[8]

TYRANNY OF THE SHOULD

The tyranny of the should frequently invites projection. It directly hinders mature obedience when those driven by perfectionism blame others for these inner demands. In some cases, these expectations may in fact originate from individuals who impose their demands for perfection onto others. However, when no one in the person's present or past environment can be identified as the source of these felt demands, the person may be projecting.

God, parents, and superiors are prime targets for projection by neurotic personalities, who are unaware of the overexacting demands of perfectionism originating in the self and who are searching for a source of these demands outside of themselves. Some Christians drive themselves too hard in order to please some inner voice demanding perfection. This voice may be their own demands or the residue of childhood training, but it is unlikely to be the voice of the power behind the universe.

The pivotal question for those driven by perfection is "Where are the shoulds coming from?" If they experience these demands as coming from some outside source, they may very well be victims of authority figures who themselves are plagued by an idealized self and the tyranny of the should. These authority figures may fit Horney's description of the neurotic whose drive for perfection is externalized and imposed on others: "[this] person may primarily impose his standards upon others and make relentless demands as to their perfection. The more he feels himself the measure of all things, the more he insists— not upon general perfection but upon his particular norms being measured up to. The failure of others to do so arouses his contempt or anger."[9] If this is the situation, clearly no projection is involved, and those in authority need to be confronted. If, however, the source of the shoulds is within, the perfectionist needs to confront himself or herself with that truth.

Those driven by the tyranny of the should often feel that their despotic dictates come from outside (from God, superiors, parents, spouses, or others in the community). They frequently react in one of two ways, both of which indicate a compulsive overreaction rather than a free and mature response to authority. They either swallow the self through a compliance that is childish and self-depreciating or they try to salvage the self through a rebellion that is adolescent and self-defeating. Both reactions preclude the possibility of mature obedience and affective maturity.

Presented here are three awareness exercises designed to deal with projection in one's obedience or to help others to do so in spiritual direction or religious formation. The first is a fantasy exercise useful to illustrate how susceptible we all are to using the defense mechanism of projection. The second, an exercise on images of God, is intended to help uncover projected images that demean religious obedience. The third is a clarification exercise aimed at helping people understand the various inner demands that, if left unexamined, can diminish their freedom.

A GROUP PROJECTION FANTASY: "THAT MAN IS YOU" (2 SAM 12:7)

Purpose

To understand through a personal experience the dynamics of projection.

Procedure

(1) In small groups of 4–5 people, ask for a volunteer to take on the role of focus person.

(2) Instruct the remainder of the group to create a fantasy revolving around the focus person. Each person is to fantasize an episode in which the focus person is the central character.

(3) Each person then shares his or her fantasy with the focus person and the rest of the group.

(4) After each person has shared his or her fantasy, the facilitator addresses the following questions:

(a) To the focus person: "Which part(s) of the fantasy can you identify with and own? Which part(s) can you not identify with and own?"

(b) To the creators of each fantasy: "Which part(s) can you identify with and own?"

(5) Discuss the responses to the questions above.

Comments on the Exercise

This fantasy exercise frequently shocks people into realizing how prone they are to projection. More often than not, participants will be forced to admit that many parts, if not all, of their fantasy had little to do with the focus person. Rather it represented projected materials from their own lives, such as their own needs, desires, and feelings.

This experiential awareness provides the participants with a fresh opportunity to live with greater responsibility, which according to Fritz Perls, the founder of Gestalt Therapy, means simply to be willing to say "I am I" and "I am what I am." To be a responsible self is to admit to one's projections and to reidentify with them. Honest admission of our condition contributes to growth by freeing us to perceive alternative responses to our lives.

WINDOW ON GOD: MAKING IMPLICIT IMAGES EXPLICIT

Purpose

To raise to explicit consciousness the images of God that influence one's life and behaviors.

Procedure

(1) Divide a sheet of paper in half with a straight horizontal line, and then in quarters with a straight vertical line down the middle. The sheet should now resemble an old-fashioned window with four panes.

(2) In the first pane, express God with a drawing, symbols, or words as he has been presented or taught to you by parents, teachers, and friends.

(3) In the second pane, express (once again through a drawing, symbols, or words) the image of God you have formed from your own experiences or personal search. Here you might describe moments when you experienced God in prayer, whether in happy or difficult times.

(4) In the third pane, express the image of the God whom you obey.

(5) After finishing the three panes, study your page and note what the juxtaposition of the three images gives rise to in you in terms of insights, questions, and feelings.

(6) In the fourth pane, jot down how your images of God affect your life of obedience.

Comments on the Exercise

The value of this exercise is that it can help us see how inconsistent we often are in the way we view God. At times, our image of God reflects the maturity of adult faith because it is based on personal religious experience and theological reflection. At other times, our conception of God is still influenced by the outdated notions of God that we acquired uncritically in early childhood and adolescence. Realization of this discrepancy can foster adult obedience by ensuring that the image of the God we obey matches more closely our adult understanding rather than that acquired as children. In the ordinary course of faith development, maturity comes when our image of God is less filled with projected matter from the past, and more flexibly formed by the present revelation of the living God, who is "beyond all knowledge" (Eph 3:19).

THE "CROCK OF SHOULDS": RESISTING THE TYRANNY OF SHOULDS

Purpose

First, to help a person to become more aware of the shoulds he or she is experiencing in the present; second, to recognize the source of these inner dictates; and third, to clarify how he or she wishes to respond to each of them.

Procedure

(1) Make a list of the shoulds you are experiencing in your life in the present. Make your statements brief and simple, expressing directly what you feel you ought to be doing and feeling without giving any reasons or explanations. Give life to your pen. Be as spontaneous as possible, trying not to filter or censor what automatically surfaces in your consciousness. Merely record what occurs at each moment. Continue to list these "I shoulds" for 10–15 minutes. Write down whatever comes to mind, even if it means repeating yourself.

(2) Look over the list and put a plus (+) next to the statements about which you feel positive, an "x" next to those about which you feel negative, and a question mark (?) next to those about which you have ambivalent feelings.

(3) Try to identify the source of the shoulds that stir up negative feelings by asking "Where is this should coming from?" Can you associate any of these negative shoulds with a face or voice? Are these shoulds being imposed from someone in the environment or do they originate in yourself? Perhaps they originally came from someone in the environment, but have since been internalized to such a degree that it would be truer to say that the source is within yourself.

(4) Once the source of the negative shoulds is identified, ask yourself how you want to respond to each at this time in your life. If the source is someone other than yourself, it could be someone close by, distant, or even dead (since death ends a life, not a relationship). Knowledge of the source will help you decide how you want to and can respond.

Comments on the Exercise

The value of this exercise is that it can clarify, for those driven or paralyzed by the tyrannical voices of inner shoulds, where the battle for personal freedom is to be fought—with someone in the environment or within oneself. If the source of shoulds is actually within oneself and being projected onto others, it would be fruitless and destructive to look for a solution outside oneself.

This exercise also helps a person to recognize shoulds that elicit positive feelings. Perhaps it would be more proper to label these as "wants" rather than "shoulds." Desires must be seriously respected in the discernment that accompanies Christian obedience. Writing about the connection between our spontaneous desires and finding God's will, Thomas Merton states "we must be prepared to take responsibility for our desires and accept the consequences . . . Such real, genuine aspirations of the heart are sometimes very important indications of the will of God."[20]

Through this exercise, we can also examine those shoulds that stir up mixed feelings within us. By reflecting more concretely on our ambivalent reactions to these shoulds, we can gradually clarify our feelings and decide how we want to respond to them.

RECONCILING AUTONOMY AND OBEDIENCE

When the use of projection prevents us from responsibly directing our own lives, it retards genuine spiritual growth. It also caricatures Christian obedience, which requires all of us to seek and do the will of God as autonomous adults. Mature Christian obedience entails:

(1) being prayerfully open to the presence of God in all the concrete circumstances of our lives;
(2) heeding earnestly the promptings of God who, being dissatisfied with loving us from a distance, has become flesh and drawn near to us;
(3) following trustingly wherever the Lord leads.

Lay Christians and religious share the same call to imitate the obedience of Jesus. What is distinctive about the obedience lived by religious is their desire and commitment to search for the will of God in the context of a religious community. Their search is not completely handed over to their superiors. Rather, adult living of the vow acknowledges that the search for God's will is shared equally by the individual and the superior who represents the community. Similarly, lay Christians acknowledge that their search for God's will also lies within the context of their community of family, friends, and colleagues.

Personal autonomy is incompatible with Christian obedience only when people abdicate responsibility through projection and blaming. Christian obedience requires persons who are truly self-possessed and spiritually mature. The more securely autonomous Christians feel themselves to be, the more ably they will dedicate themselves through obedience to the will of God. As Jesuits were told by their Thirty-First General Congregation in 1966, mature Christian obedience demands the constant cultivation of a spirit of initiative and responsibility.[21]

CHAPTER SIX

SEXUALITY IN THE SERVICE

OF LIFE AND LOVE

"I tend to gaze quite closely at the faces of priests I meet on the street to
see if a lifetime of love has marked them noticeably. Real serenity or
asceticism I no longer expect, and I take for granted the beefy calm that
often goes with Catholic celibacy, but I am watching for the marks of
love and often see mere resignation or tenacity."
EDWARD HOAGLAND

ALL CHRISTIANS, not only celibates, are challenged to live a lifetime
noticeably marked by love. Everyone is called to be chaste. Although
that goal is accomplished differently in marriage, celibacy and the
single state, it calls all of us to appreciate, integrate, and order our
sexuality. Likewise, no way of life, whether religious or lay, is free
from the pitfalls that produce lives marked more by mere resignation or
tenacity than by love. Nevertheless, all Christians are called to imitate
Jesus, whose love led him to lay down his life for his friends. The night
before he faced death, Jesus told his intimate companions gathered
together for a final meal: One can have no greater love than to lay
down one's life for one's friends. "You are my friends" (Jn 15:13–14).
The gospel command to love as Jesus did requires us to commit ourselves seriously to the love of friendship. It challenges us to encounter
our sexuality and to use our sexual energies to foster friendship and
other relationships of love.

Traditionally, Christians have distinguished between two aspects of love, *eros* and *agape*. *Eros* refers to the sexual, passionate, sensual aspects of love. *Agape* links love to the kind of self-transcending and sacrificial commitment that roots life giving relationships. A holistic approach to sexuality seeks to affirm and integrate both these aspects of love. To use the biblical metaphors suggested by theologian James B. Nelson, holistic sexuality entails an appreciation for two gardens: the Erotic Garden that is depicted in the Song of Songs and the Garden of Eden that is described in the Yahwist creation account in Genesis 2–3. Employing these images, Nelson succinctly describes the context in which we as Christians must strive to love chastely.

The Erotic Garden represents sexuality before the Fall. In this garden there is no bodily shame and its inhabitants are thoroughly sensual.

> The woman and the man delight not only in each other's embodiedness but also in the sensuous delight surrounding them—trees, fruits, flowers, fountains of living water. In this garden there is no sexist dualism, no hint of patriarchy, no dominance or submission. The woman is fully the equal of the man . . . Each exults in the body and beauty of the other, and together they embrace their sexuality without the guilt of exploitation.[2]

The image of the Erotic Garden reminds us of the radical goodness of human embodiment and the erotic. Christian philosopher John Giles Milhaven celebrates this goodness when he asks rhetorically: "Why then do lovers—spouses, for instance—happily and wisely will bodily excitement and satisfaction for its own sake, and not just for what it may express and serve? What is there in this turbulent, fleshy need and in this opaque, overwhelming pleasure that God sees is good?"[3]

The Garden of Eden, on the other hand, symbolizes the struggle that sexuality presents. The results of the Fall of our first parents manifest themselves in the shame that accompanies nakedness, the pain that marks childbirth, and the curse that turns human work into a burden. In short, Eden reminds us of our sexual alienation.

> Realistically, we know that sexual alienation abounds. It is alienation from ourselves (bodies feel foreign, or bodies are used as pleasure machines). It is alienation from others (we fear intimacy and vulnerability; we use sexuality in patterns of domination and submission). It is alienation from God (sexuality seems alien to "true spirituality").[4]

We Christians today, states Nelson, "live between the gardens."[5] To affirm the value of these two gardens is to acknowledge the beauty and possibilities of *eros* as well as to admit the challenge of ordering *eros* towards life-giving ends. We must renew our appreciation of *eros* because erotic love fuels our need for intimate communion with others and with God. Thus *eros* fosters authentic humanness which is achievable only in relationship. We must also creatively direct our sexual energies in ways that affirm our own and others' dignity and equality. In an age when so much suffering results from the misuse of sexuality —rape, incest, sexual abuses of all types, divorces and estrangements due to infidelity, diseases spawned by promiscuity—the virtue of chastity, which challenges us to love as Jesus did, must certainly be central to a holistic spirituality. As people living between both gardens, we need to be aware of both the promise and the challenge of sexuality. As Nelson puts it, "Sexual expression still needs ordering and discipline, yes, but that is quite different from the denial of the spiritual power of sexuality itself."[6]

CHASTITY AS A WAY OF LOVING

Sexuality is a relational power because it bonds us with others in affection and mutual care. When it is repressed, so is the energy for relating and loving. Chastity, the virtue that affirms the radical goodness of human sexuality as a gift from God, frees us to use our sexuality to make intimate contact with others. Genuine chastity is the fruit of an honest encounter with our sexuality, and is not easily come by. It is the result of a strenuous struggle with the fierce forces of sexuality and comes only when the raw power of our sexual drive has been tamed and converted for loving use. Chastity seeks to produce lives that are noticeably marked by love.

Chastity means simply that sexuality and its physical expressions are viewed as good insofar as we put our sexuality at the service of love in our personal relationships. So much more than genital activity, sexuality lets us enter the lives of others as friends and encourages them to enter our lives. It can link us to others in ways that bring understanding and sensitivity, warmth and acceptance, compassion and mutual support. It can energize us and unleash human creativity. Causing us to be attracted and vitalized when others come near, sexuality is a source of life-giving power not only for procreation, but also for ordinary human relationships. We glorify God and become more like our creator when we create the loving, other-centered relationships which also give us such human satisfaction and personal fulfillment.

But sexuality can also be a destructive power. The sexual drive, like any of our powers, can turn into a disintegrating force due to lack of concern, weakness, or even well-intentioned error. Nevertheless, we should not fear our sexuality, but embrace it. What we should fear at times is our own inability to think as highly of the gift as does the creator who made us sexual beings.[7]

ENCOUNTERING THE EROTIC

When people spurn their sexuality, they become cut off from its vitalizing power. There are no simple shortcuts to a chastity that brings wholeness. A continuing process of development, mature love involves a lifelong struggle of becoming more and more chaste, of growing gradually in appreciating, integrating and ordering one's sexuality. It also necessitates a sometimes bruising encounter with the erotic. "Out of this encounter," states theologian John Courtney Murray, "comes life that is human" because "untamed life in the bones" is "disciplined unto integrity."[8] This integrity constitutes chastity, which is the freeing of all the forces of life by their coordination by a self that is governed by deeply held values and desires.

This forging of integrity from the untamed life in the bones requires a holistic form of knowing that goes beyond cold rationality. To embody *eros* and *agape* in a mature way, we must rely on an awareness that comes from the integration of thinking, feeling, and sensing. This mode of knowing is reflected in the Hebrew verb *yadah,* signifying the kind of knowledge that results from the unification of intellect, feeling, and action. The disciplining of sexuality for the sake of integrity relies on this kind of holistic knowing that enables people to "listen to the messages from all the self's aspects: the mind, the heart, the genitals, the viscera, the spiritual sensitivities."[9] The awareness that results from this process of listening will allow people to direct their sexual energies along the lines of freely chosen values and deeply felt desires.

The marriage of knowing and valuing with the forces of life is the process by which our sexual passions are shaped for love and integrated into our personalities. Some people so fear their sexual feelings that they endeavor to cap them through denial. For them, erotic feelings are like potential terrorists threatening to hijack the ship of self and steer it uncontrollably into dangerous waters. Consciously or unconsciously, they feel that the best way to avoid this danger is to pretend that these potentially disruptive forces are not present. When this denial is done unconsciously, it is called repression. Through the defense mechanism of repression, individuals block from their consciousness unwanted feelings and impulses. But both denial and repression are ineffective ways of coping with sexual feelings because they exclude awareness. Knowing what we are experiencing enables us to bring some order and harmony to passion which relies on personal awareness and choice for direction. Thus, denial of the sexual and erotic ironically destroys the control it seeks.

Those who seek to achieve purity by denying their sexuality and avoiding the erotic endanger themselves psychologically and spiritually. Psychologically, they run the risk of becoming rigid, listless, or angry people, whose frustrated sexual drive leads more often to neurotic symptoms than to loving behaviors.[10] Spiritually, they run the risk of pride. A person who copes with his or her sexual urges through denial or repression, as Murray points out, risks "becoming a disembodied head, that fancies itself a whole thing when it is not; when it denies its dependence on the body and all that the body stands for; and therefore risks denying its dependence on God who made it dependent on the body. The pure spirit can readily be the proud spirit." This conceit consists in "a certain hardness of spirit, a withdrawal of reason into a world of unreality because it is isolated from the facts and forces of life, and therefore unable to be integral."[11] Purity based on the denial of sexuality is specious. Sexual denial hardens the heart and makes it arrogant. It closes the heart to mercy, renders it incapable of understanding the weak, and powerless to pronounce the words of Jesus to the woman caught in adultery. Such a purity is too glacial to be compassionate. Thus, the denial of sexuality leads to a hardness that is poor material for fostering the kind of friendship that Jesus hoped would exist among his followers.

Those who flee from their sexuality to avoid being overwhelmed and tyrannized by it need to stop running. Only by encountering the erotic directly can they hope eventually to overcome their sexual fears. Direct confrontation of their worst fears can have the beneficial result of allowing them to see these erotic forces in real life proportions rather than in the exaggerated dimensions fashioned by the imagination. Then they will know what they are really up against and not succumb so easily to panic. This confrontation is like that of the young boy walking home alone at night, growing increasingly frightened by a clinking sound that seems to be following him. The sound grows progressively menacing as his imagination fuels his fear with terrifying images of the danger that is catching up to him. If he runs blindly off, his fear will increase. If he turns to confront the threatening sound, he may discover it is only a lost puppy following him home, dragging a chain in its mouth. When we encounter our sexuality directly, we too may be pleasantly surprised that it is not as intimidating or omnipotent as we feared. Even those who experience a self-destructive addiction to sex find themselves able to control their sexuality and restore harmony to their lives, often with the help of a twelve-step program called Sex and Love Addicts Anonymous (SLAA). SLAA support groups function very much like Alcoholics Anonymous groups in their encouragement of individuals to face their problems squarely and to rely on God's power to bring about wholeness and recovery.

Freud's influence has so permeated modern thought that sex is sometimes perceived to be larger than life, a despotic determiner of all things, a tyrannical tail wagging the dog. Parodying this reductionistic notion of human motivation as sexual sublimation, John Barth states:

> The dance of sex: If one had no other reason for choosing to sub-
> scribe to Freud, what could be more charming than to believe that
> the whole vaudeville of the world, the entire dizzy circus of history,
> is but a fancy mating dance? That dictators burn Jews and business-
> men vote Republican, that helmsmen steer ships and ladies play
> bridge, that girls study grammar and boys engineering all at behest of
> the Absolute Genital? When the synthesizing mood is upon one,
> what is more soothing than to assert that this one simple yen of

humankind, poor little coitus, alone gives rise to cities and monasteries, paragraphs and poems, foot races and battle tactics, metaphysics and hydroponics, trade unions and universities? Who would not delight in telling some extragalactic tourist, "On our planet, sir, males and females copulate. Moreover they enjoy copulating. But for various reasons they cannot do this whenever, wherever, and with whomever they choose. Hence all this running around that you observe. Hence the world"? A therapeutic notion![12]

In reaction to Freud, humanistic psychology emphasizes that human beings are multi-motivated and that sex, while a strong influence on human behavior, is not always the pivotal, decisive factor. In calling for a demythologizing of the omnipotence of the id, humanistic psychologists argue that meaning, values, and goals can outweigh the desire for sexual gratification in influencing people's choices and actions. Neither repression nor denial of the erotic is necessary for maintaining order in one's life. The desire for fidelity to a spouse or the pursuit of meaningful goals, for example, can govern sexuality and provide some discipline without doing violence to the person and without denying sexuality its important place. Then, instead of being an incorrigible part that disturbs the equilibrium of the whole, sexuality becomes integrated with the rest of one's personality and works for the well-being of the total person.

Suppression is the term used to describe this kind of conscious control over one's sexual appetite for the sake of clearly chosen goals and values. Psychologist William Kraft puts it succinctly when he says: "Suppression is a 'no' that is based on a more fundamental 'yes.' "[13] A wife who is experiencing erotic feelings toward a coworker at the office, for example, suppresses her desire by first acknowledging her feelings as a natural part of her sexuality and then choosing not to act on them. Suppression differs from repression because it entails conscious awareness and personal choice. Unlike repression, it allows us to affirm our sexual feelings and to decide how we want to respond to them. By enabling us to have more alternatives for action, it expands our freedom.

Suppression may be appropriate in many situations when sexual urges can disrupt what is going on. A student studying for an exam, a therapist attending to an attractive client, or a lonely minister counseling a recently divorced person may need to suppress their sexual fantasies and feelings in order to function effectively. This suppression entails placing them on the back burner until they can be dealt with more reflectively. Sometimes treating these distracting thoughts with benign neglect naturally defuses the sexual tension, because they seem to recede when they are met with inattention. Because sexuality involves an appetite as strong as the need for food and sleep, it is natural that fleeting sexual fantasies are daily customers queuing up at consciousness's counter. Suppression permits us to give them the attention that is their due, but does not allow them to cut in line and disrupt the business of life.

In an ironic way, when we try to escape a direct encounter with the erotic, we can become preoccupied with it. Denial, in other words, can lead to fixation. As with other kinds of fixation, sexual obsession causes a myopia which blinds people to the broad purposes of sexuality which have to do with giving life and building relationships. Some Christians are unconsciously ashamed of their sexuality. Embarrassed by sexual feelings, they are incapable of integrating them in ways that promote their overall health and development. Such people suffer from a form of puritanism that requires the projection of unwanted sexual desires and urges onto others. Sex is then seen to be "out there" and everywhere! Acceptance of sexuality as a natural part of life fosters harmonious development; denial leads to distorted preoccupation with sex.

The story is told of two monks—one young and one old—walking through a forest in medieval France. Upon reaching a river, they encountered a shapely young maiden with golden hair stranded on the bank, unable to ford the river by herself. Without a moment's hesitation, the old monk lifted the young lass into his arms and carried her across. Miles later, as they continued their trek through the forest, the young monk confronted the old one. Recalling the incident with the girl at the river, the young monk confessed his utter disillusionment with his supposedly more experienced brother in religion. Complaining, the young monk asked in righteous indignation, "How could you, a religious bound to the vow of chastity, be so casual and unguarded in your contact with such a beautiful woman?" The wise old monk responded calmly, "Yes, but I left her back there at the bank of the river. You are still carrying her with you."

AVOIDING EROTICISM

Fixation leads easily to eroticism. The impersonal use of others for the sake of one's own gratification, eroticism is sexuality severed from relational concerns and isolated from interpersonal love. It is a corruption of the gift of sexuality because it leads to interpersonal alienation rather than interpersonal intimacy. It diminishes persons by treating them as objects to be used for selfish pleasure rather than as irreducible subjects to be loved.

That eroticism runs rampant in today's society is manifested by the fact that sex is big business, whether it takes the form of prostitution, pornography, or advertisement. The Christian challenge to live chaste lives takes on greater import when seen in the context of this exploitation of sex for profit. Jesuits were reminded of this when they were told by their governing body meeting in Rome in 1974 that chastity "has a special apostolic value in our time, when [people] tend to put whole classes of their fellow human beings beyond the margins of their concern, while at the same time identifying love with eroticism. In such a time, the self-denying love which is warmly human, yet freely given in service to all, can be a powerful sign leading [others] to Christ who came to show us what love really is: that God is love."[4] The chaste love of Christians today, therefore, must witness to Christ's universal love and stand as a prophetic condemnation of the eroticism of our times.

Chaste love challenges us to be like the old monk who carried the woman across the river. Without inhibiting self-consciousness, we need to reach out to others in care and service. Chastity should free us to engage women and men without fear, viewing them as total persons and not as sexual objects. Due to fear, many of us allow our sexuality to separate, rather than to unite, us with others. Some of us have been trained to keep our distance, lest being too warm and friendly gets us into destructive entanglements. The story of a priest whose ministry to a dying AIDS patient became an experience of having his own fractured sexuality healed into greater wholeness illustrates how fear can condemn us to superficial relationships devoid of intimacy. Approached by Bobby, darkly handsome and dying of AIDS at 25, the priest was asked to stand by him as he broke the news to his parents, who knew neither that he had AIDS nor that he was an active homosexual. In the course of many hours of conversation, the priest came to some painful realizations:

> We talked many hours . . . and I managed to pry open, with his help, a steamer trunk of past regrets—of relationships I had run away from because my training taught me that any relationship could become sexual. It also taught me to fear homosexual men, and so I dealt with them as nonpersons; I did the same with women . . . I always suspected that drawing close to a man or a woman would automatically lead to sexual involvement. One learned to avoid involvement . . . In his pajamas, with tubes running into his body, Bobby became a healer for me . . . Bobby helped me to realize that I was starving even as he lost more weight than he could possibly afford.[15]

The story of Bobby and the priest helps us to understand that the essence of chastity is loving people. Chaste persons are those who appreciate what it is to be sexual and have learned, with time and effort, how to put their sexuality at the service of love and integral development. The more chaste people are, the more capable they are of establishing and maintaining good relationships with others, without having them damaged by disordered and unruly sexual instincts. As a result, they are capable of greater commitment and openness towards others. Viewing others as irreducible wholes, they find themselves increasingly incapable of abusing others for their own selfish sexual interests. Chastity is the measure of one's capacity as a woman or a man to love others as women and men. To gauge how chaste we are, a good practical guideline is the depth and quality of our friendships. To remain at a safe distance from others is not a sign of chastity. On the contrary, it is a kind of unchastity if it prevents us from involving ourselves deeply and caringly in others' lives.

THE HUMAN EXAMPLE OF JESUS

Jesus exemplifies chastity as responsible engagement rather than flight from interpersonal involvements. Throughout the gospels, Jesus' stance towards others is not aloof, cold, or indifferent. A truly chaste person, he is loving, warm, and affectionate. He is capable of responding sensitively to both men and women, without fearing tenderness or being overwhelmed by sexual passion.

The evangelist Luke portrays Jesus as a person comfortable with his humanity and capable of relating deeply with others. The gospel contains an incident that is very instructive about the nature of chaste love. It is the story of Jesus' intimate encounter with the woman "who had a bad name in the town" (Lk 7:36–50). Hearing that Jesus had been invited to dine at a Pharisee's house, she crashed the party bringing with her an alabaster jar of ointment. "She waited behind at his feet, weeping, and her tears fell on his feet, and she wiped them away with her hair; then she covered his feet with kisses and anointed them with the ointment." At the sight of this, the Pharisee grumbled to himself, "If this man were a prophet, he would know who this woman is that is touching him and what a bad name she has."

This well-known story has been used traditionally to illustrate the relationship between forgiveness and love: that a person who has been forgiven much loves much. But if we consider the intimate contact between Jesus and the woman, it also reveals a dramatic example of two people loving each other chastely.[6] The physical contact was highly sensual: the woman anointed Jesus' feet with oil, covered them with kisses, and wiped away her tears with her hair. Although intensely sensual, there was not the slightest indication of anything sexually inappropriate. What the Pharisee objected to was not the nature of the contact, but that Jesus allowed the sinner any contact at all. The intimacy between Jesus and the woman was also affective, since the woman bared her soul to Jesus by crying. Jesus too was direct in communicating his feelings to the woman and the Pharisee.

What does this passage tell us about chaste love? The woman was able to be open and emotionally vulnerable because she discovered in Jesus a chastity that could be trusted. Possessing a peaceful acceptance of his embodiment as a person, Jesus seemed at ease with a woman who showed her feelings in such sensuous ways. Not put off by her reputation, Jesus was comfortable with letting her come close to shed her tears of sorrow. By allowing her to show her love in the way that she knew how, Jesus respected her integrity and enabled her to feel whole and good about herself. In contrast to the Pharisee who disdained the woman who had "a bad name in town," Jesus' love was shown to be universal and available to anyone seeking it. For her part, the woman was chaste in her treatment of Jesus. Despite her profession and reputation, she revealed no trace of seductiveness or manipulation. Confronting the condemning Pharisee, Jesus was eloquent in her defense.

> "Simon," he said, "you see this woman? I came into your house, and you poured no water over my feet, but she has poured out her tears over my feet and wiped them away with her hair. You gave me no kiss, but she has been covering my feet with kisses ever since I came in. You did not anoint my head with oil, but she has anointed my feet with ointment" (Lk 7:44-47).

What might have been an awkward situation for someone uncomfortable with physical contact and the show of feelings was for the chaste Jesus a moment of successful ministry. Through this intimate interaction, he achieved his goal of mediating the forgiving love of God. By focusing on his mission, Jesus was undeterred by the social complications of the situation, and communicated to the penitent woman through word and touch that her sins were forgiven. "Your faith has saved you; go in peace."

The encounter of Jesus with the penitent woman was sensual, but not unchaste. Sensuality is the appreciation of our bodily existence, an enjoyment of the pleasures of earthly life and the beauty of the body. When linked exclusively to lust, as in certain periods of the past, sensuality is seen as a negative aspect of life, something to be eliminated through bodily mortification and ascetical practice. Yet sensuality, in and of itself, is not negative. It is a natural part of being human; its source is the very fact of our embodiment. Full acceptance of our humanity requires that we accept our ability to delight in sensible reality. However, sensuality can become negative when we are preoccupied with pleasure for pleasure's sake, no matter what the cost—even if it involves the exploitation or neglect of others and their needs. Sensuality militates against chastity when it makes sexuality a depersonalized source of personal pleasure.

Trying to live chastely in imitation of Jesus requires discipline, honesty, and awareness. All of our interactions with others contain a sexual element because we are embodied beings. As Jesuit psychiatrist James Gill states, "It is impossible for us to be non-sexual in anything we think or say or do—even in our communication with God! All of us in the church owe it to ourselves and to . . . our creator, to accept the maleness or femaleness [God] has given to us, and to accept the reality of the presence of a sexual aspect in all that goes on within and among us, especially within the context of our interpersonal relationships."[7] It is not surprising that at times we can become sexually stimulated or that genital feelings spontaneously arise. Such moments are inescapable for anyone—whether married, celibate or single—trying to be open, warm, and loving. However, this should not scare us off from close involvement with others. As Gill counsels, at times like this "We strive to gain, with the help of God's grace, such deep convictions about the value of our chastity and such strength of motivation to observe it, that we can withstand the attractiveness of whoever or whatever might strongly appeal to our genitality."[8]

Honest awareness and discipline at these moments can help us to do what is appropriate for ourselves as well as for others. If we pay attention to our emotional and physiological reactions to sexual stimuli, we will know when we are getting aroused and when we need to retard our actions for the sake of reflection. Reflection allows us the chance to decide what we want to do about our growing sexual arousal and what behaviors would bring about what we want. We need to be knowledgeable about our patterns of sexual arousal and of responsible ways of responding, if we are to love chastely. We need to know how our sexual arousal is influenced by such factors as our moods and fantasies, or alcohol and other drugs. Feeling aroused, a bored office worker for example, might need to stop fantasizing sexually about his married colleague at the next desk, or a marriage counselor attracted to a client may decide that it is inappropriate to imagine him as a potential sexual partner. Awareness brings about "response-ability." And the greater our response-ability, the greater our ability to live according to our values as Christians.

FROM FOOT WASHING TO FRIENDSHIP

The centrality of friendship in Christian life is emphasized in another foot washing scene in the New Testament. In the solemn context of the last supper, Jesus explained to his followers the meaning of his life and death, as well as the nature of Christian community and service. In a dramatic gesture, he got up from table, rolled up his garment and, taking a towel and a basin of water, he washed the feet of his disciples.

The significance of that action is lost if it is viewed solely as a lesson in humility. What Jesus did in the foot washing was of far greater significance than that, for by it he defined the meaning of service in the Christian community. Theologian Sandra Schneiders provides an exegetical explanation of John 13 that supports this view.[19] Jesus' intention in the foot washing was to introduce a model of service that would speak neither to the superiority of the giver nor to the inferiority of the recipient. What Jesus desired was a mode of service that involved the mutual sharing of gifts among friends. By washing the feet of his disciples, Jesus did something beneath his dignity as master that jarred established sensitivities. That this was the case is verified by the sharp protest of Peter who cried out, "You shall never wash my feet." His protest, however, was met with an equally strong response from Jesus: "If I do not wash you, you can have nothing in common with me." The strength of the Lord's response is understood when we grasp the full meaning of his words. Jesus is saying to Peter: "If you refuse to go along with this action of mine, you can have nothing further to do with me. Our relationship would be forever severed."

How can we explain the severity of Jesus' reaction to Peter? Peter's refusal is symbolic insofar as it pertained to more than the simple action of having his feet washed. It represented Peter's attachment to the status quo and to a model of service in which the strong give to the weak, the rich give to the poor, and the intelligent give to the ignorant. This way of viewing service is based on domination because service here expresses the superiority of the server, while reinforcing the inferiority of the one served. By behaving as an inferior, Jesus upset the established order to which Peter was strongly attached. Hence, Peter's stubborn resistance. Schneiders concludes:

> Peter was not merely objecting to having his feet washed by another but specifically to the reversal of service roles between himself and Jesus ... his protest was not simply an embarrassed objection to Jesus' action but a categorical refusal to accept what this reversal of roles implied ... In some way, Peter grasped that complicity in this act involved acceptance of a radical reinterpretation of his own life-world, a genuine conversion of some kind which he was not prepared to undergo.[20]

Jesus assumed a posture of inferiority, claims Schneiders, not to advocate it, but as a way of introducing another notion of service—one based on the mutuality of friendship, not on superiority or inferiority. "Do you understand," he said, "what I have done to you? You call me Master and Lord, and rightly; so I am. If I, then, the Lord and Master, have washed your feet, you should wash each other's feet. I have given you an example so that you may copy what I have done to you. I tell you most solemnly, no servant is greater than his master . . ." (Jn 13:12–16).

The kind of service inaugurated by Jesus calls for the free sharing of gifts among equals in a community of friends. In his eyes, the desire for first place has no function in friendship. This teaching was a bitter pill to swallow for Jesus' disciples, whose desire to dominate one another and establish their superiority over others was frequently reproached by Jesus (Mt 20:20–28; 23:1–12; Mk 9:38–41; 10:33–37; Lk 18:14; 22:24–27). The foot washing account, Schneiders argues, is a dramatic interpretation of this theme of equality among friends in the Christian community. According to her:

> In the Johannine perspective what definitively distinguished the community which Jesus calls into existence from the power structures so universal in human society is the love of friendship expressing itself in joyful mutual service for which rank is irrelevant. By the foot washing Jesus has transcended and transformed the only ontologically based inequality among human beings, that between himself and us. Peter's refusal of Jesus' act of service was equivalent, then, to a rejection of the death of Jesus, understood as the laying down of his life for those he loved, and implying a radically new order of human relationships.[21]

When as Christians we gather together at church, we represent this new order established by Jesus. In the eucharist, we celebrate his gift to us, his freely laying down his life for our sake. The meaning of eucharistic service requires Christians today to be the body and blood of Jesus for others in the world; it requires that one's body be broken and one's blood be poured out for the sake of friends. The symbolism of this commitment is translated into concrete actions in many ways. While some people literally give their lives up for others, as in the martyrdom of the four American women in El Salvador in 1980, or the assassination of Archbishop Oscar Romero, most Christians dedicate themselves to others in the quiet routine of work and domestic life. Whether dramatic or mundane, the service of Christians must be modeled on Jesus, who commanded us to love each other as he loved us, that is, as friends among whom the desire for first place has no room.

HONORING FRIENDSHIP

Jesus' commandment of love takes on special importance today. At a time when eroticism so often masquerades as love, friendship needs to be honored anew. Chaste love needs to stand up in prophetic witness to a genitally-fixated culture that prizes orgasm over intimacy, performance over sharing. Author Jane Redmont, who is at work on a book about American Catholic women, argues eloquently for the importance of honoring friendship in her critique of the first draft of the bishops' pastoral letter on women, *Partners in the Mystery of Redemption: A Pastoral Response to Women's Concerns for Church and Society.* "Friendship belongs everywhere in this document," she states, "especially in the section on relationships. I want the bishops to honor friendship and call it sacred, to give it not an ancillary place but a fundamental one."[22] Friendship must be valued because it "sustains women's lives—in neighborliness in local communities, in the women's movement, in relationship with men."

Redmont's call for a greater emphasis today on friendship is cogent and convincing because it is rooted in the heart of Jesus' teaching. In fairness, it cannot be seen merely as a sentimental, privatistic request. "To lift up friendship as the standard against which to measure other relationships," states Redmont, "is a profoundly political act and a religious one as well." With the words, "I no longer call you slaves, rather, I call you friends" (Jn 15:15), the gospel challenges our understanding of both power and holiness. As a result, both divine and human reality look different. "Surely," suggests Redmont, "this has implications for the lives of women." Indeed, the gospel challenge of chaste love as friendship among equals has important implications for both men and women.

Although the need for intimate friends is deeply felt, it is very often frustrated in today's mass society. Starving on a diet of superficial

relationships, many people seek deeper interpersonal contact in encounter groups, prayer groups, support groups for the recently divorced and separated, as well as in a wide variety of twelve-step pro-
grams dealing with addiction. Ironically, some become addicted to
group meetings because their everyday lives lack the support of intimate friends. Other people find intimacy in interminable therapy,
paying for the presence of someone who can offer them understanding
and acceptance. Many factors reinforce our sense of isolation in today's
mass society. The frenzied pace of our lives and the frantic pressures to
get ahead militate against closeness. The frequent need to move because of work also makes it difficult for families to be rooted and
involved in the local community. And the anonymity of megalopolis
where people do not know the names of even those in adjoining apart-
ments feeds the bitter loneliness of many. It seems the more we live in a
mass society, the more important are intimate friendships.

Yet, the fostering of intimate friendships is more complicated than
many think. Social philosopher Erich Fromm contends that many
misunderstand the nature of love when they place too much emphasis
on the object of love rather than on the process of loving.[23] People
think that to love is easy. It comes naturally; the big problem is to find
the right person to love. Frequently, those who have never loved
anyone are convinced that they will immediately know how to love as
soon as the right person comes along. This attitude, argues Fromm, is
both naive and untrue. Love is an art that has to be cultivated through a
lifetime of practice. Having intimate friends has more to do with our
capacity for giving and receiving love than with waiting with romantic
expectation for that special someone to appear.

Good friendships cannot happen overnight. Unfortunately, the desire for an instant cure for loneliness often results in problematic
rushed-into-relationships. Based more on egotistical need than mutual
love, these relationships are a pseudo-remedy for loneliness. More
often than not, they end in frustrating failure. Loneliness can strike any
one of us, driving us at times to search desperately for someone to
remove our pain. Knowing when we are vulnerable to these rushed-
into-relationships can save us much needless suffering. We are extremely vulnerable, for example: when we have recently lost a loved
one through death, divorce, or a move; when we experience ourselves

as sexually less attractive because of physical changes as in mid-life; when we have had a recent experience of rejection or failure; when we feel a deep emotional void within due to past experiences of physical, emotional, or sexual abuse; when we experience deep anxiety in the midst of a major career or lifestyle change. Insecure moments such as these can drive us into the arms of another. Such neediness and desperation, however, are poor conditions for building lasting relationships of intimacy. Instead, we need to learn how to foster friendships based on mutual love.

Both lay Christians and religious can be vulnerable to rushed-into-relationships because no one is immune from anxiety attacks based on feelings of insecurity, helplessness, and abandonment. The following analysis of the complexities involved in fostering friendships within religious life contains insights readily applicable to the lives of lay Christians. Many parallels exist between lay and religious life in terms of the dynamics of forming close and satisfying relationships. These parallels are real because they reflect common psychological factors that impinge on us all.

PARTICULAR FRIENDSHIP REVISITED

The love of friendship as a gospel value certainly has implications for the lives of professed religious and celibate priests. Living the vow of chastity in a healthy and growthful way does not preclude friendship, but in fact requires it. Friendship, the most accessible of relationships, can bind any one of us to any other, regardless of age, gender, race, sexual preference, physical ability, or socioeconomic class. Hence, it should be highly valued by religious and priests, whose vow of chastity is meant to symbolize and embody Christ's universal love. The collar and the habit, for example, are meant to communicate that those who don them wish to belong to all. Friendship allows two human beings —or a group of them—to experience genuine emotional and spiritual intimacy, whether or not the relationship also includes sexual intimacy.

Making and keeping friends are among the most important things people can do for themselves. Statistical research by behavioral scientists is unnecessary to verify that friendship is a major, indeed crucial, factor in emotional health and happiness. Sympathetic understanding between close friends often decreases the pressures and strains of their lives. Since friendship contributes significantly to growth and survival, one might wonder why some religious do not value and foster deep friendships.

The priest who befriended Bobby, the dying AIDS patient, points to his protective seminary training and asks, "Is it any wonder some of us became depersonalized?"

> The world we lived in was impersonal, a long black line of marching heads bent at the same angle . . . we were forbidden to visit anyone else's room without the door being ajar. Aside from the sniggering and unspoken fear of homosexuality, such arrangements also precluded intimacy. The preclusion was worse than the fear; how does one grow as a person without intimacy? We were also warned about the danger of having a "particular friendship." Particular friendships became the altar upon which intimacy was sacrificed.[24]

Persons who entered religious life even as recently as twenty years ago recall the frequent novitiate caveats against forming "particular friendships." Recreating in assigned groups, calling each other by title rather than by first names, and limiting time given to free association were some of the structures used to prevent relationships that might be detrimental to living religious life to its fullest. It was argued that these particular friendships impeded community life because they were exclusive and divisive. They threatened to impair individual growth and development because they tended to foster overdependence and emotional immaturity. It was also feared that these relationships could lead to compromises in chastity. This guarded attitude towards closeness in the novitiate made friendships at best an ambiguous value for many who sincerely wished to embrace the religious life with total commitment.

Following the Second Vatican Council, however, novitiate formation has encouraged a more unambiguous and positive view of friendships in religious life, while at the same time heeding the traditional wisdom and concerns of the past. Just as friendship needs to be honored and given a fundamental place in human life in general, so must it be honored anew among religious. For this to happen the notion of particular friendship needs to be revisited.[25]

After many years of working in novitiate formation, I have come to the realization that emotional entanglements can form very rapidly, creating so much preoccupation that the novices find it very difficult to invest in the program. Thus, I have found it helpful to discuss the topic of relationships early on in the year, even as soon as the second week after their arrival. Our discussion helps them realize that friendships are valued and respected in religious life, while at the same time enabling them to understand how to foster friendships that will help, rather than hinder, their living community life and apostolic chastity in a fruitful way.

Interpersonal bonding among our novices occurs rapidly. The first week involves a rather intense orientation program, highlighted by two to three full days of faith sharing. In the course of this faith sharing, they reveal something of their life's story—the struggles and joys of growing up in their families, dealing with personal issues, discerning their vocations—often on a very intimate and deep level. A strong feeling of camaraderie and closeness results from this intense personal sharing of their experience of the Lord's loving and merciful presence in their lives. I have always seen this as a very positive step in the process of forming the community of "friends in the Lord" called for by our recent documents. Yet, at the same time, I have come to realize that such interpersonal intensity occurring so soon after entrance also makes certain individuals extremely vulnerable to the pain and complications that come with rushed-into-relationships and instant intimacy. Before sketching my understanding of the dynamics which lead to sudden rupture and hurt feelings in these cases, I would like to discuss three factors which often account for the quick emergence in the novitiate of such friendships. I present them as my own hypotheses as to what often motivates people, either consciously or unconsciously, to rush into these unpromising relationships. I have witnessed people plunging into these relationships as an attempt: (1) to seek security in the midst of an unsettling and stressful major new beginning in their lives; (2) to fill the affective void created by the recent separation from family, friends, and native soil upon entrance into the novitiate; and (3) to compensate for severe affective deprivations and wounds from the past.

FRIENDSHIP AS A REMEDY FOR INSECURITY

Moving to a new location, separating from one's network of affective support, and initiating a major change in one's direction in life can cause stress. Because entering religious life entails all these factors, it is difficult. The shift from the lay to the religious state is still a drastic and hard transition, despite the many external changes brought to novitiate formation since Vatican II. In former times, the radical discontinuity experienced between the life of a lay person and that of a religious was clearly marked by the traditional symbols of a clerical/religious subculture: wearing distinctive religious garb, keeping silence in the house, listening to readings at meals, adhering strictly to a daily schedule which regulated one's activity from rising in the morning to retiring at night. While the disappearance of many of these practices in the modern novitiate may have lessened the initial discomfort and culture shock of entering into a new way of life, the transition can nevertheless be overwhelming.

Soon after the excitement of entrance day and orientation recedes, the novices start to be bombarded with some basic personal questions: Who am I in this group? Do I want to belong? Did I make a mistake in joining? Will I fit in? How close do I want to be with others in this group? How do I go about relating affectively and physically with the others, now that I am committing myself to a life of celibate chastity? What is the place of friendship and relationships in this new life? The literature on the psychology of small groups indicates that such questions concerning one's identity and affiliation are inevitable whenever one joins a new group. To lessen the novices' anxiety, I try to validate their experience as normal and understandable by discussing the findings of group psychologists regarding entry-level issues and anxieties. I then, suggest that they give the process time, since only interaction within the group and extended reflection can settle their concerns. People eventually either find their place in the group or leave.

Most novices are able to live with the temporary ambivalence created by the these entry-level concerns and to continue the process without excessive anxiety. However, certain personalities, insecure in new and ambiguous situations, may latch on to a friend as a quick remedy for feelings of disequilibrium and insecurity. Based on desperation and dependence, these relationships usually result in problems and call for clarification.

FRIENDSHIP AND AFFECTIVE SUPPORT

The ability to make friends to satisfy one's legitimate need for affective support is a sign of maturity and should be encouraged in the novitiate. When people leave their family and friends to join religious life, they naturally feel the pain of loss or experience homesickness, especially if this is the first such move for them. So it is not uncommon that novices sometimes experience an affective void. Reaching out and investing in new relationships as time goes on will usually alleviate this initial feeling of emptiness. Nevertheless, there are certain individuals who continue to be troubled by a deep, persistent loneliness. This aching emptiness drives them into a desperate search for someone who will be the final answer to their loneliness. Such relationships are doomed to fail because they rest on false assumptions and unreasonable expectations.

First, there is the false belief that a single individual can satisfy all the affective needs which formerly were met by a network of parents, relatives, friends, and associates. Marriage counselors often advise clients that no one individual can wholly fulfill the affective needs of another. To demand this of a spouse is to demand the impossible and to risk rupturing the relationship. The same is true for friendships in religious life. Failure to recognize this fact leads some individuals to move serially from one frustrating and stormy relationship to another.

Closely related to this search for that special friend who will provide for all of one's emotional needs is an often unconscious attempt to turn a friend into a surrogate spouse. Aspirants to religious life enter the novitiate having made a conscious decision to give up a life mate in order to live and love in a celibate fashion. Yet, on an unconscious and emotional level, a need to have a deeply intimate and intense relationship which will substitute for what one forgoes in not having a spouse sometimes exists. The psychological phenomenon at work here is called displacement. Originally part of Freud's theory, displacement involves the shifting of emotional energy from its original connection with an unacceptable idea into connection with an acceptable idea. In the context of the novitiate, spousal affection and intimacy are sometimes displaced onto a friend in the community. This displacement obstructs healthy friendship because it entails the redirection of romantic, and sometimes erotic, feelings that are appropriate when directed to a spouse or lover, but inappropriate when directed to a fellow religious. To expect a member of the community to be the center of one's affective universe as a spouse might be is unrealistic and unworkable. The dynamics of celibate love, symbolizing the universal love of Christ, ideally move toward ever greater inclusiveness of others. While characterized by exclusiveness, a marital relationship that is deeply loving also provides the foundation for greater openness to others. The ideal of celibate love is stated well in a work commissioned by the Bishops' Committee for Priestly Formation, entitled *Spiritual Renewal of the American Priesthood:*

> Celibacy promotes a radical Christian style of interpersonal relationships, namely, one that rests on the universal character of charity. The charism of celibacy allows the individual to love deeply and warmly yet without finding it necessary to move toward exclusivity . . . If marital love is characterized as a focus on the one, while being open to the many, celibate love is characterized as a focus on the many, while being open to everyone . . . The priest wishes to be brother to everyone and spouse to no one.[26]

Thus, a friendship that consciously or unconsciously seeks to find a spouse surrogate in a fellow religious is doomed to frustration. It can also lead to an obsessiveness that makes it very difficult for the novice involved to participate fully and peacefully in the training program.

A third factor that threatens the establishing of healthy, long-lasting friendships is the illusion that there is someone who can eradicate the essential aloneness or ontological loneliness that is part of the human condition. According to spiritual writer Henri Nouwen, people operating out of the illusion that the final solution to their loneliness is to be found in human togetherness tend to lay heavy messianic expectations on their friends. The end result is always disappointment and collapse of the friendship. In his words:

> When our loneliness drives us away from ourselves into the arms of our companions in life, we are, in fact, driving ourselves into excruciating relationships, tiring friendships and suffocating embraces. To

wait for moments or places where no pain exists, no separation is felt and where all human restlessness has turned into inner peace is waiting for a dreamworld. No friend or lover, no husband or wife . . . will be able to put to rest our deepest cravings for unity and wholeness. And by burdening others with these divine expectations, of which we ourselves are often only partially aware, we might inhibit the expression of free friendship and love and evoke instead feelings of inadequacy and weakness. Friendship and love cannot develop in the form of an anxious clinging to each other.[27]

When these "divine expectations" become obvious, people generally experience an urgent need to renegotiate or to terminate the relationship for fear of disappointing or hurting the other. Those who are experienced in interpersonal relationships can generally articulate precisely where the problem lies and try to bring about a gradual and gentle realignment based on more realistic expectations. However, those who are inexperienced will bolt in panic and confusion. This sudden rupture of the relationship is then experienced by the other, who is often just as confused, as rejection. Thus occurs the mental suffering referred to by Nouwen. Rejection triggers a variety of negative feelings: hurt, anger, resentment, jealousy, possessiveness, and depression. Star-struck infatuation quickly gives way to negative-fixated disillusionment. The pain at this point can be so preoccupying that the persons involved can concentrate on little more than their relational difficulties.

FRIENDSHIP AND PAST AFFECTIVE DEPRIVATIONS

Another potential pitfall to building healthy friendships stems from severe affective deprivations experienced in the past. Some people enter the novitiate starving for affection and affirmation because of a long history of deprivation often traceable to early childhood. According to psychiatrists Conrad Baars and Anna Terruwe, these individuals suffer from what they label "deprivation neurosis." "The mere fact that a child is frustrated in its natural need for love, tenderness, and unconditional acceptance," they suggest, "is sufficient to produce a neurosis."[28] Whenever the unmet need occurred in the past, such neurotics continue "to search restlessly for the gratifications that are rightfully theirs for they feel a deep-seated dissatisfaction and unrest which affect their entire psychic being."[29]

Those who enter religious life with such a history of neglect often experience huge emotional gaps that cry out to be filled. They feel imprisoned in the pain of past hurts. Such persons may have been sexually abused, physically brutalized, emotionally suppressed or abandoned outright as children. In the supportive environment of a novitiate community of attractive peers, they frantically search out friendships that will compensate for the deprivations of the past. Unfortunately, these relationships are fragile and frustrating because they originate, not out of freedom and mutuality, but from compulsion and self-centeredness. The help they seek in a friend would be better sought in a therapist.

Those who insist that celibates should be intimate with everyone, but with no one person in particular, misunderstand the nature of human intimacy. It is impossible to be intimate in general without first experiencing the intimacy of friendship with one person. For religious, however, relationships with particular persons should be deepened in such a way that will enable them to relate more authentically with all of the people they encounter. The exclusive coupling of two friends is incompatible with the stance religious are called to have toward others. The boundaries that set off their relationships should be permeable by all who enter their lives so that more and more people can come to find a place in their hearts. The love between husband and wife must be equally permeable so that children and others can partake of that love. As psychiatrist Sr. Anna Polcino notes, "Coupling cannot be the model for religious and clergy. For us, the model must be intentional friendships, whereby the two establish an open bonding, relinquishing possessiveness . . . The friendship is always open to others; it is not exclusive, but rather inclusive. . . ."[30]

REAFFIRMING FRIENDSHIP'S VALUE

It is important to assert unambiguously the value of friendships in religious life. By giving flesh and blood reality to God's love and care, friends enable us to believe more strongly in a God who refuses to love us at a distance, but is incarnately involved in all that we do. Without doubt, life-giving friendships must be counted as part of the hundred-fold promised those who leave everything to follow Christ (Mk 10:30).

Healthy friendships should be actively fostered in the novitiate for a variety of reasons. Some reasons relate to the nature of religious life in general and others flow from the dynamics of the formation process itself. Religious life by its very nature is communitarian. Men and women join religious communities because they feel called to work for the kingdom of God with collaborators in companionship rather than in isolation. Moreover, religious are being challenged these days to go beyond colleagueship to friendship. The Thirty-Second General Congregation of the Jesuits directed these words to its members:

> From the union with God in Christ flows, of necessity, brotherly love. Love of the neighbor, which union with Christ implies, has for its privileged object in our case, the companions of Jesus who compose our Society. They are our companions; and it is our community ideal that we should be companions not only in the sense of fellow workers in the apostolate, but truly brothers and friends in the Lord.[31]

Therefore, an enlightened understanding of the vow of chastity affirms the importance of friendships for the full living of celibate love. Only a truncated and narrow view of the vow would see deep friendships as inimical to religious life. Celibates are not exempted from Christ's commandment to love their neighbor as they love themselves. Thus, the celibate way of life can only be justified if it is seen as a way of loving. Religious are not exempted from the lifelong human process of learning how to love with integrity, fidelity, and care. Like all human beings, they must be committed to learning from their interpersonal experiences. It is in their intimate relationships that they come to know the meaning of what is involved in loving as Jesus did. In this sense, friendships serve as a school of love because friends can help one another grow as loving persons. Living integrated and vibrant celibate lives is not simple, but involves a lifelong process of learning. Good friends can support, encourage, and sustain the sometimes ambivalent commitment of those struggling to live out the ideals of apostolic celibacy.

Finally, religious formation is most effective when it is experiential. I believe strongly that learning is most lasting and significant when it comes through personal experience and trial and error. While the path to integrated and authentic celibate love entails risks, it is mainly through personal experience that lifelong lessons will be appropriated. An effective formation program must create an environment in which religious: (1) can feel free to learn from their experiences; (2) can feel hopeful that much can be learned from their mistakes; and (3) can experience deeply the faithful love and unconditional acceptance of God made manifest in the enduring love of good friends. Good friends, like good wine, can only develop at a natural pace over time.

A LIFE MARKED BY LOVE

Chastity is a way of loving that belongs to all Christians. Its goal is to produce lives that are noticeably marked by love. This broad understanding of chastity stands in contrast to a view that restricts chastity's function to the control of sexual passion. This narrower understanding has prevailed in the church and in secular society for many centuries. It is a negative notion insofar as it emphasizes chastity's role of regulating our sexual appetite, particularly our appetite for sexual pleasure. This is a one-sided understanding and needs to be complemented by a fuller view of chastity in line with a renewed appreciation of sexuality as the God-given power for the sake of loving others and forming fruitful relationships.

Positively, chastity is the virtue that helps us appreciate our own and others' sexuality in all its aspects. Chastity seeks to integrate sexuality and to place it at the service of love in personal relationships. An important function of chastity is to order our sexual activity in such a way that it will promote our own welfare as well as those with whom we are in relationship. Thus, chastity goes far beyond the physical. If we are not reaching out to others in friendship in imitation of Jesus, we cannot really be chaste in the full sense, no matter how successful we may be in avoiding selfish sexual behavior. Genuine chastity should allow all Christians—married, celibate, and single—to live lives of passionate love, not resignation. Carmelite William McNamara remarks that "Married lovers are not sexual and passionate enough. And what's more, neither are celibate lovers, who should be at least as sexual and passionate as married people. There is no other way to be a really great lover. And if religious men and women are not great lovers, what hope is there for Christianity?"[32]

CHAPTER SEVEN

BLESSED ARE THE POOR:
ENRICHMENT IN THE MIDST
OF PRIVATION

Poverty as such has no value; it becomes meaningful insofar as it enriches
others, after the example of Christ, who, "though he was rich, for your
sake became poor, so that by his poverty you might
become rich" (2 Cor 8:9).[1]
LADISLAS M. ORSY

MANY SOCIAL ILLS such as crime and violence are rooted in the
degradation that results from poverty. Poverty often destroys individual dignity and like a cancer it can threaten human community. It is no
wonder that it is seen as a public enemy and a disease we must battle.
How, then, can poverty be regarded as a Christian virtue and an aid in
our spiritual journey? What is the nature of the poverty that followers
of Christ are called to practice? Certainly, poverty cannot pose as a
value if no enrichment accompanies it. According to theologian Ladislas Orsy, the poverty that the gospel promotes "is first a great
enrichment, and secondly, a measure of sacrifice . . . If the element of
enrichment is not there, poverty is not desirable."[2] Orsy emphasizes
the positive without minimizing the reality of sacrifice. How poverty
can be understood and practiced in ways that enhance Christian maturity is the focus of this chapter.

THE MANY FACES OF CHRISTIAN POVERTY

Like other complex realities, gospel poverty eludes a simple definition. And because it does not admit to a univocal understanding, heated debate easily erupts when anyone attempts too facilely to pinpoint its nature. Rooted in our personal experience of Jesus, Christian poverty finds diverse exemplars in such persons as Francis of Assisi, Mother Teresa, Dorothy Day, and Pope John XXIII. Thus, it is a rich spiritual reality that is embodied in varied and multiple forms.[3] A survey of its various modes reveals that reality from different perspectives.

POVERTY OF SPIRIT

A fundamental understanding of Christian poverty is called poverty of spirit or spiritual poverty. Acknowledging that to be human is to be poor before God and to rely radically on the Lord alone, poverty of spirit refers to our human condition, not to our economic state. It calls for a humble admission of our human limitation in the face of such existential realities as death, change, and loneliness. By stripping us of our illusion of self-sufficiency, spiritual poverty turns us toward God in expectation and trust.

It is based on the first of the Beatitudes, which contains Christ's promise that those who trust in God will be blessed, and on the texts that speak of the providence of God who knows what we need even before we ask (Mt 6:25–34; Lk 12:22–32). These passages invite us to surrender our lives into God's care. "Now if that is how God clothes the grass in the field which is there today and thrown into the fire tomorrow, how much more will he look after you, you . . . of little faith" (Lk 12:28). It challenges us to place ultimate trust in divine reliability, not on human resources. While not denying the importance of responsibly using our human talents and abilities to care for our world, it repudiates a godless mentality that relies more on military arsenals, savings accounts and insurance policies for security than on the living God. Spiritual poverty does not necessarily require living in destitution or neglecting to provide for the future. It means simply that our resources are not amassed in order to establish an arrogant self-sufficiency, but are allotted in a planned manner to enhance our relationship with God and others.

Poverty of spirit frees us from the idolatry of mammon, preventing us from making money and possessions false gods in which we entrust our total welfare. Christians ought not make wealth, or any other created thing, an absolute value. Theologian Karl Rahner warns of the danger of making absolute what is only relative, eternal what is merely transitory, and infinite what is of only finite worth. We lose our perspective on created things and no longer "take creatures seriously within the horizon of the Absolute."[4] Only God is absolute; all created things are good insofar as they help us reach the end for which we were created. A blind side exists in all of us that makes us fall for "this particular thing" as if our very life depended on it. "I just couldn't live without it!" is something we hear frequently. When we hear this from others, we recognize how silly it is to regard as ultimate what is ephemeral. Yet, we are often oblivious to this same foolishness when it afflicts us. We must always guard against this loss of perspective because it jeopardizes our journey back to God. It would be tragic to allow our attachment to a limited good to alienate us from infinite Goodness. The poor in spirit are blessed because they know that God alone can satisfy their hungry hearts.

Spiritual poverty is attained when our love relationship with God influences our attitude towards the material world. "Our personal relationships," states Orsy, "always affect and transform our relationship to the material world around us."[5] An ordinary meal becomes a festive event at a family reunion. A loaf of homemade bread takes on special meaning when received as a gift on Valentine's Day. An ordinary wine is savored as if it were of vintage stock when shared by old friends at a school reunion. These examples show how the material world is transformed by personal relationships. In a similar way, God's love for us has an effect on our relationships with all other creatures. When there is a great love between God and us, our relation to the material world also undergoes a transformation. Some things lose their importance; others become rich in meaning. When God is our supreme value, all created beings are defined in reference to the divine, and our love of God determines the meaning and value of created goods. When creatures help us praise, reverence, and serve God, they are deemed good for us because they unite us to our Lord and creator. When they threaten our union with God, they become snares which endanger our spiritual growth.

LOVE FOR THE POOR

Solidarity with the poor and the exploited is another form of Christian poverty. This mode of poverty invites us to emulate Yahweh's love for the poor, the *anawim*. Because Yahweh has shown a special love for the poor and the oppressed (Is 61:1–2; Lk 4:18–19), we who strive for closeness to God must also keep the poor close to our hearts. In the New Testament, Jesus openly declared that he came to bring good news to the poor, and exhibited a special concern for those marked by deprivation (Mt 11:4–5). In the Beatitudes, he does not try to spiritualize away poverty which is a form of suffering. Given Jesus' compassionate care for the poor, we who wish to be imitators of Christ must also embrace those who claim such a tender spot in his heart. Moreover, our love for Christ must be demonstrated in our concrete acts of love for the poor and "the least" among us, with whom Christ identifies (Mt 25:31–46). As the Johannine teaching states, it is impossible to love God whom we have never seen, if we do not love our sisters and brothers whom we can see (1 Jn 4:20).

Union with the poor and the oppressed requires a commitment to combat poverty as an evil that degrades the lives of many people. Material poverty is not a Christian ideal, but is rather a subhuman condition caused by our sinfulness and the selfish exploitation of the weak. Social injustice is therefore something to be eradicated through our efforts on behalf of the *anawim*. When we love the poor, our identification with them will grow; this increased identification will then rouse us from apathetic slumber and move us to act on their behalf. Identifying with others gives us a new vision. But this new vision involves a risk, for, as psychologist Robert Kegan puts it, "what the eye sees better the heart feels more deeply." He goes on to say, "We not only increase the likelihood of our being moved; we also run the risks that being moved entails. For we are moved somewhere, and that somewhere is further into life, closer to those we live with."[6] Christians will be unable to hear the "cry of the poor" (Ps 9:13; Job 34:28; Prov 21:1), unless they have greater personal experience of their miseries and distress.

Solidarity with the poor necessitates viewing reality from their perspective. It is only by removing the filters that influence our perceptions of social reality that we will truly be able to understand the plight of the poor. This empathic understanding is difficult to attain because our reactions to events are very much conditioned by our own class mentality. "One who claims to be free from class mentality," argues Jesuit Pedro Arrupe, "is rightly suspect. Only with great difficulty do we escape from the claims of class."[7] Only close association with people outside of our own socioeconomic class can liberate us from being encapsulated by the mentality and ethos of our milieu.

In order to help us cross the mental barriers that imprison us, Arrupe emphasizes the importance of close contact with the poor by inserting ourselves into their context at least for a while. This experience will "enable us, at least for a time, to get away from a world in which we feel secure, perhaps even comfortable, and experience in our own flesh something of the insecurity, oppression and misery that is the lot of so many people today. Without such an experience, we cannot really claim to know what poverty is."[8]

Furthermore, we must enter these insertion experiences with a poverty of mind and heart that allows us to be receptive to new ideas and emotions. If our minds and hearts are already "preoccupied," there will be no room for receiving what others have to give us. Our humble openness creates a vacancy for others to enter our lives and to have a possibly transforming influence on us. A famous professor of religion at Tokyo University once approached a Zen master (*roshi*) and asked for instructions in meditation. Consenting to the request, the roshi first asked the professor to sit and have tea. The Zen master then began to fill the professor's cup halfway, then all the way to the brim. When the roshi continued to pour even after the tea began to overflow, the professor looked up with confusion. The Zen master then said, "If you really want to learn, you must bring an empty cup." If we want to learn from the poor about their plight, we too must bring an empty cup to our encounters with them.

SIMPLICITY OF LIFE AS WITNESS

Simplicity of life is another form of poverty closely associated with poverty as union with the poor. It fosters a singularity of focus making the advance of God's kingdom one's central concern. Preoccupation with doing the Lord's work frees those who practice simplicity of life from narcissistic concerns for a comfortable and easy lifestyle. Dorothy Day, founder of the Catholic Worker movement, makes clear the practical benefit of poverty to those trying to serve others:

> Once we begin not to worry about what kind of house we are living in, what kind of clothes we are wearing, we have time, which is priceless, to remember that we are our brother's keeper, and that we must not only care for his needs as far as we are immediately able, but try to build a better world.[9]

Describing the rise of the Catholic Worker movement in the early 1930s, historian Mel Piehl comments on how the Workers were helped by their voluntary poverty. Poverty sharpened their immediate sense of identification with the downtrodden, which, in turn, greatly intensified radical commitment. Moreover, their sense of sharp departure from the whole cluster of American values surrounding abundance and consumption constituted a significant critique of American society and made them less vulnerable to distraction and compromise.[10]

Poverty as simplicity requires that we do not confuse the necessities of life with what is luxurious. Quoting St. Ignatius, Arrupe warns that "we must take care not to start substituting the superfluous for the necessary, confusing what pleases us with what is good for us, and thus converting measures of prudence to excuses for self-indulgence."[11] Entitled "The Luxuries We Can't Do Without," an article reports the findings of a survey recently done for the Doyle Graf Raj advertising agency by the Roper Organization. Of the 600 adults surveyed (representing 100 households apiece in San Francisco, New York, Chicago, Washington, D.C., Houston, and Los Angeles), 57 percent said they could not live without a microwave oven, 59 percent called their answering machines a necessity, 54 percent said they absolutely needed their home computers, and 36 percent considered their videocassette recorders indispensable. "What just a few years ago were clearly novelties or luxuries have today become necessities of speed and convenience," said the president of the company that initiated the study of households with annual incomes above $100,000.[12]

As a form of Christian poverty, simplicity stands as a counter-cultural challenge to a society steeped in the pursuit of comfort, power, and riches. It is an indictment of consumerism which implies that accumulating possessions is a good in itself. We are constantly barraged by this philosophy through advertising that invites us to surround ourselves with the newest and best of everything, as if salvation and happiness are only one more purchase away. The consumeristic spirit exposes how flawed our relationship to created things has become: what was meant by God to be a means to an end has become an end in itself. To curtail this distorted spirit, we must allow our personal relationship to God and our needy sisters and brothers around the world to transform our attitude toward the material world. Seeing the starvation and malnutrition of fellow human beings should move us from stockpiling to sharing.

In the gospels, Jesus states clearly that wealth is a serious obstacle to entering the kingdom of God (Lk 6:24; 12:16–21; 16:20f). Why does Jesus say this? It is not because he is trying to promote poverty for its own sake. Nor is it because he is trying to suggest contempt for the goods of this world. Rather, Jesus presents a straightforward message. What he says about riches follows from the commandment to love. It has to be very difficult for the wealthy to enter the kingdom of heaven because we must love our neighbor in order to gain eternal life; and when we do that, we do not have riches left over.

SHARING IN COMMUNITY

Communitarian sharing is another form of Christian poverty that is rooted in the experience of the early church: "The whole group of believers was united, heart and soul; no one claimed for his own use anything that he had, as everything they owned was held in common" (Acts 4:32; also 2:44–45; 4:36–37; 5:1–11). This shared ownership ensures its practitioners that no one is left in need and fosters a community whose members genuinely feel a close union of minds and hearts.

There is an "all for one and one for all" spirit associated with this ideal of Christian community. Its aim is to eliminate the difference between rich and poor and it emphasizes the equal worth of persons in the eyes of God. People are valued not because of their possessions, but their intrinsic worth grounded in God's love.

The common ownership of property in religious orders illustrates this form of Christian poverty. Without it, the bonds that unite religious communities would be eroded by privatistic and individual concerns. Thus, Ignatius of Loyola called poverty the firm wall of religion. The general erosion of community in modern life testifies to the fact that private ownership tends to separate. "Private Property. Keep Out!" not only keeps us from trespassing onto others' property, it also prevents us from entering each other's lives in friendship and mutual care. Common ownership, on the other hand, fosters community by placing the common good at the center of our concern.

Lay Christians in increasing numbers are seeking to experience deeper forms of community living. Charismatic households and covenant communities, as well as communities of Jesuit volunteers, L'Arche members and Catholic Workers are examples of such lay groups. From their struggles they have gradually realized the importance of poverty as communitarian sharing, as well as the debilitating effects of an excessive emphasis on individual ownership. Though not bound by a vow of poverty, they try to embody concretely the form of Christian poverty that calls for the sharing of goods and a concern for all in the community. It seems that it is precisely this spirit of communal love that continues every year to attract young people to join these groups.

POVERTY AS READINESS TO SERVE

Lastly, Christian poverty can take the form of apostolic availability or a readiness to help others. Service is the heart of this mode of poverty which invites us to put ourselves at the beck and call of others in need. The underlying attitude is that our possessions equip us to share and to serve. Recognizing a broader aspect of poverty than just what involves material goods, apostolic availability consists in placing our knowledge, talents, energy, and time at the disposal of others.

A dramatic illustration of poverty as availability can be seen in the story of Brian Willson who lost the lower portions of both legs when he was run over by a munitions train on September 2, 1987. Willson and a group called Nuremberg Actions were trying to block munitions trains leaving the Concord Naval Weapon Station in Northern California. The trains, they claim, carry arms shipments bound for Central America. Feeling strongly that the sending of arms to Central America is "madness," Willson, who had just toured Nicaragua, protested, "If they want to murder they should go to Central America and look into the eyes of the mothers and children being killed with American bombs."[3] Brian Willson, a Vietnam veteran and practicing attorney, well exemplifies poverty as readiness for service because he was willing to give up so much for the lives of people unknown to him, solely on the principle that "the lives of Central Americans" are "no less important than his."[4] Whether one is sympathetic to his political views or not, it must be admitted that his willingness to give up what he possessed, even his very life, for the welfare of others represents the spirit of poverty as apostolic availability. Many others, such as dedicated teachers and social workers who forsake larger salaries for the chance to serve, exemplify this form of poverty in daily and less dramatic ways.

Some religious view their vow of poverty as an avenue to increased availability for ministry. By dispossessing themselves of property and possessions, they hope to be free for the ready service of others. As Jesuits were reminded by a document on religious poverty, voluntary poverty is an attempt "to achieve that liberty from inordinate attachments, which is the condition of any great and ready love . . . this very liberty to love is in the service of the apostolate."[5] Freedom to love is the ideal of poverty as apostolic availability. Of course, this ideal greatly depends on a spirit of interior detachment, which entails possessing a heart that is not captivated by created things. Detachment empties the heart of greed and makes it single-mindedly set on being sent to do the Lord's bidding.

In summary, a common characteristic of all forms of Christian poverty is its interpersonal nature. The meaning of created goods for Christians cannot be understood apart from our relationship to God and others. The significance of material things, for example, becomes clear when seen in reference to God. When we view created things in terms of our relationship to God, they can be regarded simultaneously as gifts from a loving creator, the means to attaining union with the

Lord, and possible snares that retard our pilgrim's progress. Our attitude toward the material world is also shaped by our relationship with others. As dwellers of the earth, we were created, not to live in isolation, but to be united as grateful recipients of a common divine benefactor. Christian poverty requires us to acknowledge that all people on earth are brothers and sisters and to allow this familial connection to transform our appreciation and use of material goods. As members of the human community, we must enjoy the goods of the earth with an alert eye to the needs and welfare of others. In short, underlying all the modes of poverty we have discussed is the conviction that the things of the earth are for the sake of fostering union—our union with God and with each other. Hence, our relationship to the material world must be both aesthetical and ascetical. The aesthetical aspect ensures that we delight in the goodness and beauty of all created things. The ascetical aspect ensures our freedom to say "no" to certain material objects because of a "yes" we want to say to deeper desires. By preserving this freedom to say "yes" or "no" to created goods, we strengthen our ability to use creatures only in ways that deepen our relationship of love with God and others.

POVERTY, DEVELOPMENT, AND MATURITY

As with other virtues, growth in Christian poverty involves a gradual process, and is not something achieved all at once. Progress in living Christian poverty is often blocked by psychological immaturity. For example, neurotic insecurity and narcissism foster hoarding rather than sharing. On the other hand, growth in Christian poverty will not only make us better Christians, but can also contribute to our psychological development as persons—a clear instance of how holiness and wholeness need not be incompatible. By examining some of the findings of developmental psychology, we can deepen our appreciation of how Christian poverty contributes to healthy development.

A basic issue that divides developmental psychologists into clearly distinct schools of thought revolves around a fundamental question: Is there a general and universal trajectory that self-changes and "growth" follow over the span of a lifetime? One group's answer is negative. These psychologists such as L. Edward Wells and Sheldon Stryker rest their position on the presumption "that the evolution of selves through the life course is characterized by variability and fluidity."[16] What is usually presented as the generalized life course, they argue, merely represents a rather idealized summary of the numerous and diverse patterns out of which individuals construct their lives.[17] Another school of thought, however, maintains that there are distinct and universal sequences of stages, crises, and forms through which all normal selves develop. In this group of structural-developmental psychologists are such names as Jean Piaget, Erik Erikson, Lawrence Kohlberg, and Robert Kegan. Erikson and Kegan have articulated theories that assert an invariant, underlying order for changes in self-concept during one's life—self-concept being, in Kegan's phrase, "a more or less consistent sense of a me." They argue, in other words, that there is a natural "deep structure" of self-development.

Kegan has suggested what that underlying structure is by indicating six different levels of subject-object relations throughout the lifespan. According to him, we are never just individuals, but people always embedded in a "holding environment."

> The person is an "individual" and "embeddual." There is never just a you; and at this moment your own buoyancy or lack of it, your own sense of wholeness or lack of it, is in large part a function of how your own current embeddedness culture is holding you.[18]

Subject-object relations refer to the individual's relationship to his or her holding environment, the psychosocial setting that at each stage sustains the construction of the self. Development involves a sequence of six stages or "evolutionary truces" by which we try to find the proper balance between being distinct as individuals and being embedded in a holding culture. These structural stages describe the way we currently make meaning of our experiences. Stages are benchmarks, and we live in the motion around these benchmarks. Kegan sheds light on the self-in-motion in those transitional moments in our lives when our meaning-structures begin to slip and we find ourselves caught in the balance between our "new" and our "old" selves. At these inevitable moments in the course of development when we begin to outgrow our ways of making meaning, we become vulnerable to a breakdown in meaning that may occasion a crisis in the very construction of self.

Through case studies, Kegan shows concretely how these stage transitions show up in real life. For instance, Terry, a 16-year-old who has been hospitalized, illustrates someone defending a rigid "imperial" construction of self (the second stage in Kegan's developmental scheme). She frustrates her therapists by refusing to join in milieu therapy because it requires a sharing of feeling that threatens the integrity of her current, constricted way of making meaning. At the third stage, Kegan presents Eric, a depressed college freshman who wants to escape from his dormitory room and return home to his parents. His "interpersonal" construction of self is so embedded in his relationship with his family that he feels rejected and confused when his parents suggest that he remain at college even though he is homesick.

Kegan believes that growth along the developmental stages occurs when we are able to let go of our present holding environment and move beyond to another one which is broader and allows for more personal expansion. In other words, the self grows by its emergence from embeddedness. Some examples of these cultures of embeddedness from which we must advance are: our mother or primary caretaker in infancy; parents in the family triangle in early childhood; authority figures and peers in school; friends, colleagues at work and love relationships. As we develop, we need to dis-identify ourselves from our embedded culture or holding environment by a shift in self-consciousness. We need to shift from "I *am* my family" to "I *have* a family," from "I *am* my relationships" to "I *have* relationships." Throughout life, we are "hatched out" over and over again from one holding environment to another. One of the powerful features of Kegan's constructive-developmental approach to the study of the person is that it "reconceives the whole question of the relationship between the individual and the social by reminding that the distinction is not absolute, that development is intrinsically about the continual settling and resettling of this very distinction."[19]

Each of the developmental stages, Kegan maintains, is an evolutionary truce, setting the terms on the fundamental issue regarding how distinct we are from our life surroundings and how embedded. It is a temporary solution to the lifelong tension between the yearning we all experience for inclusion and for distinctness.[20] Throughout the course of life there is a continual moving back and forth between resolving the tension slightly in favor of autonomy at one stage, and in favor of inclusion at the next. However, the desirable direction of development, according to structural-developmentalists, is clearly towards new forms of openness and inclusion.

Because his model recognizes the equal dignity of the human yearning for both autonomy and inclusion, Kegan feels that it can be "a corrective to *all* present developmental frameworks which univocally define growth in terms of differentiation, separation, increasing autonomy, and lose sight of the fact that adaptation is equally about integration, attachment, inclusion."[21] Along with Kegan, feminist psychologists like Carol Gilligan criticize the myopic outlook that would identify differentiation (the stereotypically male overemphasis in the human ambivalence between autonomy and inclusion) with growth and development, while viewing integration (the stereotypically female overemphasis) as dependency and immaturity.[22]

That the overemphasis on autonomy in self-development needs to be redressed by placing greater value on communion with others is supported by the findings of Abraham Maslow. The father of humanistic psychology, Maslow did extensive research on healthy people who were thriving in their lives and work. In his study of these "self-actualizing" persons, he discovered that the move toward self-actualization involves a move toward becoming, among other things: more possessed of *gemeinshaftsgefuhl* (a feeling for the worldwide familyhood of all); more deeply experiencing of interpersonal relationships; more transcendent of particular culture.[23] That such people are especially capable of practicing poverty as compassionate solidarity with the poor and the oppressed could be easily argued.

GROWTH AS REBIRTHING

This brief excursus into developmental theory enables us now to see how striving to live gospel poverty not only makes us better Christians, but also stimulates our upward movement on the developmental ladder. Kegan understands "person" to refer as much to an activity as to a thing—"an ever progressive motion engaged in giving itself a new form."[24] Personal development thus requires the continual acquisition of "a new form" by which the self is understood. Growth toward maturity, according to Kegan, can be seen when individuals abandon the limited holding environment which has influenced their present self-definition and acquire a wider holding environment which challenges them to redefine themselves in broader ways—ways that allow for more attachment and inclusion, while preserving one's autonomous identity.

Similarly, Jesus identified spiritual growth with the acquisition of new forms through a process of rebirth. In challenging Nicodemus to be born again or from above (the Greek word, *anothen,* can mean both), Jesus outlined the nature of growth for all Christians (Jn 3:1–10). Kegan's developmental theory supplies concreteness to what this continual rebirth entails for us who are striving to enter the Kingdom of God. The Spirit of God must be allowed to penetrate our hard-shelled encapsulation and shatter our self-containment so that new life can sprout forth at developmental intervals. Rebirth, at each point, comes with the death of the encapsulated ego.

Long associated with Kegan at Harvard Graduate School of Education, developmentalist Lawrence Kohlberg is widely known for his stages of moral reasoning. Unlike Kegan's wider focus on ego development, Kohlberg restricted his research to the development of moral reasoning. Although the important question of whether people tend to exercise moral judgment in real life situations as they do in paper-and-pencil interviews was not fully addressed by Kohlberg, his developmental scheme is useful in spelling out what the Christian rebirthing process entails in terms of moral development. When we examine his six stages, we can see a movement from egocentric reasons for moral decisions in stages one and two (avoiding punishment and benefitting from pragmatic exchange) to social reasons in stages three, four, and five (having a reputation as a "good person," upholding the social order, and fulfilling one's social contracts) to motives based on universal ethical principles like justice in stage six. In this movement, the dynamic flow is from encapsulated self-concern, to concern for the social order based on self-interest, and finally to concern for what is right based on universal principles without any reference to subjective factors of personal gain.

Similar to the developmental schemes of both Kegan and Kohlberg, Christian poverty in its various forms calls for a progressive expansion of our self-understanding. For example, poverty of spirit, born out of an honest self-assessment done in the solitude of one's soul, is our humble acknowledgment that each of us relies radically on God for existence and happiness. However, poverty as communitarian sharing, by introducing a social dimension to poverty, turns our gaze from ourselves to others. Its requirement of communal sharing requires that we move from seeing ourselves as isolated, atomized selves to appreciating our essential connection with others in the Christian family. Then, when poverty as solidarity with the poor and the oppressed is taken seriously, we are challenged to an even broader self-definition. The holding environment from which our new self-definition is to come expands from our local Christian community to the community of the global village. The movement required by these various forms of Christian poverty necessitates an ever-expanding sense of self: from being an isolated individual to being a member of a nuclear family to being a member of a Christian community related by belief, not blood, and finally to being a member of a universal family founded on the Fatherhood and Motherhood of God. The self expands because it is progressively defined in relation to ever larger entities.[25] "Psychological and spiritual health," states Sam Keen, "does not consist in having no self but in keeping the process of self-formation flowing, of continually enlarging the images by which we understand ourselves and our world."[26] Faith assures us that the ultimate holding environment destined for all who love God will be the community constituted by a triune God in whom we will be forever blissfully embedded. The call to Christian holiness, then, is an invitation to be embedded in God. Jesus' principal mission was to lead us to holiness, to show us the way to this embeddedness in God. The pedagogy used by him to teach us the path to life with God is well illustrated in the "Two Standards" meditation of Ignatius' *Spiritual Exercises*.[27] An analysis of this meditation will show the key importance of poverty in the pedagogy of Christ.

POVERTY AND THE PEDAGOGY OF CHRIST

The meditation on the Two Standards is basically an instruction on the discernment of spirits. It contains Ignatius' understanding of how Christ leads people to holiness and how Lucifer, "the deadly enemy of our human nature," ensnares them. Ignatius' insights into the process of Christian growth have for centuries been recognized by the church as a perennial wisdom transcending the limitation of his own religious culture. Thus, modern readers should not become distracted by his historically conditioned language. As a contemporary spiritual writer states:

> The theology of the *Exercises* is not dependent on Ignatius' medieval world-view of angels and devils. His use of the two spirits struggling for dominance in the soul is the imagery of the times. But the meaning is the biblical struggle between . . . grace and sin . . . the inevitable war between the forces of good and evil. Ignatius' angelology and demonology are beside the point.[28]

The term "standards" is best understood here as placards or banners, such as those used by opposing forces in a medieval battle. In this meditation, Ignatius illustrates how Christ attracts followers to join him and how Lucifer allures through artifice.

Ignatius lays out the opposing strategies of these two leaders this way. On the one hand, Lucifer entices people to his cause by tempting them "to covet riches . . . that they may the more easily attain the empty honors of this world, and then come to overweening pride." Through these three steps of riches, honor, and pride, the evil one leads us to all other vices. On the other hand, Christ encourages those who desire holiness to seek poverty and "a desire for insults and contempt, for from these spring humility." Corresponding to the three-prong attack of Lucifer, Christ's counterattack calls for three steps: poverty as opposed to riches; insults as opposed to worldly honor; and humility as opposed to pride. Through these three steps, Christ leads us to all other virtues.

An analysis of this meditation reveals the psychological and spiritual wisdom contained in Ignatius' insight into the opposing pedagogies of Christ and Lucifer. Christ's goal is to unite us to God, while Lucifer's aim is to sever the bonds that link us to God. Christ leads us to God by helping us come to a true understanding of our identity as people who are absolutely dependent on and unconditionally loved by God. On the other hand, Satan alienates us from God, by deluding us into thinking of ourselves as totally self-sufficient entities who are neither dependent nor indebted to God for anything. In essence, what is involved is a matter of self-definition. Do we see ourselves as creatures and therefore as correlative beings, whose identity cannot be understood apart from a creator? Or do we see ourselves as freestanding entities, definable in a way that is totally independent of God? A brief look at the process of self-definition will help us understand the underlying dynamics of the opposing strategies of Christ and Satan.

THE PROCESS OF SELF-DEFINITION

The process of self-definition enables us to know that we are who we are and that we are of some worth. We have to use conceptual terms to describe this process, but it is not primarily an intellectual operation. Rather, it is more a psychological experience that is very much bound up with the sentiments, images, and emotional responses that spontaneously define us for ourselves. None of us comes into the world with a subjective knowledge of ourselves, much less with an appreciation of ourselves. This knowledge emerges gradually over time, as Kegan and other psychologists illustrate through their various theories of ego development.

In the process of coming to know who we are and of feeling ourselves as distinct from all our experiences, the initial experience is that of the domination of the material. Observing an infant, we see that the baby can shove and kick the blanket and the blanket cannot kick back. The beginning of growth of the ego consists in this experience of domination and then possession of the material. "That's mine!" is a constant refrain of the two-year-old child. For the child, "That's mine!" means at the same time "I am." In this early stage, the definition of the ego is in terms of material possessions. In other words, the "I am" is defined in terms of the "I have."

A further experience in the definition of the psychological ego comes with the experience of being loved. As children we come to know that we amount to something and are valuable, because the world of adults, which is our criterion of knowledge, bends down in affection upon us. We know that we are lovable because we are loved. It is no wonder that children who suffer severe affective deprivation at the hands of frigid or psychologically disturbed parents barely know that they exist. Some of these unaffirmed people later seek to validate themselves through various means: by amassing material riches, by striving for achievement in work and community affairs, or by acquiring status symbols ranging from cars to academic degrees. "But all these attempts at self-affirmation," contend psychiatrists Conrad Baars and Anna Terruwe, "are futile."[29]

These attitudes about ourselves originating from our infantile existence are transferred to our lives as adults. As adults, then, we find ourselves inhabiting hostile worlds, or challenging worlds, or kind worlds—depending on how our initial experiences have shaped our attitudes about ourselves. This step in the definition of self is profoundly modified for Christians who live according to their faith. This is because the central message of Jesus is that all of us are called to experience ourselves of worth because of our realization of God's love for us.

TO BE EMBEDDED IN GOD

This realization of God's love is the final step in the process of self-definition for Christians. Here we ground our value on the very basis of who and whose we are, as those loved by a God whose faithfulness is unshakable: "Does a woman forget her baby at the breast, or fail to cherish the son of her womb? Yet even if these forget, I will never forget you. See, I have branded you on the palms of my hands" (Is 49:14–16). God's love is what causes us to be and to be of worth. Our experiences of possessing things or being loved by others may reassure us of our value as individuals; but they neither constitute our value nor account for our existence. Only God's love does both. Therefore, we can define ourselves adequately only in reference to our relationship to God. This is the truth of our lives. To be is to be embedded in God, for it is in God that "we live, and move, and exist" (Acts 17:28).

Given this process of self-definition, the logic of Satan's seductive scheme for alienating us from God can be laid out clearly. Basically, what the evil spirit does is to appeal to the remnants of our infantile stages. Satan tempts us by urging us to continue to define ourselves in terms of material possessions and social recognition. By tempting us to amass great wealth, which leads to our growing in stature in the eyes of the world, Satan's strategy is ultimately to push us to the point of pride. Pride consists in defining ourselves and human values in a way that is independent of God. The logic of Satan is clear: riches will lead to honors, which, in turn, will delude us into thinking that we are totally sufficient unto ourselves. Pride is essentially the building of a false self. The falsest thing that we can say about ourselves as creatures is that we are independent, that all we are and all we hope to be does not depend upon God. But, by keeping our attention on riches and honors, the two pillars upon which our false personality is constructed by pride, the evil spirit keeps us from the truth of our dependence on God. When we become forgetful of God, we have been effectively entrapped by the evil spirit.

Strangely, the opposing strategy of Christ to protect us from "the enemy of our human nature" is one that goes against all of our natural inclinations. Christ calls us to poverty, humiliations, and a knowledge of God's love. Christ's strategy involves a double emancipation. Poverty emancipates the ego from dependence upon material things. Humiliations emancipate the ego from dependence upon the recognition and approval of others. This twofold emancipation enables us to base our definition of ourselves on the realization of God's love. When we have done this, we have arrived at the ultimate truth about ourselves: that we have life and are valuable as persons because of God's unconditional love for us. As scripture attests, God's love upholds our being. If God did not deem us worthy, he would not sustain us in existence. "Yes, you love all that exists, you hold nothing of what you have made in abhorrence, for had you hated anything, you would not have formed it. And how, had you not willed it, could a thing persist, how be conserved if not called forth by you? You spare all things because all things are yours, Lord, lover of life!" (Wis 11:24–27). The pedagogy of Christ thus leads us to humility, which is a grateful acknowledgment that God, in Kegan's phrase, is the ultimate holding environment in which we can truly understand who we are. In this Ignatian scheme, Christ-like poverty is the gateway to the truth of our identity as people called to exist in loving relationship to God.

Poverty, by stripping us of all the facades that we use to buttress an insecure sense of self, enables us to be simply who we are and to receive God's gratuitous love as unearned gift. Paradoxically, this childlike simplicity takes a lifetime to achieve. As human beings, we are so radically beset by self-doubt about our essential goodness and value that we are constantly fortifying a weak self-worth by identifying with "other things." These things are of infinite variety. They can be our looks, talents, degrees, possessions, reputations, careers, performance and even our health. We glory in these things that seem to bolster our worth. Some workaholic adults, for example, may at first glance seem to illustrate Erikson's stage of generativity. But a closer look often reveals that they are really in the pre-adolescent stage of industry because they are identifying with their work to compensate for a poor sense of personal identity. We cling to things that seemingly assure our worth. Poverty requires our giving up this desperate clinging. It requires an ongoing dis-identification, whereby we say, "I *have* talents (looks, possessions, etc.), but I *am not* my talents (looks, possessions)."

As Christians, we must separate ourselves from these things that conceal the essential self. While these "other things" are deeply personal, they nonetheless are still other than who we are at the very core of our being. As theologian Karl Rahner puts it, "This type of separation from self is one of the main tasks of the Christian—and it takes a whole life to complete it. It is a necessary part of the road to Christian sanctity."[30] This letting-go process allows us to enjoy a peaceful kind of freedom in our relationship to the material world. We can be at peace in having or not having. An Indian tale told by Anthony de Mello captures the nature of this letting-go process and the rich freedom it begets.

> The sannyasi had reached the outskirts of the village and settled down under a tree for the night when a villager came running up to him and said, "The stone! The stone! Give me the precious stone!"
>
> "What stone?" asked the sannyasi.
>
> "Last night the Lord Shiva appeared to me in a dream," said the villager, "and told me that if I went to the outskirts of the village at dusk I should find a sannyasi who would give me a precious stone that would make me rich forever."
>
> The sannyasi rummaged in his bag and pulled out a stone. "He probably meant this one," he said, as he handed the stone over to the villager. "I found it on a forest path some days ago. You can certainly have it."
>
> The man looked at the stone in wonder. It was a diamond. Probably the largest diamond in the whole world for it was as large as a man's head.
>
> He took the diamond and walked away. All night he tossed about

in bed, unable to sleep. Next day at the crack of dawn he woke the sannyasi and said, "Give me the wealth that makes it possible for you to give this diamond away so easily."[31]

When we relinquish all that is not essential to our basic identity as people utterly cherished by God, we slay the dragon of compulsive acquisition and free ourselves to receive the wealth of God's affirming love.

POVERTY AND NECESSARY LOSSES

In our discussion of poverty as a stimulus to human growth, much reliance was placed on the findings of developmental psychologists such as Kegan and Kohlberg. Recently, however, Judith Viorst, writing from a psychoanalytic background, has expounded a theory that provides further psychological endorsement of Christian poverty as a growthful stance in life. "The road to human development," states Viorst, "is paved with renunciation. Throughout our life we grow by giving up."[32] Her central thesis is that loss is a far more encompassing theme in our lives than we realize. We deal with loss not only through the death of people we love, but we also lose through separations and departures from family and friends. Furthermore, our losses include "our losses of romantic dreams, impossible expectations, illusions of freedom and power, illusions of safety—and the loss of our own younger self, the self that thought it always would be unwrinkled and invulnerable and immortal."[33] Unavoidable and inexorable, these losses are a part of life. The beginning of wisdom and hopeful change, Viorst contends, comes with recognizing that growth comes from responding to these losses in constructive ways. Peaceful acceptance of these inevitable losses leads to the possibility of creative growth. Resentment and resistance, on the other hand, inevitably lead to despair in the face of the fleeting and ephemeral nature of our human condition.

The story of the Taoist farmer, recounted in the writings of Lao-Tzu, illustrates well the dance of life's events and how losses can yield new gains. For Christians, the story serves as a reminder of the need to stay open always to our mysterious God, who often writes straight with crooked lines.

The farmer's horse ran away. That evening the neighbors gathered to commiserate with him since this was such bad luck. He said, "Maybe." The next day the horse returned, but brought with it six wild horses, and the neighbors came exclaiming at his good fortune. He said, "Maybe." And then, the following day, his son tried to saddle and ride one of the wild horses, was thrown, and broke his leg. Again the neighbors came to offer their sympathy for his misfortune. He said, "Maybe." The day after that, conscription officers came to the village to seize young men for the army. But because of the broken leg the farmer's son was rejected. When the neighbors came to say how fortunately everything had turned out, he said, "Maybe."[34]

Throughout the vicissitudes of life, "we grow by losing and leaving and letting go."[35] A more explicitly Christian formulation of this philosophy is one of the most well-known adages of Alcoholics Anonymous: we grow by "letting go and letting God." This conviction of recovering alcoholics stems from a deep sense of spiritual poverty. Step One of the 12-step recovery program is a frank admission that "we were powerless over alcohol—that our lives had become unmanageable."[36] Step Two states that "we came to believe that a Power greater than ourselves could restore us to sanity." And step Three involves a "decision to turn our will and our lives over to the care of God." Although not every Christian suffers from an addiction to alcohol, all are nonetheless called to stand before God with the same kind of spiritual poverty and humble admission of the need for God's saving power. Dealing with the inevitable losses of our lives can easily make our situation seem unmanageable and even bring us to the brink of despair. At such times, we must remember that the pattern of death and resurrection is to be the form of our lives—just as it was in Jesus' life. Jesus promised that if we submit with faith to diminishment and death, God will always bring about enrichment and new life:

> I tell you, most solemnly, unless a wheat grain falls on the ground and dies, it remains only a single grain; but if it dies, it yields a rich harvest. Anyone who loves his life loses it; anyone who hates his life in this world will keep it for the eternal life (Jn 12:24–25).

While Viorst provides a good phenomenological description of the necessary losses of human life, it is the gospel that proclaims the good news of God's intervention to renew life wherever there is loss in any form. As Christians we are not left merely with loss, but always with new life. Our experiences of loss serve to deepen a longing rooted in the human spirit—a yearning that will only be satisfied when we see God face to face in the heavenly Jerusalem, where "there will be no more death, and no more mourning or sadness" (Rev 21:4).

CONCLUSION

In the Constitutions of their order, Jesuits are told by their founder, St. Ignatius, to "love poverty as a mother, and . . . when occasions arise, feel some effects of it."[37] Viewing poverty as a mother serves to highlight the fact that Christian poverty is meant to be a practice that is productive. Authentic Christian poverty should not diminish the joy in living but add to it by giving birth to new forms of sharing, caring, and community. If striven for with an attitude of faith and love, poverty should, in the course of a lifetime, stretch us from the narrow egocentrism of an infant to the universal altruism of a Mother Teresa of Calcutta. The effects of voluntary poverty—in all its various forms as poverty of spirit, simplicity of life, communitarian sharing, union with the poor and oppressed, and readiness for service—can, with the help of grace, transform us into the image of Christ, who though rich became poor for our sakes, so that by his poverty we might become rich. In this transformation, we will be enriched by mother poverty.

CHAPTER EIGHT

CONCLUSION: "BEING
ON THE WAY IS
A WAY OF ARRIVING"

"In our era, the road to holiness necessarily passes
through the world of action.'"
DAG HAMMARSKJOLD, *Markings*

THE METAPHOR OF a journey captures well what most adults come
sooner or later to realize about spiritual and psychological growth: it is
a never-ending series of changes and struggles. In a word, it is a hard
road to travel. It is tied to the ways we respond to the crises of human
life. These crises are both predictable and unpredictable. The predictable ones have been outlined in the literature of developmental psychology, which depicts the pattern of adult growth, not as an undis-
turbed straight line, but as a zigzag process often full of setbacks and
frustrations. The unpredictable crises are easily recognized: sudden ill-
nesses, career disappointments, interpersonal misunderstandings, the
loneliness of ruptured relationships, the separation of death or divorce.
When faced with the struggles that are the inescapable conditions of
growth, people frequently ask themselves: "Why go on? Why keep
trying, if there is no chance of success? What difference does it make
anyway?" The frustrations of seemingly endless change—new jobs,
new residences, new relationships—force many to question whether it
is worth all the effort. These are not theoretical or abstract questions.
They emerge from the concrete experience of striving to grow in

holiness and wholeness. These quandaries frame the struggle to love as Jesus commanded.

In this book I have sought to fashion a spirituality that strengthens the individual's commitment to the ongoing process of sanctification and maturation. Central to this spirituality is the firm belief that God is always close by with divine love and power to help us in our struggles. Followers of the risen Christ are called to believe that "the power by which life is sustained and invited toward wholeness is no human creation and abides and remains steadfast even in a world where death does have dominion over every individual."[2]

As in other human journeys, we reach the destination of our spiritual pilgrimage only gradually. However, there is a paradoxical nature to the spiritual sojourn. While alive, we will never fully reach our goal of union with God and others. Yet, being on the spiritual path is already a way of attaining that end. God is to be enjoyed not only at the end of the search, but all along the way. The Christmas story of the magi illustrates this truth. God was present to them not only when they joyfully arrived at the cave in Bethlehem, but also in the original stirrings that sent them off in search of the promised messiah. God's presence was also experienced in a guiding star that directed them through dark nights and in a dream that warned them of Herod's threat. They experienced God's support, too, in the encouragement they gave each other throughout an uncharted search that took them miles from home. God is more present to us than we think.

Our search for union with God is lifelong, often a strenuous trek punctuated by dark passages. If we are to persevere, we must take courage in God's abiding presence all along the way. Even as we are traveling toward God as destiny, Emmanuel is already with us in man-ifold ways. The disciples of Jesus were once given a dramatic lesson about how Christ is ever-present. One day they were crossing the Lake of Galilee when a fierce storm enveloped their little boat. Frightened by violent winds, the apostles were stricken with panic. Suddenly, Jesus appeared to them walking on the water. "It is I," he told them, "Do not be afraid" (Jn 6:21). Jesus then calmed the storm, and the boat quickly came to shore. The significance of Jesus' words is clear when we look at the original text. The Greek has Jesus saying *ego eimi* which literally means "I am." In the Septuagint, the Greek translation of the Old Testament, the phrase *ego eimi* is used as a surrogate for the divine name (Ex 3:14). It is Yahweh's response to Moses' question, "Who shall I say sent me?" In placing these words in Jesus' mouth, John expresses the early church's belief in the divinity of Christ. The good news affirmed in this Johannine passage is identical to that contained in Matthew's story of the magi: God is always with us in our journeys through life. This truth must permeate our consciousness, especially when our fragile boat is rocked by waves of worry and troublesome torrents. In our fear and confusion, we need to recognize the presence of the risen Jesus drawing near to us to still the storm. Calm will descend on us when we hear Jesus say, "Do not be afraid. It is I."

LETTING GO OF FLAWLESS IMAGES

The journey metaphor most accurately reflects reality when it is seen as a zigzag path rather than as an undeviating straight course. Not a process that moves relentlessly ahead in a single direction, human growth is a mixture of progressions and regressions. At times, we experience forward movements; on other occasions, slips indicate regress; and sometimes, no matter how much effort we expend, we find ourselves at a standstill, seemingly stuck at a developmental plateau. Is this wrong? On the contrary. Accepting the jerky aspect of growth and relinquishing the illusion of a forever smooth-flowing journey is not only necessary but will bring serenity to our striving for maturity. Failures should not produce despair; temporary plateaus need not trigger paralysis. The expectation of a flawless journey is counterproductive because it misrepresents the process of developmental growth.

It also distorts the truth of what it means to be a human being. A view of the human person that does not acknowledge that sinfulness casts a shadow on every person is unrealistic. Such a notion can also have harmful effects. Our sinful condition renders us radically weak. In an ironic way, not to admit to our weakened capacity leads us to a sense of perversity and guilt rather than worthiness and self-acceptance. The refusal "to recognize the persistent ambiguity and the final impotence of our lives tantalizes us with an optimistic promise of self-evolved becoming," concludes theologian LeRoy Aden. It also "stands in danger of giving us a sense of failure and despair to the extent that we do not achieve it."[3] Thus, failure to acknowledge the shadow aspect of human personality diminishes, not enhances, self-esteem.

Aden elaborates on the harmful effects of a naively optimistic view of human development in the context of a critique of Carl Rogers, the father of client-centered therapy and a major influence in the field of pastoral counseling. Aden objects to a basic hypothesis of client-centered therapy: the belief that persons have within themselves the ongoing capacity to reorganize their lives in the direction of maturity and fulfillment if the proper psychological climate is present. Concretely, this hypothesis presupposes that if the counselor communicates empathy, warmth, acceptance, and genuineness, a client will naturally begin to manifest behavior that enhances the true self. According to Aden, "Rogers' faith in the individual's ability to choose the good is absolute. He entertains no qualifications. He allows no doubts. In fact, therapists who begin to question the hypothesis and who shift to another mode of interaction only confuse the client and defeat their own purpose."[4]

Rogers clung tenaciously to his belief in the individual's absolute capacity for constructive and enhancing behavior. Aden recounts an incident in Rogers' life in which he nearly destroyed his own psychic health by maintaining at all cost this article of faith. Rogers once dealt with a very disturbed woman who continually demanded more of him—more time, more warmth, more realness. Although he began to doubt his own adequacy and to lose the boundaries between himself and the client, Rogers was very reluctant to let go. Finally, when he realized that he was on the edge of a personal breakdown, he swiftly referred the client to a psychiatric colleague and left town for an extended period. He eventually sought therapy to overcome feelings of complete inadequacy as a therapist and deep worthlessness as a person.

According to Aden, this "event shows that Rogers would doubt himself as a therapist and as a person before he would question his basic faith in the individual."[5] Rogers had provided his disturbed client with understanding and acceptance over an extended period of time. Nevertheless, she got progressively more dependent and sicker, bordering on psychosis. Her behavior explicitly challenged the very foundation of his theory. Thus, it was easier for him to doubt his own worth as a clinician than to re-examine the linchpin of his therapeutic creed.

Belief in the individual's indomitable capacity for ongoing growth and actualization had to be maintained at all cost.

FORGIVENESS: THE END POINT OF LIFE

Carl Rogers has made many contributions to pastoral counseling, but his trust in the absolute ability of individuals to grow continually toward fulfillment is a harmful assumption for Christians. It contradicts Christianity's deepest insight into the human person as radically good yet burdened by sinfulness. This sinful condition impedes our struggle for growth in holiness and maturity. It often leads to imperfect fulfillment. Unlike the contemporary tendency to absolutize fulfillment as the basic truth and the final goal of human existence, Christian faith reiterates the good news proclaimed by Christ: forgiveness is the end point of human life.

Thus, faulty fulfillment and incomplete development need not worry those who trust in the forgiving love of God. In the end, we will fully enjoy the unconditional acceptance of God, not because we are flawless, but *in spite of* our imperfections. Our merciful God's gift of forgiveness means that we "cannot and need not measure up to any conditions of worth."[6] When forgiveness, and not fulfillment, is seen as the end point of our lives, we can live with greater acceptance of our weaknesses and with greater hope in God's power to complete what grace has started. No longer will the ambiguity of our fulfillment judge us nor the impotence of our efforts condemn us. With St. Paul, we are "quite certain that the One who began this good work" in us "will see that it is finished when the Day of Christ Jesus comes" (Phil 1:6). As Aden states beautifully, the promise of ultimate forgiveness "allows us to be incomplete and yet complete, estranged and yet related, distorted and yet fulfilled." When our journey reaches its termination, we will be wrapped in God's merciful arms, like the prodigal son.

Because "You are forgiven" will be the final words we will hear, we are freed from the compulsive need to actualize perfectly our human potential and are released from the guilt that accompanies falling short of that goal. "Success and failure are accidental," writes one spiritual writer. "The joy of the Christian is never based on . . . success but on the knowledge that [one's] Redeemer lives.'"[7] Thus, the author encourages us to learn to live peacefully to the end of our lives with a certain imperfection:

> The Lord will never ask how successful we were in overcoming a particular vice, sin, or imperfection. He will ask us, "Did you humbly and patiently accept this mystery of iniquity in your life? How did you deal with it? Did you learn from it to be patient and humble? Did it teach you to trust not your own ability but My love? Did it enable you to understand better the mystery of iniquity in the lives of others?[8]

Our lack of perfection will never separate us from God because the Lord's forgiveness is always perfect and total.

WHAT TO DO UNTIL THE MESSIAH COMES

Until that day of Christ Jesus, when we will receive "the perfection that comes through faith in Christ, and is from God," we are called to strive for the goal without ceasing (Phil 3:9-10). We are to imitate St. Paul in his deep yearning "to have Christ and be given a place in him" (Phil 3:9). We have not yet won, but are still running, trying to capture the prize for which Jesus captured us. We, too, must forget the past and strain ahead for what is still to come. We must, in Paul's words, race "for the finish, for the prize to which God calls us upward to receive in Christ Jesus" (Phil 3:14).

Paul's expression of the Christian goal is beautifully poetic. This book has spelled out some of the practical dimensions of that vision. We have discussed ideals about how to love God and each other by the practice of prayer and the gospel values of poverty, chastity, and obedience. These ideals are meant to help Christians finish the spiritual race and to receive a place in Christ. They can be useful in our spiritual odyssey. Like the stars, they may never be reached; but they are helpful to steer our lives by. Ideals can hinder us, however, and discourage us from trying when the fear of performing poorly paralyzes us. The French saying, "The best is the enemy of the good," illustrates this attitude of fearfulness. Ideals impede our spiritual progress when we use them as an excuse for mediocrity, thinking to ourselves: "Christian holiness is something for saintly people, not ordinary folks like us." Furthermore, ideals are injurious when they lure us into thinking that we can earn God's approval by doing everything perfectly. Paul refers to this as seeking a perfection that comes from the Law rather than on faith in Jesus (Phil 3:9). When striving for holiness deceives us into thinking that we can stand in pharisaical judgment over others, we have been seduced by pride. Finally, ideals are harmful when they lead to cynicism and disillusionment. That no one fully lives up to espoused values should not undermine the importance of having high aspirations. The failure of sincere efforts should not disillusion us, but the apathy of not trying should appall us.

Dreaming is not the same as doing. Ideals should inspire us to act, not merely to dream. Thoughts of what could be tomorrow should lead us to do what we can today. When lofty aspirations lead to romantic preoccupation rather than realistic pursuits, they retard our spiritual development. In a letter to a friend, C.S. Lewis makes this point nicely:

> We read of spiritual efforts, and our imagination makes us believe that, because we enjoy the idea of doing them, we have done them. I am appalled to see how much of the change which I thought I had undergone lately was only imaginary. The real work seems still to be done. It is so fatally easy to confuse an aesthetic appreciation of the spiritual life with the life itself—to dream that you have waked, washed, and dressed and then to find yourself still in bed.[9]

No matter how grand our ideals, they can only be achieved through small but steady steps. As the Chinese sage Lao-Tze stated centuries ago, "The journey of a thousand miles begins with one step." We must bear this wise saying in mind as we let the star of idealism lead us, like the magi, to the messiah.

ACTIVITY AND PASSIVITY IN SPIRITUAL STRIVING

Striving for spiritual maturity is paradoxical. It requires us to be simultaneously active and passive. We are called to exert our efforts and use our God-given talents to develop ourselves. And, at the same time, we must remember that our efforts alone can never bring us to holiness and wholeness; only God's grace can effect our transformation into Christ. While we ultimately cannot save ourselves, we must nevertheless co-operate with divine grace. We must dispose ourselves to be receptive to the sanctifying action of God's touch. In our spiritual journey we have to negotiate a delicate passage between the Scylla of presumption and the Charybdis of despair. Presumption, according to St. Thomas Aquinas, is "an unwarranted dependence upon God."[10] It is the attitude that God will do it all and that our efforts are not important. Fostering irresponsible inaction, it keeps us from doing our part. Despair, on the other hand, is losing hope in God's saving power. It stems from an exclusive reliance on our efforts, without any trust in God's power to make up for our human limitations. It results from thinking that every-thing depends on us alone. Only ongoing discernment can help us maintain the right balance in our spirituality between personal effort and trusting reliance on God. Both dynamics are encouraged by scripture.

Many New Testament passages attest to the need to rely on God's power in order to bear spiritual fruit in our lives. A beautiful expression of this is the Johannine image of God as the vinedresser. Jesus is the vine and we are the branches. The Father prunes us so that we might bear fruit (Jn 15:1–2). Spiritual growth is passive in the sense that purification and progress are the direct results of God's action upon us.

The evangelist Mark reinforces the centrality of God's action in his parable about the seed growing by itself.

> This is what the Kingdom of God is like. A man throws seed on the land. Night and day, while he sleeps, when he is awake, the seed is sprouting and growing; how, he does not know. Of its own accord the land produces first the shoot, then the ear, then the full grain in the ear. And when the crop is ready, he loses no time; he starts to reap because the harvest has come (Mk 4:26–29).

Notice that the farmer's work is described with a minimum of words. The emphasis falls on the mysterious process of growth. Just as the earth produces fruit spontaneously, so God's reign comes by divine power alone. Once the seed is planted, the result is as sure, as depend-able, and as silent as the forces of nature. Stage by stage—first the green shoot, then the spike of corn, and then the full grain in the ear—the seed of God's reign grows to harvest in a way that the farmer does not understand. This parable reminds us that nature (God's creation) contains a power that humans do not make or direct. Similarly, God's grace will bring about conversion and growth in us in ways we may not understand. In human lives, the spirit of Jesus is the divine power that brings God's kingdom from seed to harvest. When we remember that God's "working in us, can do more than we can ask or imagine" (Eph 3:20), we will be protected from the pride and anxiety that stem from the myth of total self-sufficiency.

But scripture also stresses the importance of human effort. Luke's gospel strongly urges followers of Christ to translate words into action. "Why do you call me 'Lord, Lord,' " asks Jesus, "and not do what I say?" (Lk 6:46).

> Everyone who comes to me and listens to my words and acts on them
> . . . is like the man who when he built his house dug, and dug deep,
> and laid the foundations on rock; when the river was in flood it bore
> down on that house but could not shake it, it was so well built. But
> the one who listens and does nothing is like the man who built his
> house on soil, with no foundations: as soon as the river bore down on
> it, it collapsed; and what a ruin that house became! (Lk 6:47–49).

Jesus not only challenges us to practice his teachings, but also warns that our very hearing of his word must be done with care. In the parable of the sower and the seed, he describes the fragility of the seed of God's word. If it is not received by the right soil, it will not take root and grow. Grains that fall on the edge of the path represent people who have heard the word of God, but have it stolen from their hearts by the forces of evil. Seeds that fall on rock are like people who receive the word in a superficial way, and give up in time of trial. Those that fall in the midst of thorns are Christians who let worries, riches and pleasures of life choke their growth, preventing it from reaching maturity. Grains that fall in the rich soil signify those of generous hearts who have let the word take deep roots in themselves and have yielded a harvest through their perseverance (Lk 8:11–15). Emphasizing the importance of human effort in disposing the soil of the inner self for receiving the word, Jesus concludes with a warning: "So take care how you hear" (Lk 8:18). While Mark's parable of the seed growing by itself stresses the power of God actively bringing about growth, Luke's parable emphasizes the necessity of energetic human cooperation.

Another Lukan parable about a fruitless fig tree highlights the importance of personal effort. When its owner realized that his tree had been barren for three years, he ordered his gardener to remove it. Instead, the caretaker pleaded, "Sir, leave it one more year and give me time to dig round it and manure it: it may bear fruit next year; if not, then you can cut it down" (Lk 13:8–9). We too are called to tend actively the seed of God's word so that it can take deep root in our souls and can bear fruit for the world.

A classical biblical text used to illustrate the need for receptivity to God's formative action in our lives is Jeremiah's visit to the potter. Watching the artisan working at his wheel, the prophet noticed that he continued to shape and reshape the clay until he created what he was envisioning. Then the word of Yahweh came to Jeremiah as follows: "House of Israel, can not I do to you what this potter does? . . . Yes, as the clay is in the potter's hand, so you are in mine, House of Israel" (Jer 18:1–6). While the image of the human person as clay being shaped by the divine potter testifies beautifully to God's active involvement in our spiritual development, it should not be used to justify excessive passivity or infantile irresponsibility. While trying to be malleable to the fashioning influence of God, Christians are called to take adult responsibility for their growth. This means taking active means to deepen one's love for God and neighbor.

Activity and passivity must coexist in dynamic tension if we are to remain spiritually healthy. In describing her Jeremiah-like visit to a potter at work in Provincetown, situated at the tip of Cape Cod, Massachusetts, a recent writer shed light on the active-passive dimension of spiritual formation. The observer discovered that the artist, a woman of over 70 years, was a wise person as well as a potter. After conveying her belief in the direct relationship between the pliability of the clay and its strength, the artisan added, almost as an aside, "If you can't bend a little and give some, life will eventually break you. It's just the way it is, you know."[11] The visitor noticed that the potter worked with both hands: one placed inside, applying pressure on the clay; the other on the outside of the gradually forming pot. Too much pressure from the outside would cause the pot to collapse, while too much pressure from the inside would make the pot bulge outward. The old potter spoke wisely about life:

Life, like the pot I am turning, is shaped by two sets of opposing forces . . . Sadness and death and misfortune and the love of friends and all the things that happened to me that I didn't even choose. All of that influenced my life. But, there are things I believe in about myself, my faith in God and the love of some friends that worked on the insides of me.[12]

Like Jeremiah, this modern day potter sheds light on the Lord's ways of dealing with us. The Lord who calls us to be holy is also the one who forms us into the image of Jesus, the living icon of God. This divine artist works on us with two hands: one shaping us from the inside and another molding us from the outside. Like the clay pot, we need to be malleable. And, paradoxically, our pliability will give us strength to persevere actively in the process. Knowing how to bend a little will keep us from breaking.

EXPERIENCE AS MANURE IN THE SPIRITUAL FIELD

In the spiritual project of transformation into Christ, effort is what counts, not unremitting success. Acclaiming the value of practice in spiritual growth, the Eastern guru Chogyam Trungpa speaks of the "manure of experience and the field of bodhi."[13] Bodhi represents the search for enlightenment. If we are skilled and patient enough to sift through our experiences and study them thoroughly, we can use them to aid our enlightenment. Our experiences, our mistakes and even our failures function like fertilizer. According to Trungpa, to deny or cover up our errors is a waste of experience. When we do not scrutinize our failures for the lessons they contain, we miss an opportunity. What appears to be useless trash contains potential nutrients for life. But, to convert our deficiencies into positive value, we need to pile them on a compost heap, not sweep them behind a bush. Hiding failure is to store it like rubbish. "And if you store it like that," the guru remarks, "you would not have enough manure to raise a crop from the wonderful field of bodhi."[14]

In a parallel way, experience can be said to be manure in the field of Christian development. Like manure, past experiences must be plowed into the ground to enrich the inner soil of the self, making it more receptive to the seed of God's word. Then we will reap an abundant harvest based on our perseverance. Mistakes need not ruin our spiritual journey, if we learn from them. Even great saints like Augustine of Hippo and Ignatius of Loyola learned how not to make mistakes by making many. The Lord who desires our holiness can bring good out of everything, can work in any and all of our experiences to transform us. In our fragmentation, we rejoice in the power of God to bring wholeness. If we bring our weakness before the Lord, humbly asking for the help of enabling grace, we can then trust that the Lord will produce an abundant harvest.

SPIRITUAL GROWTH THROUGH TRIAL AND ERROR

The ideals of holistic spirituality cannot be achieved without immersing ourselves in the messiness of nitty-gritty experience. Learning how to love God and others in an integrated way comes only through daily practice. The way of trial and error, not book learning alone, will teach us how to fashion a dynamic and balanced life in which there is room for solitude and community, ministry and leisure, autonomy and intimacy, personal transformation and social reform, prayer and play. Striking the right balance is a highly personal matter. No one can attain it for us; we must discover it ourselves through personal experience. As theologian John Dunne states, "Only one who has tried the extremes can find this personal mean . . . on the other hand, trying the extremes will not necessarily lead to finding the mean. Only the [person] who perceives the shortcomings of the extremes will find it."[15]

BLESSINGS FOR THE JOURNEY

Achieving wholeness and holiness requires traversing the difficult terrain of real life with all its challenges and crises. Even at the end of a lifetime of effort, we will still need to be completed by the finishing touch of the divine artist. God will then bring to completion in us the eternal design of people destined to love wholeheartedly. While awaiting that unifying touch of divine grace, we pilgrims are called to follow the way of Jesus. And the Lord who walks with us assures that we will always be blessed. The blessings sent our way may not always be enjoyable, but they will always nudge us forward in our efforts to love as God intended.

A rabbi was once asked, "What is a blessing?" He prefaced his answer with a riddle involving the creation account in chapter one of Genesis. The riddle went this way: After finishing his work on each of the first five days, the Bible states, "God saw that it was good." But, God is not reported to have commented on the goodness of what was created on the sixth day when the human person was fashioned. "What conclusion can you draw from that?" asked the rabbi. Someone volunteered, "We can conclude that the human person is not good." "Possibly," the rabbi nodded, "but that's not a likely explanation." He then went on to explain that the Hebrew word translated as "good" in Genesis is the word *tov,* which is better translated as "complete." That is why, the rabbi contended, God did not declare the human person to be *tov.* Human beings are created incomplete. It is our life's vocation to collaborate with our creator in fulfilling the Christ-potential in each of us. As the medieval mystic Meister Eckhart suggested, Christ longs to be born and developed into fullness in each of us.[16] A blessing is anything that enters into the center of our lives and expands our capacity to be filled with Christ's love. Therefore, a blessing may not always be painless, but it will always bring spiritual growth. Being blessed does not mean being perfect, but being completed. To be blessed is not to get out of life what we think we want. Rather, it is the assurance that God's purifying grace is active in us, so that our "hidden self [may] grow strong" and "Christ may live in [our] hearts through faith." In this way, we will with all the saints be "filled with the utter fullness of God" (Eph 3:16–19).

NOTES

Introduction

1. Thomas A. Hand, *Saint Augustine On Prayer* (Westminster, Maryland: Newman Press, 1963), p. 71.

2. Richard John Neuhaus, "Religion and Psychology," *National Review* (February 19, 1988), p. 46.

3. Ibid. See Paul Vitz, *Psychology as Religion: The Cult of Self-Worship* (Grand Rapids, Michigan: Eerdmans, 1977).

4. Brendan Kneale, F.S.C., "Superiority of the Religious Life," *Review for Religious* 47 (July/August 1988): 506.

5. John M. Lozano, *Life as Parable: Reinterpreting the Religious Life* (Mahwah, NJ: Paulist Press, 1986), p. 52. In using the word "parable," Lozano means more than a simple story used as a pedagogical tool to embellish a point. According to him, parables for Jesus "were not just an additional embellishment, but the very substance of his preaching. He proclaimed the kingdom of God and confronted his listeners with it through his parables." Jesus used the poetic language of parables "not to offer a rational explanation of the kingdom of God, but to bring his listeners face to face with it." The genre of parables extends itself beyond oral language to include actions of Jesus, gestures that certainly inform, but at the same time that challenge, invite and surprise us, as parables do. Furthermore, Lozano points out that the very life of Jesus during his ministry is in itself a parable. "Through the veiled language of his own life, he spoke to his contemporaries about God and his saving love" (p. 51). It is with these extended senses of parables that Lozano conceives of the religious life of the vows as a parable.

6. Ibid., p. 53.

7. Sandra M. Schneiders' explanation of the "difference" between religious and other Christians is cogent and precise: "Our reason for speaking of some people as 'religious' in a special sense is not that any Christian can be non-religious but that this designation captures the peculiar gift by which the religious dimension of human experience exercises a dominant and organizing role in their lives and brings about a permanent, active, full-time commitment to the movement generated by this special gift" (pp. 41–42). Thus "what makes religious 'different' is *neither* the specifically Christian character *nor* the peculiarities of lifestyle that congregations develop but a need to respond to a particular gift, a special vocation, that consists in an absorption, for the sake of

the whole community of believers, in the religious dimension of life." *New Wineskins: Re-imaging Religious Life Today* (Mahwah, NJ: Paulist Press, 1986), p. 44.

8. *Dogmatic Constitution on the Church (Lumen Gentium)* in *The Documents of Vatican II,* ed. Walter Abbott (New York: America Press, 1966), paragraphs 39–42.

9. Schneiders, *New Wineskins,* p. 89.

10. Suzanne M. DeBenedittis, *Teaching Faith and Morals: Toward Personal and Parish Renewal* (Minneapolis, MN: Winston Press, Inc., 1981), p. 8.

Chapter One

1. Martin Buber, "Heart-Searching," in *The Way of Man According to the Teaching of Hasidism* (Secaucus, NJ: The Citadel Press, 1966), pp. 9–14.

2. That is, proved true; so the leaders of the Hasidic communities are called.

3. Hugo Rahner, S.J., *Ignatius the Theologian,* trans. Michael Barry (New York: Herder and Herder, 1968), p. 207.

4. George I. Brown, *The Live Classroom: Innovation through Confluent Education and Gestalt,* ed. George I. Brown with Thomas Yeomans and Liles Grizzard (New York: The Viking Press, 1975), p. 3.

5. David Nyberg, "The Progress of Our Stupidity About Students' Intelligence," *The Chronicle of Higher Education* (March 26, 1986), 96.

6. Ibid.

7. George I. Brown, *The Live Classroom,* p. 3.

8. Charles Silberman, *Crisis in the Classroom* (New York: Random House, 1970), p. 8.

9. DeBenedittis, *Teaching Faith and Morals,* p. 9.

10. Ibid.

11. John Carmody, *Holistic Spirituality* (Mahwah, NJ: Paulist Press, 1983), p. 3.

12. Decree 16, "Chastity in the Society of Jesus," 31st General Congregation in *Documents of the 31st and 32nd General Congregations of the Society of Jesus* (St. Louis: The Institute of Jesuit Sources, 1977), No. 249, Par. 6.

13. Gregory Baum, "Reply and Explanation," in *Ecumenist* 9 (Nov.–Dec. 1971), 18.

14. Leo P. Rock, S.J., "The California Province Novitiate: What We Do and Why" (A Statement to the California Province of the Society of Jesus, September, 1973), p. 4.

15. See Josef Goldbrunner's *Holiness Is Wholeness* (New York: Pantheon, 1955).

16. See Barry McLaughlin, *Nature, Grace, and Religious Development* (Westminster, Maryland: The Newman Press, 1964).

17. Gregory Baum, "Reply and Explanation," p. 17.

18. Ibid.

19. James Gill, M.D., in William A. Barry et al., "Affectivity and Sexuality: Their Relationship to the Spiritual and Apostolic Life of Jesuits—Comments on Three Experiences," *Studies in the Spirituality of Jesuits* X:2–3 (March–May, 1979), 47.

20. Ibid., pp. 47–48.

21. See Donald Goergen, *The Power of Love: Christian Spirituality and Theology* (Chicago: The Thomas More Press, 1979), p. 21.

22. Ibid., p. 39.

Chapter Two

1. Ann and Barry Ulanov, *Primary Speech: A Psychology of Prayer* (Atlanta: John Knox Press, 1982), p. 57.

2. Erich Fromm, *The Art of Loving* (New York: Harper & Row, 1956).

3. Martin Buber, "Resolution," in *The Way of Man*, pp. 21–25.

4. Ibid., p. 21.

5. Ibid., p. 22.

6. Søren Kierkegaard, *Purity of Heart Is To Will One Thing*, trans. Douglas V. Steere (New York: Harpers, 1938), p. 3.

7. Martin Buber, *The Way of Man*, p. 23.

8. Johannes B. Metz, *Poverty of Spirit*, trans. John Drury (Mahwah, NJ: Paulist Press, 1968), p. 7.

9. Ibid.

10. Ibid., pp. 7–8.

11. Paul Tillich, *The Courage To Be* (New Haven: Yale University Press, 1952), pp. 164–5; 172–3.

12. Paul Tillich, "You Are Accepted," in *The Shaking of the Foundations* (New York: Charles Scribner's Sons, 1948), Chapter 19.

13. Ibid.

14. Alice Walker, *The Color Purple* (New York: Washington Square Press, 1982), p. 178.

15. Bernard J.F. Lonergan, S.J., *Method in Theology* (New York: Herder and Herder, 1972), p. 130.

16. Ignatius of Loyola, *The Spiritual Exercises of St. Ignatius*, trans. Louis J. Puhl (Chicago: Loyola University Press, n.d.), No. 323. 10.

17. Ibid., No. 328. 8.

18. Paul Tillich, "You Are Accepted," in *The Shaking of the Foundations*, Chapter 19.

19. See William Karel Grossouw, *Spirituality of the New Testament,* trans. Martin W. Schoenberg (St. Louis: B. Herder Book Company, 1961).

20. Ibid., p. 69.

21. Ibid.

22. See Regina Bechtle, S.C., "Reclaiming the Truth of Women's Lives: Women and Spirituality," *The Way,* 28:1 (January 1988), 50.

23. Joseph Powers, *Spirit and Sacrament: The Humanizing Experience* (New York: Seabury Press, 1973), p. 23.

24. Regina Bechtle, "Reclaiming the Truth of Women's Lives," p. 50.

25. *Dogmatic Constitution on the Church,* paragraphs 30 and 33.

26. *Sharing the Light of Faith: National Catechetical Directory for Catholics of the United States* (Washington, D.C.: United States Catholic Conference, Department of Education, 1979), p. 2.

27. Alice Walker, *The Color Purple,* p. 176. In quoting from Walker's work, I have retained her use of the masculine pronoun in reference to God in order to preserve the integrity of her artistic style. Believing that our God encompasses the richness of both male and female, I have deliberately attempted in my own writing, however, to use nonsexist language. Only when referring to Jesus the Lord and the one he called "Abba" have I used masculine forms when talking about God.

28. See John A. Sanford, *Ministry Burnout* (Mahwah, NJ: Paulist Press, 1982) for a straightforward treatment of some of the factors that lead to burnout in ministry.

29. "It is a mark of the evil spirit to assume the appearance of an angel of light. He begins by suggesting thoughts that are suited to a devout soul, and ends by suggesting his own. For example, he will suggest holy and pious thoughts that are wholly in conformity with the sanctity of the soul. Afterwards, he will endeavor little by little to end by drawing the soul into his hidden snares and evil designs." St. Ignatius of Loyola, "Rules for the Discernment of Spirits," in *The Spiritual Exercises,* No. 332.4.

30. John Sanford, *Ministry Burnout,* pp. 5–16.

31. Ignatius of Loyola, *Spiritual Exercises,* No. 236.

32. Monika K. Hellwig, "A Royal Priesthood," *America,* 156:18 (May 9, 1987), 393.

33. Monika Hellwig, "Royal Priesthood," p. 393.

34. Belden C. Lane, "Rabbinical Stories: A Primer on Theological Method," *Christian Century* 98:41 (December 16, 1981), pp. 1307–8.

35. Decree 11, "The Union of Minds and Hearts," in *Decrees of the 32nd General Congregation of the Society of Jesus* (St. Louis: The Institute of Jesuit Sources, 1977), No. 14.

36. Erik Erikson, *Identity, Youth, and Crisis* (New York: Norton, 1968), p. 138.

37. As quoted in Harold Kushner, *When All You've Ever Wanted Isn't Enough* (New York: Summit Books, 1986), p. 172.

38. Kurt Vonnegut, *Cat's Cradle* (New York: Dell Publishing, 1963), pp. 64–65.

39. Donald Goergen, *The Power of Love*, pp. 170–71.

40. John Carmody, *Holistic Spirituality*, p. 51.

41. Teilhard de Chardin, "The Grand Option," in *The Future of Man* (New York: Harper and Row, 1964), p. 46.

42. John Carmody, *Holistic Spirituality*, p. 53.

43. Thomas Merton, *Contemplative Prayer* (Garden City, New York: Doubleday & Company, Inc., 1969), p. 23.

44. Henri Nouwen, *Reaching Out: The Three Movements of the Spiritual Life* (Garden City, New York: Doubleday & Company, 1975), p. 30.

45. Anthony de Mello, *One Minute Wisdom* (New York: Doubleday, 1988), p. 68.

Chapter Three

1. Henri Nouwen, *Reaching Out*, p. 27.

2. As quoted in James W. Fowler, *Becoming Adult, Becoming Christian: Adult Development and Christian Faith* (San Francisco: Harper & Row, 1984), p. 93.

3. Anthony de Mello, *One Minute Wisdom*, p. 15.

4. Walter Brueggemann, "Covenanting as Human Vocation," *Interpretation* 33(2), 115–129.

5. St. Ignatius of Loyola, "Principle and Foundation," *The Spiritual Exercises of St. Ignatius*, No. 23.

6. Ibid., No. 169.

7. James Fowler, *Becoming Adult*, p. 92.

8. Ibid., p. 95.

9. Martin Buber, *The Way of Man*, p. 15.

10. Rainer Maria Rilke, *Letters to a Young Poet* (New York: Norton, 1954), pp. 18–19.

11. R.D. Laing, "Violence and Love," *Journal of Existentialism* 5 (1965), 417–422.

12. Frederick Perls, Ralph Hefferline, and Paul Goodman, *Gestalt Therapy: Excitement and Growth in the Human Personality* (New York: The Julian Press, 1951), p. 189.

13. Fritz Perls, *The Gestalt Approach and Eye Witness to Therapy* (Ben Lomond, California: Science & Behavior Books, 1973), p. 34.

14. Rainer Maria Rilke, *Letters,* pp. 46–47.

15. Thomas Merton, *Raids on the Unspeakable* (New York: New Directions, 1964), pp. 85–86.

16. William F. Lynch, *Christ and Prometheus: A New Image of the Secular* (South Bend, Ind.: University of Notre Dame, 1970), p. 130.

17. Edith Genet, "Images of God," *Lumen Vitae* XXXIV:1 (1979), 72.

18. Ron DelBene with Herb Montgomery, *The Breath of Life* (Minneapolis, MN: Winston Press, 1981), pp. 8–9.

19. John H. Wright, *A Theology of Christian Prayer* (New York: Pueblo Publishing Company), p. 134.

20. Ibid., pp. 134–135.

21. Alice Walker, *The Color Purple,* p. 176.

22. John Wright, *A Theology of Christian Prayer,* p. 134.

23. Genet, "Images of God," pp. 67–68.

24. Thomas Merton, *Spiritual Direction and Meditation,* pp. 30–33.

25. Ibid., p. 31.

26. Ibid.

27. Ibid.

28. E. Edward Kinerk, S.J., "Eliciting Great Desires: Their Place in the Spirituality of the Society of Jesus," *Studies in the Spirituality of Jesuits,* XVI:5 (Nov. 1984), 2.

29. Thomas Merton, *Spiritual Direction,* p. 31.

30. Kinerk, "Eliciting Great Desires," pp. 3–4.

31. Ibid., p. 4.

32. Ibid.

33. Robert Johann, "Wanting What We Want," *America* 117 (Nov. 18, 1967), 614.

34. St. Ignatius of Loyola, *Spiritual Exercises,* No. 175.

35. Ibid., No. 176.

36. Ignatius states in No. 335.7 of *The Spiritual Exercises,* "In souls that are progressing to greater perfection, the action of the good angel is delicate, gentle, delightful. It may be compared to a drop of water penetrating a sponge. The action of the evil spirit upon such souls is violent, noisy, and disturbing. It may be compared to a drop of water falling upon a stone." See also Nos. 328 and 329.1.

37. Ibid., Nos. 77–87.

38. Ibid., #23.

39. Michael J. Buckley, "Rules for the Discernment of Spirits," *The Way,* Supplement No. 20 (Autumn, 1973), 25–26.

40. Ibid., p. 26.

41. St. Ignatius of Loyola, *Spiritual Exercises,* No. 183.

42. William Peters, *The Spiritual Exercises of St. Ignatius: Exposition and Interpretation* (Jersey City, NJ: The Program to Adapt the Spiritual Exercises, 1967), p. 127.

43. John Futrell, "Ignatian Discernment," *Studies in the Spirituality of Jesuits,* II:2 (April 1970), 57.

44. James Simkin, "The Introduction of Gestalt," in *Live Classroom: Innovations Through Confluent Education and Gestalt Therapy,* Ed. George Brown with Thomas Yeomans and Liles Grizzard (New York: Viking Press, 1975), pp. 38–39.

45. Carl Rogers, *On Becoming a Person: A Therapist's View of Psychotherapy* (Boston: Houghton Mifflin, 1961), p. 22.

46. Ibid., pp. 22–23.

Chapter Four

1. Diane M. Connelly, *All Sickness Is Homesickness* (Columbia, Maryland: Center for Traditional Acupuncture, 1986), pp. 30, 33.

2. Ann and Barry Ulanov, *Primary Speech: A Psychology of Prayer* (Atlanta: John Knox Press, 1982), p. 7.

3. Elizabeth Barrett Browning, *Aurora Leigh and Other Poems,* ed. Cora Kaplan (London: The Women's Press, Ltd., 1978).

4. Gerard Manley Hopkins, "God's Grandeur," in *The Poems of Gerard Manley Hopkins* (Fourth Edition), eds. W.H. Gardner and N.H. Mackenzie (London: Oxford University Press, 1967), p. 66.

5. Belden C. Lane, "Rabbinical Stories," p. 1307.

6. Henri de Lubac, *Teilhard de Chardin: The Man and His Meaning* (New York: New American Library, 1967), p. 34.

7. Ibid., p. 35. Emphasis in the original.

8. Ann and Barry Ulanov, *Primary Speech,* p. 2.

9. St. Ignatius of Loyola, *The Spiritual Exercises,* Annotation #6.

10. *The Cloud of Unknowing and the Book of Privy Counsel,* ed. William Johnston (New York: Doubleday & Company, Inc., 1973), p. 54.

11. For a fuller description of this method of praying with scripture, see Anthony de Mello, *Sadhana: A Way to God* (Garden City, New York: Doubleday & Company, Inc., 1978), pp. 107–111. This work is one of the best practical guides to using Eastern forms in prayer.

12. William C. Spohn, "The Biblical Theology of the Pastoral Letter and Ignatian Contemplation," in *Studies in the Spirituality of American Jesuits* (St.

Louis: The American Assistancy Seminar on Jesuit Spirituality, 1985), Vol. XVII, No. 4, pp. 8–9.

13. Ibid., p. 10.

14. Abraham J. Heschel, *God in Search of Man: A Philosophy of Judaism* (New York: Harper and Row, 1955), p. 46.

15. Sam Keen, *Apology for Wonder* (New York: Harper and Row, 1969), p. 34.

16. Ibid., p. 35.

17. Abraham Heschel, *God in Search,* p. 108.

18. Ludwig Wittgenstein, *Tractatus Logico-Philosophicus* (London: Routledge & Kegan Paul, 1961), p. 44, as quoted in Keen in *Apology,* p. 22.

19. Abraham Heschel, *God in Search,* p. 45.

20. Ibid., p. 106.

21. Ibid., p. 108.

22. Dag Hammarskjold, *Markings,* trans. Leif Sjoberg and W.H. Auden (New York: Alfred A. Knopf, Inc., 1964), p. 46.

23. *The Cloud of Unknowing,* p. 55.

24. M. Basil Pennington, "Centering Prayer: Refining the Rules," *Review for Religious* 46:3 (May–June, 1986), 386–393.

25. Ibid., p. 390.

26. William Johnston has been a prolific writer on the topic of mysticism and contemplative prayer. His *Christian Zen* (New York: Harper & Row, 1971) would be a helpful introduction to how Zen can be profitably adapted for use by Christians. Kakichi Kadowaki, *Zen and the Bible,* tr. Joan Rieck (Boston: Routledge & Kegan Paul, 1980) provides an understanding of the similarities between Christian asceticism and the way of Zen.

27. For a brief description of sitting postures, see William Johnston, *Christian Zen,* pp. 105–109.

28. Anthony de Mello, *Sadhana,* pp. 37–39.

29. Robert F. Morneau, *Mantras for the Morning: An Introduction to Holistic Prayer* (Collegeville, Minnesota: The Liturgical Press, 1981), p. 10.

30. Some examples given by R. Morneau in *Mantras.*

31. Ignatius of Loyola, *The Spiritual Exercises,* #43.

32. See George Aschenbrunner, "Consciousness Examen," *Review for Religious* 31 (1972).

33. For a discussion of the importance of the consciousness examen as a tool for growth, see John Govan, "The Examen: A Tool for Holistic Growth," *Review for Religious* (May–June, 1986), pp. 394–401.

34. St. Teresa, *Interior Castle,* trans. Kieran Kavanaugh and Otilio Rodriguez (Mahwah, NJ: Paulist Press, 1979), No. 7, p. 70.

Chapter Five

1. Dag Hammarskjold, *Markings,* p. 99.

2. Robert Kegan, *The Evolving Self: Problem and Process in Human Development* (Cambridge, Massachusetts: Harvard University Press, 1982), pp. 159–160.

3. Gordon W. Allport, "Motivation in Personality: Reply to Mr. Bertocci," *Psychological Review* 47 (1940), 545.

4. Brian O'Leary, S.J., "Christian and Religious Obedience," *Review for Religious* 44:4 (July/August 1985), 518.

5. Carroll Stuhlmueller, C.P., "The Gospel According to Luke," in *The Jerome Biblical Commentary,* ed. Raymond Brown, S.S., Joseph A. Fitzmyer, S.J., and Roland E. Murphy, O.Carm. (Englewood Cliffs, New Jersey: Prentice-Hall, 1968), p. 143.

6. David M. Stanley, S.J., *"I Encountered God!": The Spiritual Exercises with the Gospel of John* (St. Louis: The Institute of Jesuit Sources, 1987), p. 233.

7. Francis Baur, *Life in Abundance: A Contemporary Spirituality* (Mahwah, NJ: Paulist Press, 1983), p. 112.

8. Thomas Merton. *Thoughts in Solitude* (Garden City, New York: Doubleday & Company, Inc., 1968), p. 81.

9. Belden C. Lane, "Rabbinical Stories," pp. 1308–09.

10. John Courtney Murray, S.J., "The Danger of the Vows," *Woodstock Letters* (Fall, 1967), 421.

11. Decree 8, "The Spiritual Formation," 31st General Congregation in *Documents of the 31st and 32nd General Congregations of the Society of Jesus* (St. Louis: The Institute of Jesuit Sources, 1977), No. 23.

12. Decree 17, "The Life of Obedience," 31st General Congregation in *Documents of the 31st and 32nd General Congregations* (St. Louis: The Institute of Jesuit Sources, 1977), Nos. 11 and 12.

13. John C. Futrell, S.J., *Making an Apostolic Community of Love: The Role of the Superior According to St. Ignatius of Loyola* (St. Louis: The Institute of Jesuit Sources, 1970), p. 143.

14. James Simkin, "An Introduction to Gestalt Therapy," in *The Live Classroom,* p. 41.

15. J.B. Phillips, *Your God Is Too Small* (New York: The Macmillan Company, 1961), p. 54.

16. Karen Horney, *Neurosis and Human Growth* (New York: W.W. Norton & Company, Inc., 1950), p. 23.

17. Ibid., pp. 23–24.

18. Ibid., pp. 64–65.

19. Ibid., p. 78.

20. Thomas Merton, *Spiritual Direction,* p. 33.

21. Decree 17, "The Life of Obedience," 31st General Congregation in *Documents of the 31st and 32nd General Congregations* (St. Louis: The Institute of Jesuit Sources, 1977), Nos. 11 and 12.

Chapter Six

1. Edward Hoagland, "The Urge for an End: Contemplating Suicide," *Harper's Magazine* 276:1654 (March 1988), 51.

2. James B. Nelson, *Between Two Gardens: Reflections on Sexuality and Religious Experience* (New York: Pilgrim Press, 1983), p. 7.

3. John Giles Milhaven, "Sleeping Like Spoons: A Question of Embodiment," *Commonweal* CXVI:7 (April 7, 1989), 205.

4. James B. Nelson, *Between Two Gardens,* p. 6.

5. Ibid., p. 7.

6. Ibid., p. 9.

7. Anthropologist Michael S. Patton hypothesizes that traditional Catholic teaching regarding sexuality has resulted in "sexophobia" in Catholics and causes pathology in various Catholic cultures in the United States. According to him, "Traditional Catholic education . . . taught the ordinary Catholic to distrust his or her sexual feelings and all erotic behavior. Sexophobia resulted. Simultaneously, Catholics generally became fearful of God, since God was perceived as someone to fear, especially when one broke a sex law of the church . . . Sex was the ticket to hell and the wrath of divine displeasure. The result was many unhealthy attitudes towards sex in Catholicism. Catholics have suffered from high levels of stress because of their sexual religious beliefs, attitudes, and mores, with the origin of their suffering diagnosed inaccurately . . . Limited scientific research indicates there is a problem with suffering and damage in Catholic sexuality, but much more research is necessary to document this problem accurately." "Suffering and Damage in Catholic Sexuality," *Journal of Religion and Health* 27:2 (Summer 1988), 139–140.

8. John Courtney Murray, S.J., "The Danger of the Vows," *Woodstock Letters* (Fall 1967), 424.

9. James B. Nelson, *Between Two Gardens,* p. 10.

10. According to researcher Michael Patton, "The Catholic repression of sex may be hypothetically correlated to various forms of antisocial behavior." Ibid., p. 139.

11. John Courtney Murray, "The Danger of the Vows," p. 426.

12. John Barth, *The End of the Road* (Garden City, New York: Doubleday & Company Inc., 1958), p. 93.

13. William F. Kraft, "Celibate Genitality," *Review for Religious* 36:4 (1977), 605.

14. Decree 11, "The Union of Minds and Hearts," 32nd General Congregation in *Documents of the 31st and 32nd General Congregation of the Society of Jesus* (St. Louis: The Institute of Jesuit Sources, 1977), No. 26.

15. Charles R. Burns, "A Priest's Painful Choice," *Newsweek*, February 2, 1987, p. 6.

16. The hermeneutical presuppositions that support my understanding of this passage are stated succinctly in Sandra M. Schneiders, "The Foot Washing (John 13: 1–20): An Experiment in Hermeneutics," *The Catholic Biblical Quarterly* 43 (Jan. 1981) 76–80. Two of these presuppositions are: First, that, "as a work, the text mediates a meaning which is not behind it, hidden in the shroud of the past when the text was composed, but ahead of it in the possibilities of human and Christian existence which it projects for the reader." Second, that "the meaning of the text is not limited to what the author intended even though it was produced in function of such an intention. The text, in being exteriorized and established in independent existence by writing, open to anyone who can read, means whatever it actually means when validly interpreted, whether or not the author intended such a meaning" (p. 70).

17. James Gill, M.D., in William A. Barry et al, "Affectivity and Sexuality," *Studies in the Spirituality of Jesuits* X:2–3 (March–May, 1979), 49.

18. Ibid., p. 50.

19. Sandra Schneiders, "The Foot Washing," pp. 76–92.

20. Ibid., p. 83.

21. Ibid., p. 87.

22. Jane Redmont, "Sexism, Sin, and Grace: Responses to the Bishops' Letter," *Commonweal* CXV:12 (June 17, 1988), 362.

23. Erich Fromm, *The Art of Loving* (New York: Harper and Row, 1956), pp. 1–4.

24. Charles R. Burns, "A Priest's Painful Choice," p. 6.

25. For a recent treatment of friendships in religious life, see Douglas A. Morrison, "Friendships in Religious Life—A Formational Issue," *Journal of Pastoral Counseling* XXII:1 (Spring–Summer 1987), 77–86.

26. Ernest Larkin (ed.) and Gerald Broccolo, *Spiritual Renewal of the American Priesthood* (Washington, D.C.: United States Catholic Conference, 1973), p. 37.

27. Henri Nouwen, *Reaching Out*, p. 19.

28. Conrad Baars and Anna Terruwe, *Healing the Unaffirmed: Recognizing Deprivation Neurosis* (New York: Alba House, 1972), p. 4.

29. Ibid., p. 6.

30. Anna Polcino, "Belonging-Longing To Be," in *Belonging,* ed. C.J. Franasiak (Whitinsville, Massachusetts: Affirmation Books, 1979), p. 86–87.

31. Decree 11, "Union of Minds and Hearts," No. 14.

32. William McNamara, *Mystical Passion* (Mahwah, NJ: Paulist Press, 1977), p. 3.

Chapter Seven

1. Ladislas M. Orsy, "Poverty: The Modern Problem," *The Way,* Supplement No. 9 (Spring 1970), 15.

2. Ibid., p. 14.

3. For an excellent presentation of the diverse forms Christian poverty can take, see Gerald R. Grosh, "Models of Poverty," *Review for Religious* 34:4 (1975), 550–558.

4. Karl Rahner, *Spiritual Exercises* (New York: Herder and Herder, 1966), p. 18.

5. Orsy, "Poverty," p. 11.

6. Robert Kegan, *The Evolving Self,* p. 16.

7. Pedro Arrupe, "Change of Attitude Towards the Underprivileged," in *Challenge to Religious Life Today: Selected Letters and Address,* Vol. II, ed. Jerome Aixale (St. Louis: The Institute of Jesuit Sources, 1980), pp. 249–50.

8. Pedro Arrupe, "Exposure to and Insertion Among the Poor" in *Challenge to Religious Life Today,* Vol. II, p. 309.

9. Dorothy Day, unpublished manuscript, Catholic Worker Papers, W-3.1. See also *Catholic Worker* 17:1 (September 1950). Quoted in Mel Piehl, *Breaking Bread: The Catholic Worker and the Origin of Catholic Radicalism in America* (Philadelphia: Temple University Press, 1982), pp. 99–100.

10. Piehl, *Breaking Bread,* p. 100.

11. St. Ignatius of Loyola, Mon. Ign. Epp. XI, p. 374, as quoted by Pedro Arrupe, "The Mystery of Poverty," in *Center for Ignatian Studies* III:4 (1973), 45.

12. *San Francisco Chronicle,* 28 February 1989, p. A2.

13. Quoted in Kevin Fagan, "Confrontation at RR Tracks During Willson Observance," in *The Tribune* (Oakland), 2 September 1988, p. C-5.

14. *Los Angeles Times,* 2 September 1987, Part I, p. 3.

15. Decree 12, "Poverty," 32nd General Congregation in *Documents of the 31st and 32nd General Congregation of the Society of Jesus* (St. Louis: The Institute of Jesuit Sources, 1977), No. 9.

16. L. Edward Wells and Sheldon Stryker, "Stability and Change in Self Over the Life Course," in *Life Span Development and Behavior,* Vol. 8, eds. Paul

B. Baltes, David L. Featherman, and Richard M. Lerner (Hillsdale, New Jersey: Lawrence Erlbaum Associates Publishers, 1988), p. 207.

17. Ibid., p. 208.

18. Robert Kegan, *The Evolving Self*, p. 116.

19. Ibid., p. 115.

20. Ibid., p. 108.

21. Ibid., p. 108.

22. Ibid., pp. 108–09.

23. See Abraham H. Maslow, *Motivation and Personality* (New York: Harper and Row, 1954), pp. 153–174.

24. Robert Kegan, *The Evolving Self*, p. 8.

25. Using philosophical rather than psychological terms, author Sam Keen describes the desired movement in spiritual growth as that from "ego-exclusiveness consciousness" to "self-inclusiveness consciousness." "Manifesto for a Dionysian Theology," in *New Theology No. 7,* eds. Martin E. Marty and Dean G. Peerman (New York: Macmillan, 1970), p. 92. The defining boundaries of the self, in other words, keep expanding to encompass more and more, without losing its own unique identity. When this happens, fewer people are alien to the self; more are brought into the core of the self through identification and solidarity. While the self/non-self distinction perdures, what constitutes the self incorporates more reality. However, as long as this distinction remains, only the penultimate stage of development has been reached. The ultimate stage, argues Keen, requires an "un-self consciousness," and "a life beyond character." Sam Keen and James W. Fowler, *Life Maps: Conversations on the Journey of Faith,* ed. Jerome W. Berryman (Waco, Texas: Word Books, 1978), p. 117. For the "saint" or "lover" who has reached this ultimate stage of growth "the seeming plurality of things only masks a deeper unity. The communion of all beings is the hidden truth . . . The lover is animated by a life that is deeper than the ego or personality. In traditional terms, s/he is moved by grace" (Ibid., p. 123). The person who has reached this stage has ceased to be concerned with the question "Who am I?" and has been invaded by a conviction that we are all one.

26. Sam Keen, "Manifesto," p. 92.

27. Ignatius of Loyola, *Spiritual Exercises,* Nos. 136–148. My analysis of the Two Standards meditation relies heavily on the unpublished class notes of Joseph B. Wall, S.J., who devoted much of his life to sharing his penetrating insights into Ignatian spirituality with Jesuit seminarians.

28. Ernest Larkin, O. Carm., *Silent Presence: Discernment as Process and Problem* (Denville, New Jersey: Dimension Books, Inc., 1981), p. 16.

29. Conrad W. Baars, M.D. and Anna Terruwe, M.D., *Healing the Unaffirmed,* p. 189.

30. Karl Rahner, *Spiritual Exercises,* p. 19.

31. Anthony de Mello, *The Song of the Bird* (Anand, India: Gujarat Sahitya Prakash, 1982), pp. 182–183.

32. Judith Viorst, *Necessary Losses: The Loves, Illusions, Dependencies, and Impossible Expectations that All of Us Have To Give Up in Order To Grow* (New York: Ballantine Books, 1986), p. 3.

33. Ibid., p. 2.

34. As told by Alan Watts and quoted in Diane M. Connelly, *All Sickness Is Homesickness,* pp. 24–25.

35. Judith Viorst, *Necessary Losses,* p. 3.

36. *Alcoholics Anonymous: The Story of How Many Thousands of Men and Women Have Recovered from Alcoholism,* 3rd Edition (New York: Alcoholics Anonymous World Services, Inc., 1976), p. 10.

37. St. Ignatius, *Constitutions of the Society of Jesus,* trans. George Ganss (St. Louis: Institute of Jesuit Sources, 1970), No. 287.

Chapter Eight

1. Dag Hammarskjold, *Markings,* p. 103.

2. Sam Keen, "Manifesto," p. 97.

3. LeRoy Aden, "On Carl Rogers' Becoming," *Theology Today* XXXVI:4 (Jan. 1980), 558.

4. Ibid., p. 557.

5. Ibid.

6. Ibid., p. 558.

7. Adrian van Kaam, *Religion and Personality* (Denville, New Jersey: Dimension Books, 1980), p. 15.

8. Ibid.

9. C.S. Lewis, *They Stand Together: The Letters of C.S. Lewis to Arthur Greeves,* ed. Walter Hooper (New York: The Macmillan Co., Inc. 1979), p. 361.

10. Saint Thomas Aquinas, *Summa Theologiae, Latin Text and English Translation, Introductions, Notes, Appendices, and Glossaries,* Vol. 33 (Blackfriars, with New York: McGraw-Hill and London: Eyre & Spottiswoode, 1966), II–II, Q 21, a 1, ad 1.

11. Paula Ripple, *Growing Strong at Broken Places* (Notre Dame, Indiana: Ave Maria Press, 1986), p. 68.

12. Ibid., p. 69.

13. Chogyam Trungpa, *Meditation in Action* (Boston: Shambhala, 1985), p. 26.

14. Ibid.

15. John Dunne, *The Way of All the Earth* (New York: MacMillan Company, 1972), pp. 37–38.

16. Meister Eckhart once said: "What good is it to me if Mary gave birth to the son of God fourteen hundred years ago and I do not also give birth to the son of God in my time and in my culture?" As quoted in Matthew Fox, *Original Blessing: A Primer in Creation Spirituality* (Santa Fe, New Mexico: Bear & Company, 1983), p. 221.